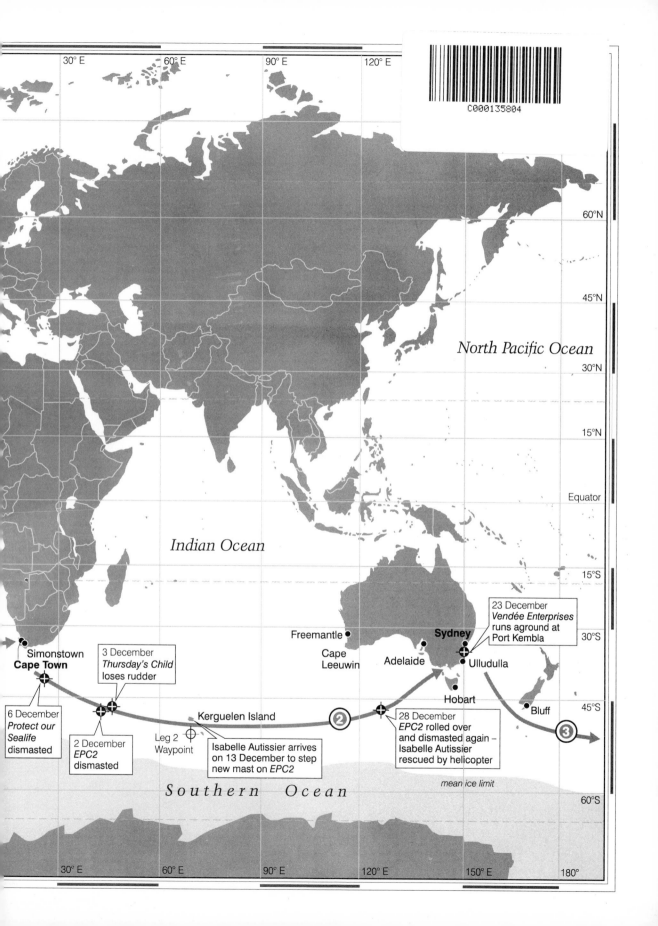

60°N

45°N

North Pacific Ocean

30°N

15°N

Equator

15°S

Indian Ocean

23 December
*Vendée Enterprises*
runs aground at
Port Kembla

30°S

Freemantle •

**Sydney**

Cape
Leeuwin

Adelaide

Ulludulla

Simonstown
**Cape Town**

3 December
*Thursday's Child*
loses rudder

②

Hobart

Bluff

45°S

6 December
*Protect our
Sealife*
dismasted

Kerguelen Island

Leg 2
Waypoint

Isabelle Autissier arrives
on 13 December to step
new mast on *EPC2*

28 December
*EPC2* rolled over
and dismasted again –
Isabelle Autissier
rescued by helicopter

③

2 December
*EPC2*
dismasted

*S o u t h e r n    O c e a n*

mean ice limit

60°S

30° E

60° E

90° E

120° E

150° E

180°

# THE LONELIEST RACE

# PAUL GELDER

# THE LONELIEST RACE

## 27,000 miles sailing alone around the world – the story of the BOC Challenge 1994–95

Sponsored by
**Autohelm**®
A **Raytheon** Company

**ADLARD COLES NAUTICAL**
London

Published 1995 by Adlard Coles Nautical 1995
an imprint of A & C Black (Publishers) Ltd
35 Bedford Row, London WC1R 4JH

Copyright © Paul Gelder 1995
Copyright of the Foreword © Josh Hall 1995
First edition 1995

ISBN 0–7136–4202–5

A CIP catalogue record for this book is available from the British Library.

Typeset in 10 on 12pt Trump Mediaeval by Falcon Typesetting
Printed and bound in Great Britain by Butler and Tanner Ltd, Frome, Somerset

# Contents

To Harry Mitchell, lost at sea,
4 April 1924 – 2 March 1995

'I would rather be ashes than dust! I would rather that my spark should be burned out in a brilliant blaze than it should be stifled by dry rot ... the proper function of man is to live, not to exist. I shall not waste my days in trying to prolong them. I shall use my time.'

JACK LONDON 1867–1916

## Foreword by Josh Hall

# The Closest Knit Team in the World

In keeping with BOC Challenge tradition, this edition of the single-handed marathon has been a melting pot of highs, lows, excitement, dramas and tragedy. I myself had experienced all these emotions by the time I gratefully stepped ashore in Cape Town at the end of leg one – my Class 1 60ft entry, *Gartmore Investment Managers*, sank in cold, four mile deep South Atlantic water over 500 miles from the Brazilian coast after colliding with a submerged object at over 10 knots in rough seas. It was probably a ship's container. The Cape Harbourmaster informed me of the thought-provoking fact that in recent years over 40,000 of them had been officially reported as lost from the decks of Atlantic container ships. How many remain semi-submerged, suspended, waiting, is anyone's guess.

I was lucky – I had superb communications on board, including a Comsat satellite phone. The skilled experience of the guys at BOC race HQ in Charleston coupled with the seamanship of Alan Nebauer aboard the 50ft *Newcastle Australia*, meant that I was plucked from the nose-diving *Gartmore* just eight hours after the collision. After spending the previous three years preparing and fund-raising for this, my second BOC, returning home for an early bath and to follow the event in the newspapers was not a thought I relished, so when Race Director Mark Schrader offered me the chance to come and work at the communications HQ in Charleston, I did not need asking twice.

Every skipper who hits the start line of this event has achieved the almost impossible. To prepare yourself physically and mentally takes a resolve and dedication that knows no boundaries; to prepare your yacht properly takes skilled management and forethought; to pull together the resources to compete, be they through sponsorship or personal input, takes unrivalled perseverance. Interestingly, the creation of the project is the best possible training for the actual adventure, during which every skill and emotion will be thoroughly tested.

Having completed 1.2 BOC Challenges as a skipper, it has been very rewarding to work on the 'other side of the fence' and help deal with all the communications issues that revolve around the race. Cyberspace has entered the sailing world in a big way with the race yachts carrying IBM Thinkpad laptop computers and having the ability to access the Internet through a Compuserve gateway. Thousands of folk and dozens of schools are following the race tack by tack, gybe by gybe through the Sailing Forum on Compuserve, where daily position updates, chart graphics, messages from skippers and even dramatic press photographs are available for download.

Information is vital these days, and its distribution even more so. Satcoms and E-mail are where the future of this type of adventure lies. If the media can follow an event easily and have direct access to the skippers, then each project will find it easier to achieve the sponsorship that it needs to campaign.

Of course the paramount issue is that of safety, and with Comsat satellite tracking and messaging capabilities, the race has never had such a sophisticated and comprehensive safety net. From Race HQ we can send and receive text messages to and from the yachts at will; we can poll any of the yachts' on board equipment at any time with no input required from the skipper, and obtain their position, speed and heading; we can tell if they have switched their equipment off and whether they did so at the terminal or at the power supply. We are an eye in the sky watching their progress, or otherwise, from satellites some 24,000 miles above the earth's surface. Quite amazing really.

The BOC Race is, always has been and always will be, a race of attrition. At the dockside before the September start I knew that fewer boats would return to a finish line gun than crossed the start line. That some skippers would eventually find the challenge too daunting, too risky, too long, too expensive, too much. Some would have success effortlessly snatched away from them by the cruel sea. Some, just when they thought things were running smoothly, would have their rigs plucked from their deck by a wind with no conscience and have to show huge reserves of fortitude and determination to stay in the race. Some would surprise everyone, including themselves, with their performance, and some would cause the world that knew them to miss a heartbeat and offer up prayers pleading for deliverance.

Despite modern technology, the sea is still the same as it has always been – relentless and unforgiving. It will, for the most part, allow us to travel across it, but sometimes it will exact a painful toll. This will never change and is both the risk and the lure for sailors. For Harry Mitchell, sailing alone around the world was a dream that simply had to be chased. Those of us who knew Harry were devastated by his loss, but we all knew that he was doing exactly what he wanted to do and would have wished to take his leave of us in no other way. Harry enriched all those who had the great fortune to meet him, and his life should be an inspiration to us all.

The overriding fact is that this is an event for adventurers; it will always attract those of a free-minded spirit, those who wish to seek out their own personal limitations and those who would probably be successful captains of industry if they did not choose to be captains of their own destiny. On this type of adventure you learn a lot about sailing, a lot about the oceans and a frightening amount about yourself. All the skippers that reached the end of this 27,000 mile, 10 month long sojourn will have the calm confidence and stature gained through

*Josh Hall.* PHOTO: GARY JOHN NORMAN

meeting every imaginable trial. They will have overcome all manner of gear failures on board their boats. They will have endured extremities of heat and cold when time will have ticked away interminably slowly. They will have developed the patience of saints through waiting in calms for wind and waiting in too much wind for calms. They will have had their personal envelopes of fear continuously pushed to new limits. They will be the closest knit team of individuals in the world because they each know what it has taken to compete and complete. They will all be winners and be recognized as such by everyone and by each other.

From my own point of view I had mixed emotions as the yachts drew closer to the finish line. I was thrilled to see my friends arriving back and to hear of their experiences first-hand, but equally it was a powerful reminder of what could have been, should have been, for Harry and those of us forced out of the race.

The awesome achievement of racing solo around the world brought an aura to Charleston City Marina that inspired hundreds of school children who came to the dockside to meet their heroes. It inspired every single person that visited, but most of all it undoubtedly inspired a few quietly observing characters who were strolling the pontoons with a sparkle in their eyes. They will be the competitors in the next BOC Challenge.

# A Voyage Round Your Soul

Captain Ahab was 58 when he chased Moby Dick. Harry Mitchell was 70 when he set off from Charleston on September 17 in his 40ft yacht in pursuit of his dream of becoming a Cape Horner and solo circumnavigator. This book was inspired by Harry and his dream. Ever since I heard about his first attempt at the age of 62 to sail singlehanded around the world I had always wanted to meet Harry, who lived in the next town along Hampshire's South Coast. His first attempt ended dramatically more than halfway round the globe on a sandbar in New Zealand in 1987. Harry was devastated. But never one to quit, even – especially – when he was behind, he bought a new boat and entered for the next BOC Challenge. This time his hopes ended prematurely a few days out of Plymouth. His yacht was struck by a cargo ship on the way to the Newport start.

In 1993 I finally got my chance to meet Harry at a BOC reception at the London Boat Show. He told me he had repaired and refitted his yacht and had sent off his entry fee for the 1994-95 BOC Challenge.

The word 'determined' is defined in the dictionary as resolute, unflinching and indomitable. Harry was all those things. The dictionary adds other words like valiant and undaunted. Harry was certainly courageous, but he was not foolish enough to be fearless and would frequently admit to being daunted. The fact that he was vulnerable but continued to try to knock down the barriers, never allowing disappointment to sway his course, was what singled him out. His courage was in acknowledging failure and fighting back, taking the setbacks in his stride. Knowing when to surrender takes courage too, of course, but keeping alive your dream to sail around the world when most 70-year-olds would be well into retirement, with slippers by the fireside, is an act of faith that deserves recognition. Harry had the motivation of a 20-year-old.

I didn't think that people like Harry Mitchell existed any more. So many characters have disappeared from the short-handed sailing scene. The professional, corporately sponsored yachtsmen have grabbed the headlines while the lone, eccentric buccaneer has become a vanishing species.

Harry re-named his yacht *Henry Hornblower* for his third attempt at a solo circumnavigation, but I soon discovered that he was the last man to blow his own horn. When I raised the idea of a book about his voyage I encountered the irascible, self-deprecating side of Harry. He missed few opportunities to make light of his endeavours, perhaps because he was always haunted by the spectre of failure. 'There's no fool like an old fool,' he would say. But Harry was nobody's fool. He was simply anxious to divert any spotlight from himself and get on quietly with what he had started.

One cold March afternoon, standing in the cabin of his yacht laid up ashore in Moody's yard at the top of the River Hamble, he did his best to discourage my intentions of writing what would have been exclusively Harry's story. With that mischievous glint in his eye and a grin on his weatherbeaten face he courteously deflected my proposal: 'You won't get much of a book out of me!' he said. 'Why not write about *all* the unsponsored Corinthian sailors in the BOC Challenge? That way if I don't finish you'll still have something to write about.'

One of the hallmarks of events like the BOC Challenge is that you don't find swaggering, gung-ho, self-promoting types. 'People who need an audience don't do this sort of thing,' Nigel Rowe once told me. 'You're out there on your own and there is no one to bullshit. People who are not comfortable with their own company don't do this race. On the other hand a high proportion of likeable and straightforward people *do*. And that's what I like about it.'

Getting Harry to open up about his BOC adventure was sometimes like cross examining the Sphinx. He was not a man to be persuaded to take centre stage, unless he could play the comedian. He didn't mind self-mockery. He admitted to having an awkward streak and could be as stubborn as he was considerate and warm-hearted. It was another side to his doggedness.

Sailors with small budgets in ocean yacht races risk a higher drop out rate than most. Pessimists said some of the Corinthian shoestring entries wouldn't reach the halfway mark in Australia. Some didn't. But fate didn't just single out the amateurs for harsh treatment. Josh Hall's 60ft yacht sank after hitting an unidentified floating object off the coast of Brazil. Isabelle Autissier, having spectacularly won the first leg to Cape Town, had to abandon her crippled yacht in the Southern Ocean. The fleet of 20 was cut by more than a third to an unlucky 13 as it set course towards Cape Horn. Almost everyone had suffered knockdowns, when the yacht is smashed so far sideways that the mast hits the sea.

Harry, setting off from Australia a day later than everyone else, ploughed on like the tortoise following the ocean hares. He certainly gave the lie to the stereotype of singlehanded sailors as neurotic loners or misfits with a masochistic streak. He was not a loner. If there was a party he would be its life and soul. He soon became a favourite with the crowds in Charleston at the start of the race. Harry was gregarious and disliked the loneliness of the long distance solo sailor more than the perils. At 70, he knew life was too short to spend so many days alone at sea and he looked forward to the camaraderie at journey's end. For Harry the reward came at each stopover. 'It's the afterwards, when it's all over and you can say you've challenged yourself,' he told me in Sydney, his voice breaking with emotion at suddenly being back from the edge of the world among friends.

Harry hated the idea that people only admired what he was doing because of his age. He didn't feel 70 and he certainly didn't act it. As reporters beat a path to his cabin hatchway he would sometimes say 'they're only interested because I'm a bit of a joke or a freak.' Reluctantly, but gracefully, he submitted to wearing the race crown of the Old Man of the Sea, recognising that clichés fitted nicely in reporters' copy and made good headlines. He even came up with a neat quote about what motivated him in the race: 'to wear a gold earring in my left ear for rounding the Horn and stay alive to a ripe old age and keep my marbles'. If he'd had a share of royalties for the quote he would have bought a new mainsail. But he wasn't sailing around the world alone to prove anything about age. In the same way that Isabelle Autissier, the only woman in the race, was labelled 'the lone woman in a battle of the sexes', so Harry was tagged as the Ancient Mariner. Isabelle's reply was, 'Maybe for some people that's important, but not for me'. She spoke for both of them.

Harry wanted to be accepted for who he was, not how old he was, but age stalked him like a shadow that eclipsed his own right to some limelight. Like Phil Weld, who at 65 became the oldest and the first American to win the Observer Singlehanded Transatlantic Race, Harry had found a sport where the accretion of wisdom could offset diminishing physical vigour.

If Harry's brand of courage was to see something through to the end, even when it might have been easier to quit, no one quite expected the end when it finally came. Luck, along with fate, is a fickle accomplice in high risk adventures like singlehanded sailing. And luck had always seemed in short supply for Harry on the BOC Challenge. It finally deserted him for the last time on Thursday 2 March when, 1,400 miles from his goal of Cape Horn, he activated his emergency position indicating radio beacon. Nobody knows why, or what happened. And speculation on the causes or outcome was as endless as it was bleak and painful. Harry's dream that became a quest and then an obsession, suddenly turned into everybody's nightmare.

As the search for Harry continued, day after day, at the bottom of the globe, his words from almost a year ago to the day echoed back ' … if I don't finish you'll still have something to write about.' It didn't feel that way. The heart went out of the project. The book had been planned as a celebration of individual achievement, courage and daring, but its reluctant luminary was lost at sea. But Harry's motto was 'Never give up'. So the story of his, and others', determination against the odds had to be told as a tribute to him.

Most of us knew Harry the solo sailor, not the husband and father of two daughters and a son, and a grandfather to four. Luck had certainly been with Harry when he met his remarkable wife Diana. 'Nothing will stop him going,' she once said with a mixture of resignation and affection, 'so I may as well help him to be as prepared as possible.' Her dignity and composure in those dark days when Harry was lost gave strength to others.

Harry had been chasing what another BOC competitor called 'the long rainbow'. His greatest fear in life had been growing old and surrendering his independence in a hospital ward or old folks' home. That Harry didn't climb his Everest to the summit did not diminish what he *had* accomplished. Of all the reasons Harry advanced for putting himself through such an ordeal (though to him the attraction lay in the adventure not the ordeal) there was, among the spurious and comic, one that seemed more measured: he felt he *'had yet to make his mark'*. As Thoreau said, 'It is as hard to see one's self as to look backwards without turning round.' In the passage of time, one man's immortal gesture soon becomes an ephemeral epitaph. How do you determine what will stick in the hearts and minds of men?

Harry found himself sailing to the ends of the earth twice in pursuit of his Holy Grail. He was so close, just 12 days away, from rounding the elusive Horn when disaster struck. The irony is – though Harry would be the last person to realise it – he had already accomplished something more durable and worthwhile than a solo circumnavigation. During his 'voyage round the soul', as he once called it, Harry left an indelible mark on everyone he encountered. He lived life to the limits and wanted no regrets or might-have-beens. For him the tragedy of life was not what we might suffer, but what we might miss. Like Herman Melville's hero in *Moby Dick*, Harry chose to test himself against the odds. He lived out his dreams not just for himself, but others. He knew that without risk there is no exhilaration.

At the end of leg three in Punta del Este, Uruguay, after the BOC fleet had set sail for the final leg home, there were those of us who gazed out to sea still hoping to see a sail on the horizon. It is hard to accept even now that *Henry Hornblower* won't be tying up at the dockside somewhere. Or that we won't see that distinctive, sturdy and straight-backed figure, with a slight limp from an old rugby knee injury, walking purposefully down the pontoon.

Paul Gelder
April 1995

*Harry and Diana Mitchell*

# *Acknowledgements*

The BOC Challenge motto is 'Around Alone' but, like the skippers who are helped by an invisible army before they cast off from the dockside, this book could not have been written without the assistance of many people. First and foremost I must thank Geoff Pack, Editor of *Yachting Monthly*, who handed me the plum assignment of covering the start of the BOC Challenge in America without realising that it would turn into a 60,000 mile travel marathon and a book. When it did, he was supportive of the project, even though every race stopover seemed to coincide with the magazine's monthly 'hotspot week'.

I am especially grateful to Nigel Rowe who, while contracted himself to write the official account of the race, gave his blessing to this project. That Harry Mitchell was the inspiration for the book is explained elsewhere. While we all suffer the anguish of Harry's disappearance, Harry's wife Diana endured the weeks of waiting and wondering with uncommon courage, dignity and grace. I was privileged that she shared with me some of her thoughts and reminiscences of the man she was married to for 43 years.

Anyone who can get away with calling Robin Knox-Johnston 'cute' to his face has my admiration. BOC Challenge Media Operations Director Dan McConnell belongs to that rare breed, a newspaperman's idea of PR man: succinct, informative and entertaining. Meeting Julia Humberstone, who works in the BOC Corporate Relations office, was an additional and delightful bonus in covering the Challenge. Julia's efficiency was as effortless as her charm, as was Jane McConnell's. BOC Race Director Mark Schrader is a man with a huge burden of responsibilities, and if getting an appointment to see him was sometimes like trying to get an audience with the Pope, the benediction was always worth waiting for. Herb McCormick, BOC Challenge Media Relations Manager, supplied me with day-to-day communication faxes from skippers. Herb co-wrote the book *Out There* with George Day, about the inaugural 1982-83 race. It was a book that set a definitive target for which to aim.

Thanks are due to all the competitors, Robin Davie, Arnet Taylor, Niah Vaughan and Neal Petersen allowed me access to their daily log reports. Isabelle Autissier, Josh Hall, Minoru Saito, Jean-Luc Van den Heede, David Adams and Floyd Romack were also extremely helpful. At Race HQ Peter Dunning was always helpful.

When she wasn't working as shorecrew on the BOC yachts (chiefly *Thursday's Child*) Kate Ford was a freelance correspondent for two New England newspapers and unselfishly shared information. Kate has an eye for detail and a talent for writing that I envy. Other dockside shorecrew to thank are Merfyn Owen, Katie Paine, Arnet Taylor Snr and wife Anne, Skip Miller, Andy Darwent and Gwen Wilkinson, and in England *Cornwall*'s Carol Cook, *Jimroda II*'s Jim Gregg and in America *Hunter's Child*'s Tony Lush.

Verity Burgess, widow of Nigel who died at sea in the 1992 Vendée Globe Challenge, discovered the Jack London quotation (which appears on this book's dedication page) on a tablet in Sydney Harbour. I copied it down with her while Harry sat opposite me at the dinner table on his first night in Sydney, never knowing it would speak so eloquently as an epitaph for him.

In Australia I had help from Andrew (Aussie) and Vicky Bray, John Hornby, Ineen and Ted Donnelly and Craig Davis. Others to thank are Robin Knox-Johnston and Barry Pickthall, who co-wrote the official book of the 1986 BOC Challenge, Tony Barteleme of the *Charleston Post and Courier*, photographers Billy Black, Patrick and Karen Roach, Jacques Vapillon, John Nash at PPL, Gary John Norman, Cedric Robertson and Mark Pepper. Andrew Bray, Editor of *Yachting World* kindly allowed me access to his picture library. Tony Garrett drew the excellent chart for the endpapers.

Janet Murphy, my book editor at Adlard Coles Nautical, was patient and encouraging. Every author relies on someone like Janet to pull him through the hard times and keep to deadlines. Autohelm's sponsorship of the book and British Airways assistance with travel helped to smooth the progress of the project. I have my father to thank for first taking me sailing on a pond in Southwold, Suffolk, and then introducing me to journalism.

Finally, thanks are due to Peter Chance, responsible for the weather routeing computer software for the race, who urged me on when I almost fell at the first hurdle after a crisis of confidence in my raw material at the Cape Town stopover. Peter was eloquent in his entreaty that the story of unsung heroes like Harry *had* to be told. My wife Anne, and daughter, Laura, endured the lost weekends as I sat at my word processor or in foreign ports. Without them to come home to I could not have finished what Harry had started.

# 20 BOC Challengers and their Boats

## CLASS I

PATRICK ROACH

**Christophe Auguin** (36) of Cherbourg, France. A professional yachtsman, he won the last BOC Challenge at the age of 30. He began sailing at five when his father took him on the family boat. He graduated to offshore events and Formula 40 catamarans before winning the Figaro, France's prestigious solo marathon, in 1986. He founded and operates Mer et Communications, a sports marketing company. His hobbies are scuba diving, skiing and paragliding.
**Yacht: Sceta Calberson**, like his previous BOC winner, is a Finot/Conq design. The 60ft sloop has a beam of 19ft and a draught of 14ft 8in.

PAUL GELDER

**Isabelle Autissier** (37) of La Rochelle, France. An engineer and marine science professor returning for her second BOC Challenge after placing seventh as the first woman ever to finish the global classic. In 1994, in her radical new yacht *EPC2*, she slashed eight days off the record of the New York San Francisco race around Cape Horn. She has sailed since she was seven.
**Yacht: Ecureuil Poitou Charentes 2** is a 60ft cutter designed by Jean Berret with a canting keel, a beam of 17ft 8in and a draught of 14ft 10in.

PATRICK ROACH

**Mark Gatehouse** (45) of Plymouth, England. The son of Richard Gatehouse, founder of the marine instrument company Brookes & Gatehouse. Mark operates Queen Anne's Battery Marina in Plymouth, and has been sailing since childhood. A veteran of many shorthanded races, including singlehanded and two-handed Transatlantics, Round Britain and Ireland, and Azores and Back, this was to be his first long distance race.

**Yacht: Queen Anne's Battery**, a 60ft aluminium ketch, built in 1986 – no stranger to the BOC having won the second (1986-87) race as *Credit Agricole III*, skippered by Philippe Jeantot.

**Josh Hall** (32) of Ipswich, England. Back for his second BOC, but competing for the first time in a Class I 60-footer sponsored by a British investment banking company. Josh raced in Class II in the last BOC Challenge in the 50ft *Spirit of Ipswich*, sponsored by 30 local businesses. He dislocated his knee in the Southern Ocean and finished the race in a surgical brace. He began dinghy sailing in childhood and helped to build the catamaran *British Airways*, spending three years sailing with Robin Knox-Johnston.

**Yacht: Gartmore Investment Managers** built in 1986 will be starting her fourth circumnavigation. She raced in the 1989 Vendée Globe non stop race as *Lada Poch III*, in the last BOC Challenge as *BBV Expo '92*, and the 1986 BOC as *Ecureuil d'Aquitaine*.

**Steve Pettengill** (43) of Newport, Rhode Island, USA. Conceived aboard a boat on Lake Michigan in 1951, he has been sailing ever since and has more than 150,000 sailing miles to his credit. He is a businessman, boatbuilder and professional ocean racer. For five years he held the New York-San Francisco sailing record with the trimaran *Great American*. He survived a trimaran capsize at Cape Horn during another record attempt.

**Yacht: Hunter's Child** serves as a floating test bed for the Hunter Marine Corporation. Designed by Bergstrom and Ridder, this high tech solo racing machine held the record for the best 24 hour run by a 60ft monohull at 344 miles. Her exotic features include an air induction venturi slot to reduce surface friction and a cantilevered rudder.

**Jean Jacques (JJ) Provoyeur** (44) of Cape Town, South Africa. Known to friends as JJ he started sailing at 13. He runs a boatbuilding company and chandlery adjacent to the Royal Cape Yacht Club and originally built *Ben Vio* for well known South African sailor Bertie Reed, who raced her as *Grinaker* in the 1989 Vendée Globe and the last BOC. JJ took over Reed's entry in the 1994 BOC six weeks before re-launching the yacht.

**Yacht: Ben Vio**, renamed *Novell South Africa*, is a Rodger Martin designed 60ft sloop with a 15ft beam and 11ft 3in draught.

CEDRIC ROBERTSON/PPL

**David Scully** (39) of Dwight, Illinois, USA. A skier, rock climber and racing car driver who once wind surfed across Lake Michigan, Scully quit his job as a commodities broker in Chicago and moved to France to pursue sailing sponsorship opportunities. He has raced in the America's Cup in Fremantle and on the record breaking trimaran *Lakota* with Steve Fosset.

**Yacht: Coyote** is a 60ft Rodger Martin design with an extreme 21ft beam and 14ft draught. Built for owner-skipper Mike Plant, she lost the bulb from her keel and capsized in mid Atlantic in 1992 on her way to the start of the Vendée Globe. Plant was lost at sea.

DAVID GILES/PPL

**Arnet Taylor** (44) of Portsmouth, New Hampshire, USA. Arnet started sailing from the age of eight on the family Sunfish. He has logged more than 30,000 miles in 20 years, much of it solo, and holds a 100 ton Master's licence. After a career in boatbuilding and fisheries management he is affiliated with a marine engineering and consulting firm as well as a company that renovates historic buildings.

**Yacht: Thursday's Child** is an earlier and legendary version of *Hunter's Child* built in 1983 and designed by Lars Bergstrom, Paul Lindenberg and Warren Luhrs for the 1984 OSTAR. The first of the Open 60 class boats, she won the OSTAR and has started two previous BOC Challenges but never finished. Named as one of the 100 greatest sailing yachts in America by *Sail* magazine. Considered a 'high tech antique' by Taylor.

MARK PEPPER

**Jean-Luc Van den Heede** (49) of Les Sables D'Olonne, France. A former maths teacher and sailing instructor for the French Glenans Nautical Centre, Van den Heede has sailed around the world three times in eight years: in the 1989-90 Vendée Globe in *Let's Go*, in the 1992-93 Vendée Globe in *Groupe Sofap Helvim* and in the 1986 BOC in *Let's Go* . His yawl is sponsored by various French businesses in the Vendée region.

**Yacht: Vendée Enterprises** a 60ft yawl built in 1991 with a beam of 12ft 6in and a draught of 14ft 2in.

## CLASS II

**David Adams** (40) of Fairlight, NSW, Australia. David is a master mariner addicted to pushing the limits at sea. Months before the BOC Challenge Adams accompanied fellow competitor Isabelle Autissier on her first attempt to break the clipper ship *Flying Cloud*'s record from New York to San Francisco via Cape Horn in *EPC2*. He also competed in the 1990 BOC in the 60 footer *Innkeeper*. He came sixth.

PATRICK ROACH

**Yacht: True Blue** is a 50 footer specially designed by Scott Jutson and built by John Sayer of Mooloolaba, north of Brisbane, Australia.

PATRICK ROACH

**Simone Bianchetti** (26) of Marchesato, Italy. Born in Cervia, a fishing village on the Adriatic Sea. Simone began sailing as a boy of 14 and served two years in the Italian military coastguard. He has twice won the Rimini-Corfu-Rimini race.

**Yacht: Town of Cervia** is a 50 footer designed by Roberto Starkel and built in Ravenna, Italy, in 1987.

**Robin Davie** (44) of St Agnes, Cornwall, England. Robin first went to sea on the sail training schooner *Sir Winston Churchill* as a 16th birthday gift. He has been a Merchant Navy Officer for 22 years and served two years in the Falklands (1982-84) with the British Task Force. He built his own 40 foot ferrocement yacht and sailed it to Cape Town to qualify for the first BOC Race, but he decided she was too slow. He raced *Cornwall* in the last BOC under the name *Global Exposure* and came second in the Corinthian Class.

BILLY BLACK

**Yacht:** *Cornwall* is a 40ft centre cockpit Hurley Tailwind, a Lars Bergstrom design built in Plymouth in 1973. The oldest and smallest boat in the BOC.

PATRICK ROACH

**Harry Mitchell** (70) of Portsmouth, England. Born April 24 1924. His adventurous roots come, perhaps, from his father, a pilot in the First World War Flying Corps, and his mother, Muriel, a qualified commercial pilot who took people up for joyrides. After a career in aviation in Canada, Harry returned to Portsmouth to help run the family car rental business and bought a 33ft yacht, becoming increasingly active in offshore singlehanded sailing. He completed the 1976 and 1992 solo transatlantic races. This is his third attempt to complete a BOC Challenge.

**Yacht: Henry Hornblower** (previously *Mitak*) is a 40ft Panic Class cutter, with lines drawn by Robert Nickerson and built in 1985 of fibreglass foam sandwich.

**Alan Nebauer** (31) of NSW, Australia. Alan began sailing dinghies at the age of 12 and joined his first ocean going 40ft yacht for the 600 mile Sydney-Hobart race when he was 16. He has sailed more than 40,000 miles, crossing the Pacific and sailing to Canada with his wife, Cindy, to study at Bible College.
**Yacht: Newcastle Australia** is a 50 footer designed by Lyons/Laubreaux and built by former BOC skipper Kanga Birtles specially for the 1994-95 BOC Challenge.

BILLY BLACK

BILLY BLACK

**Neal Petersen** (27) of Cape Town, South Africa. Born with a congenital bone disease that left him without a ball and socket joint in one hip, Neal was unable to walk until he was seven. His father, a commercial diver, taught him to swim as part of his therapy and this started his love affair with the sea. Swimming strengthened his hip and he later trained in America as a commercial diver, returning home to Africa to dive for diamonds. He is currently based in Galway, Ireland.
**Yacht: Protect Our Sealife** is a 40ft cold moulded yacht designed by Goulooze and Neal, and built in Cape Town by Neal. 'The boat is my symbol of what can be achieved,' says Neal, who sailed her in the 1992 Eurostar solo Transatlantic Race and the two-handed Round Britain and Ireland Race.

**Floyd Romack** (66) of New Jersey, USA. A pharmacist by training, Floyd runs a restaurant in Cape May, NJ, and has been trying to do the BOC for 12 years. His yacht is named after his heart attack in 1988, which postponed his last attempt. While other sailors are backed by corporate sponsors, Floyd is one of the Corinthians who took out a second mortgage to finance his dream.
**Yacht: Cardiac 88**, a 49ft cutter designed by Soveral Crealock and built by Seamaster Marine in 1990. Extensively refitted by Floyd.

TOM BENN/PPL

PAUL GELDER

**Nigel Rowe** (53) of London, England, is taking a leave of absence as the BOC Group's Chief Executive of Corporate Communications – the man responsible for the sponsorship of the BOC Challenge back in 1982. He skippered his own boats in the 1985 Round Britain and Ireland Race, and the solo and two-handed Transatlantic races in 1988 and 1990. He came to sailing comparatively late at the age of 40.
**Yacht: Sky Catcher** is a customised and stretched Hunter Legend 45, originally built in 1988 as a development project by Hunter Marine in Florida.

**Minoru Saito** (60) of Minato Ku, Japan. A native of Tokyo, Minoru is 61 and sailed his first major race in 1987 in the Melbourne-Osaka Yamaha Cup, and was placed third in the 1989 Auckland-Fukuoka Race. He completed the 1988 solo Japan-Sydney Race and, before a heart attack forced his withdrawal, was an entrant in the Around Australia Race in 1988, which he helped organise. Shuten Dohji II was a monster who lived on a mountain in Japanese mythology. The name translates as 'Son of a Drunk'.

**Yacht: Shuten Dohji II** is a 50ft centre cockpit cutter designed by Adams/Radford and built by former BOC competitor Don McIntyre in 1990 to Minoru's commission.

PATRICK ROACH

PAUL GELDER

**Giovanni Soldini** (28) of Milan, Italy. This irrepressible Italian sailed *Servant IV* (winner under Yves Dupasquier of Class II in the last BOC) in the Quebec-St Malo Race when she sank. His new 50-footer was built with the help of recovering drug addicts in a rehabilitation programme in Italy.

**Yacht: Kodak**, designed by Jean Berret is nicknamed 'The Bullet'. It is a light, simple 50-footer with a towering sail plan, minimal headroom below decks and spartan accommodation. She has a beam of 14ft and a draught of 13ft.

**Chaniah (Niah) Vaughan** (49) of Whitehaven, England. A former professional rugby league football player, Niah Vaughan came to sailing at 35 with a production Sadler cruising yacht. He has worked as a construction surveyor, diver and engineer, and is promoting historic Whitehaven's harbour redevelopment on his global voyage.

**Yacht: Jimroda II** is a Rodger Martin designed cutter starting on her third BOC Challenge. She was custom built by the late American sailor Mike Plant, who skippered her to a class victory in the 1986 BOC as *Airco Distributor*. In 1990 Josh Hall sailed her to third place in Class II as *Spirit of Ipswich*.

BILLY BLACK

# 1 · Living on the Edge

They didn't look out of the ordinary, these intrepid high seas heroes, gathered on the dockside in America's Deep South, at Charleston, South Carolina. And they were certainly too modest to lay claim to any heroics. But in a few days, at High Noon on Saturday 17 September 1994, the starting gun would sound for nineteen lone yachtsmen and one woman to set off on a 27,000 mile singlehanded round-the-world odyssey called the BOC Challenge. It is the longest race on earth for an individual in any sport. The event is sub-titled, quite simply, Around Alone.

'They all have this dream. It's an epic adventure. The problem is they might die doing it,' explained weather router Peter Chance, who thought he'd like to try it himself one day.

If you encountered any of these individuals walking down your local high street – they are aged from 26 to 70 – you'd find it impossible, as I did, to discover any distinguishing characteristics that mark them out from the crowd. The only clues that might betray their extraordinariness is an intense look in the eyes, a lean muscular fitness, and an ability to catnap and cope with a very few hours sleep in every 24. Among the competitors was a marine scientist, a grandfather, a business executive, a French ex-maths teacher, a New Jersey restaurant proprietor, a South African commercial diver and two merchant mariners.

Simply getting to the start line of the longest, loneliest yacht race is an act of courage and sacrifice that few could contemplate. A total of 40 sailors threw their hats in to the ring in advance of the entry deadline for the BOC Challenge, but only half that number made it to the Charleston start. By the finish, eight months later, the attrition rate had whittled that down to 12.

The BOC Challenge is really two races round the world by two distinct breeds of sailors scattered across the two classes: Class I, for yachts 50-60 feet in length, is where you find the superstars: professionals like Christophe Auguin, winner of the last BOC, Isabelle Autissier, Jean-Luc Van den Heede and Steve Pettengill, who get paid for sailing. They command big budgets and corporate sponsorship. They are in the race to win. Their exotic, space-age yachts are nicknamed 'aircraft carriers' or 'flying saucers' for their wide beams and flat decks and they are among the fastest monohulls in the world for their size. They can *average* speeds of more than 15 knots, with surfing speeds exceeding 25 knots. But not all Class I sailors are paid a salary and enjoy unlimited budgets. Some, like Britain's Josh

Hall, America's Arnet Taylor and David Scully sank a lot of their own money into the race and were not paid to risk their lives.

Class II, for yachts of 40-50 feet, is where you find the majority of the so-called 'amateurs' or Corinthians. Their seamanship skills may be equal to their fellow Class 1 competitors, but in almost everything else the struggle is unequal. Campaigning smaller boats helps to keep down costs, but very often they have shoestring budgets and their yachts are old boats refitted from previous races. They compete with a mixture of faith, hope and, if they can get it, charity. The best of the Class II yachts, though ten feet shorter, will give the fastest of the big boats a run for their not inconsiderable money. But while Class II also had its sponsored professionals, like Australia's David Adams and Italy's Giovanni Soldini, there are also the unpaid tail-end Charlies who have no realistic chance of winning. For them it is like setting off in the family Ford Escort saloon to race Nigel Mansell's Formula I car. These are the underdogs for whom the race is an organised adventure in which to finish is to win, thus joining the select ranks of those who have circumnavigated the globe solo.

Why do they all do it, enduring freezing cold, mountainous seas, gales, icebergs and loneliness in the spartan confines of a living area half the size of most people's kitchens? Certainly not for the money. No cash (even the quarter of a million dollars prize money) could compensate for living on a knife edge of survival. For most of the race, the nearest help will be a fellow competitor. Deep comradeship is a motivating factor for this elite group of adventurers; they fight their own battles, but they are in the war together.

Some are fugitives from the rat race, eager to escape the grinding routine and mundane responsibilities to which the rest of us submit ourselves, willingly or not. Not for them the 0820 to Waterloo, notching up commuter miles and becoming a rush-hour warrior. Others, rather than 'running away to sea' are, perhaps, running towards some inner confrontation with themselves. These solo yachtsmen are racing against the elements, against an invisible fleet somewhere over the horizon, and against their own doubts and fears. To singlehand a yacht 27,000 miles requires skill as well as daring: you have to look after yourself and your boat, navigating, cooking, trimming the sails, coping with a constant list of maintenance and repairs – all this must go on even when spirits reach their lowest ebb. There is no one to share the moment, whether everything is going right or disastrously wrong. The BOC Challenge is an endurance marathon in which everyone who finishes is a winner. There are no losers.

Ask a solo sailor why he does it and you'll get a dozen different answers, none of them satisfactory to those of us who lead conventional lives. 'I'm out there to scare the living daylights out of myself,' said Britain's Josh Hall, with uncanny prescience, on the dockside of Charleston's downtown marina a few days before the start. 'I believe we're all addicted to living on the edge sometimes.' A few weeks later Josh would be granted his 'wish' but not quite in the manner he had foreseen.

The T-shirt worn by the American skipper of *Hunter's Child*, Steve Pettengill, exclaimed: 'If you're not living on the edge, you're taking up too much space.' As journalist Kate Ford said: 'The edge is why they come, sleep-deprived, cold and wet, putting themselves in debt … '

The late solo yachtsman Phil Weld, who won the 1980 Observer Singlehanded

*The exotic space-age yachts in Class I are nicknamed 'aircraft carriers' for their wide beams and flat decks.* PHOTO: CEDRIC ROBERTSON / PPL

Transatlantic Race (OSTAR) at the age of 65, put together a list of reasons for sailing solo: 'Voyaging provides a sense of adventure that animates youthful souls. It nourishes the explorer instinct, hardens the physique ... it's a low-cost health cure ... it sharpens the perceptions ... learning new skills stimulates the brain ... it commands recognition ... one gets some hints of The Scheme. On deck alone at dawn there's time and quiet to ponder the verities.' And with humour: 'How else can a man my age get his name on the sports page?'

Three words sum up the compulsion that drives these brave souls to attempt the Everest of sailing: 'Because it's there.' The history of climbing the sailors' Everest is not yet 100 years old. The first man to reach the peak was Joshua Slocum, grandfather of singlehanders, who set off from Boston Harbour on 24 April 1895 at the age of 51 to become the first man to sail alone around the world in *Spray*. Nearly 70 years later, Francis Chichester captured everyone's imagination when, at 65, he set out in his ketch *Gypsy Moth IV* on a one-stop circumnavigation. He returned a national hero in 1967 to be knighted by the Queen at Greenwich. Chichester's voyage sparked adventure in the hearts of others who read his best-selling book *Gypsy Moth Circles the World*. His voyage became the catalyst for the first non-stop singlehanded race around the world – The Sunday Times Golden Globe.

A year after Chichester's triumphant return, a tiny 33ft teak ketch slipped almost unnoticed out of Falmouth Harbour, Cornwall. Her skipper was 30-year-old British Merchant Navy Officer Robin Knox-Johnston, who sailed himself and his yacht, *Suhaili*, into the history books after 312 days to become the first man to circle the globe non stop. There were nine others in the race, including Chay Blyth, who later went on to make the first solo voyage the 'wrong way' round the world, against prevailing winds. Stories from them and others inspired a new generation of yachtsmen. But it would be 13 years before the next solo round the world race – the BOC Challenge – was launched on 28 August 1982 at Newport, Rhode Island. The BOC Group (formerly the British Oxygen Company) is a worldwide organisation dealing in industrial gases and health care. They saw the race as an opportunity to promote business in key markets around the world.

Robin Knox-Johnston, Race Director of the first BOC Challenge, says that 'in no other challenge is a person forced to rely to such an extent on his or her own resources, or placed as far from assistance in the event of emergency. In all other sports, when the contestant gets tired or conditions deteriorate, he can drop out or camp until things improve. When conditions deteriorate at sea the sailor must stay awake and alert, handling the boat for his own preservation. Add to that the sheer mental and physical effort to survive plus the pressure of racing and the prospect becomes enough to daunt even the stoutest heart.'

In the three previous BOC Challenges, 67 sailors have crossed the start line, but only 44 have reached the finish. There have been shipwrecks, sinkings, dramatic rescues in the Southern Ocean and the death of Frenchman Jacques de Roux in the 1986-87 race. His yacht was found drifting off Australia with no one aboard. Several other skippers were lucky to be rescued from sinking yachts by fellow competitors, often thousands of miles from land at the bottom of the globe. Some exhausted skippers have slept while their vessels have run aground.

One of the endearing characteristics of the BOC Challenge is that it embraces a motley crew of competitors. As corporate sponsorship has grown, with marketing men demanding ever increasing professionalism, it is refreshing that the BOC Challenge doesn't discourage the mavericks, making room for the tortoises as well as the rocket ships. As more money is poured into sport, and high profile publicity machines get bigger, the nature of those taking part changes irrevocably. The days of Blondie Hasler's half-crown wager that led to the first single-handed transatlantic yacht race in 1960, won by Francis Chichester, are long gone. But while the gap between the sponsor-rich yachtsman and the impoverished amateur adventurer has stretched, the 1994 BOC Challenge still had its share of colourful characters. There was still something of the atmosphere of the trail-blazing OSTARs.

Seventy-year-old grandfather Harry Mitchell, personified one extreme of competitor, the Corinthian, and was everyone's favourite skipper. Sailing one of the smallest and oldest boats in the fleet, the Panic Class 40 footer *Henry Hornblower*, he had no sponsors and asked for no charity. He owed nothing to anybody but himself. Asked why he was competing he would joke: 'Somebody's got to come last, haven't they?!' His celebrated underwear dance had already gained him a reputation in Charleston at the yacht club. And when a friend's yacht had gone aground in Charleston Harbour Harry, sunbathing naked, had waved to the US Coastguard cutter as it motored past asking if he needed assistance.

Dockside spectators in Charleston who came to meet the skippers and view their boats were told by Harry, the practical joker, when they asked if he was the skipper, 'No, you want to speak to my uncle,' pointing at fellow competitor Floyd Romack working in the cockpit of his yacht opposite.

Harry's attempts to avoid publicity and throw reporters off the scent were legendary. It was typical of his modesty that he called himself a retired garage mechanic when, in fact, he had been a partner in a car hire firm. On the stern of tiny *Henry Hornblower*, Harry, along with Floyd Romack, had stencilled the letters 'OF Club' for Old Farts Club. 'The BOC is the only yacht race where golden oldies like Floyd and myself can take part and prove that youth isn't the final answer to motivation,' said Harry, who had arrived in Charleston after competing in the inaugural 3,500 mile BOC Transatlantic Challenge, a feeder race from Falmouth. Harry, the oldest competitor, had sailed in to Charleston five hours ahead of the youngest competitor, Neal Petersen. He was fourth over the line out of seven in his class, though a 22 hour penalty for reporting late to the Falmouth start gave him a corrected time of 34 days 15 hours.

Harry's romance with the sea went back to his days in the Sea Scouts in Portsmouth, on the South Coast. He used to watch the last of the clipper ships sailing up the English Channel under full canvas, knowing they had sailed around Cape Horn. 'I'd see the sailors with the golden earrings and ask them about it. They told me it was a mark of having accomplished that feat. I thought "One day I am going to wear that earring".'

Of the BOC Challenge Harry said: 'I've got two objectives. To get the earring and do it despite my age. If I fail this time maybe when I'm 74 I'll have another go!' But he also admitted: 'It's not the Challenge it once was. Too many people have done it and the professionalism now means amateurs like me stand no chance.'

His affair with sailing began in the late 1940s when he chartered yachts and sailed across the English Channel to France with friends, including a young girl, Diana, who would later become his wife. In 1963 Harry bought his first boat, a 33ft wooden sloop, *Tuloa*. His adventures came in increments as he gradually extended his experience. After crossing the Channel, the next goal he set himself was to get round Ushant, that graveyard of ships and men. Then he ventured into the Bay of Biscay. In 1970 he made his qualifying cruise for the Observer Singlehanded Transatlantic Race by sailing from the Hamble River to Lisbon, returning singlehanded and covering more than 1,600 miles on the round trip.

His first attempt to cross the Atlantic in the 1972 OSTAR ended in retirement when *Tuloa* sprang a leak. But he entered the 1976 race and this time he and *Tuloa* made it across the pond in 41 days, coming a creditable 53rd out of a starting fleet of 125. More than 50 yachts retired, with sinkings, dismastings and one boat which caught fire and sank.

The lure of a more epic passage and the rounding of Cape Horn remained. Harry had wanted to do the first BOC Challenge race in 1982, but was unable to take time off from work. When he retired in 1983, he sent off his entry fee for the 1986-87 race. He still had his old sloop *Tuloa*, which he kept undercover in a boatyard shed 'for my retirement'. But he bought Robin Aisher's famous Admiral's Cup yacht *Yeoman XX*, affectionately known as 'Kiss Kiss', to sail around the world. Harry had threatened to rename her by her nickname, but settled, instead, for *Double Cross*. The yacht was more than enough for a singlehander, having previously been raced by a crew of nine. Harry brought her halfway round the globe before going aground on a sandbar at the southern tip of New Zealand, while seeking assistance after a storm. He saved the yacht, but the race ended for him. Four years later he got himself a new boat and called her *We are Lovers* hoping that she might respond to his touch more surely. In the end he was to say that she gave him 'a bloody nose'. He was crossing the Atlantic, enroute to the start of the 1990-91 race, when he was in collision with a freighter. A damaged bow section forced his return to Plymouth and once again his hopes of rounding Cape Horn were dashed.

It typified the spirit of the event that, having repaired his yacht and renamed her *Henry Hornblower*, Harry was in Charleston to make his third attempt on the Horn. 'By the time you reach retirement age people want you to settle down to a sedate life, but I'm lucky to be fit enough to do this race,' he said. He had brought his rusty old bicycle across in his yacht to cycle around town and keep fit, too.

Down below, in the clutter of equipment there wasn't much that was high-tech or exotic about Harry's yacht. His most sophisticated electronic equipment was borrowed for the duration of the race. His basic boat had cost him some £50,000 and he had budgeted for spending another £40,000 on his campaign. His reclining navigation seat was a secondhand car seat bought in a Miami scrapyard for $75.

Corinthians like Harry Mitchell are unique because of the additional sacrifices, mental and physical endurance, they are called upon to make in a race like the BOC Challenge. Sailing smaller, slower boats, they spend twice as long at sea as the front-runners, exposing themselves to more danger and enduring more storms. For them it is the loneliest race. And when they reach port there is no paid shore crew waiting to carry out their list of repairs. They rely on volunteer help.

The twenty yachts tied up to the docks readying themselves for the start of the fourth BOC Challenge were certainly an eclectic mix: breathtaking 'higher-tech' one offs, with tilting keels and swivelling bowsprits; revamped production yachts, and one yacht that had been built in a backyard at home. And the contrasts between the competitors were as varied as their machines.

For the first time in a BOC Challenge, Britannia ruled the waves with a contingent of six British sailors outnumbering all other nations. But only three of them, Harry Mitchell, Robin Davie and Josh Hall, had faced the fury of the Southern Ocean before. After years masterminding the organisation of the race, Nigel Rowe, Chief Executive of Corporate Communications for the BOC Group, was gamekeeper turned poacher. At 53 he had decided to take a sabbatical from his six-figure salary to compete in the race himself. It was to be a punctuation point in his life – 'a chance to stop the world and get off for a year'. In a symbolic gesture to himself after hosting a BOC lunch in London's Soho for the British yachtsmen and their wives, Nigel had taken off his tie outside the restaurant and stuffed it in a rubbish bin in Tottenham Court Road. He was another man for whom a dream had turned into a consuming obsession. The ex-business executive didn't think he would be able to go back to being 'a five-days-a-week suit' after the race. But the adventurer in him wasn't quite sure how much the next eight months would be a life-changing experience. 'There are degrees of success I fantasise about and ones of failure I don't even want to think about,' he said.

Unlike most of the others Nigel had come to sailing relatively late, at 40. His first singlehanded race across the Atlantic had been six years ago. 'I'm probably the least experienced person in the race,' he said. 'I expect to be scared to death several times. But I'll try not to be last. There is, after all, a safety factor in having someone else behind you ...'

Nigel had sunk his life savings into the venture with a quarter of a million dollars tied up in his yacht, *Sky Catcher*, a heavily customised 48-footer named for her tall (72ft) rig. He called her 'a fast boat with a slow driver.' He was in the race to finish, with little thought of winning his class. But when he unexpectedly found himself the winner of the Transatlantic Challenge his competitive edge was hardened. Claiming he was no 'Mr Fixit', he had lots of built-in redundancy in his yacht, anticipating breakdowns. His back-ups included five different ways to steer the boat and four ways to generate power. He also employed a Florida marine architect, Skip Miller, as shore crew at stopovers. Nigel was the first to admit that his career had been spent in the comfort of the corporate womb of large international companies with others to take care of things for him in offices, planes and hotels around the world.

Perhaps the race was a chance to get back to basics and put aside his Armani suits, Jean-Paul Gautier spectacles and Lotus sports car. But Nigel wasn't forsaking all luxuries. He was a man who did things in style. The kettle on his galley stove came from Harrods, and along with the bland freeze-dried food he had stowed away a few extravagances from Fortnum & Mason. The connoisseur of fine wines and the opera buff also had a few select bottles and compact discs among his provisions. By the halfway stage of the race, Nigel would have surprised himself with his resourcefulness at fixing things that broke on *Sky Catcher*.

Among the Corinthian Brits, few had struggled harder to get to the start line than 43-year-old Merchant Navy officer Robin Davie, sailing the oldest boat in the race and one of the three 40-footers. Renamed *Cornwall* and painted in Cornish black and gold colours, Robin had sailed the yacht round the world in the last BOC race as *Global Exposure*. The voyage had taken 181 days. 'She's a heavy agricultural boat,' he admitted. Appropriately, he had been to horse shows and carnivals in Cornwall, towing his yacht there and selling T-shirts, posters, and postcards to raise sponsorship money. In the last race, Robin had charged five dollars for tours of his yacht in Newport, he had written to 800 companies and run 336 miles around Cornwall, all part of his fundraising effort. Once again money and sponsors were in short supply and the yacht hadn't had the refit it needed after the last race. Instead, it had been hauled out of the water and left in the boatyard for three years until it was time to give her a new paint job for the 1995 race. In the last few days in Charleston Robin sold enough T-shirts to bolt down a couple of new winches the night before the start of the race. A local dealer donated a cassette stereo with waterproof speakers so he was wired for sound on the ocean. The only thing Robin had changed on his 21-year-old Hurley Tailwind was the mast section. It was to prove an ironic piece of caution. 'I'd love to have a 60ft boat and I'm very disappointed I can't compete to win, but there's a lot of luck attached to this race,' Davie told one of his well-wishers at the dockside in America.

The other 40-footer in the race was *Protect Our Sealife*, which had been designed and built by the 27-year-old South African Neal Petersen in his grandmother's backyard outside Cape Town. More than anyone else Neal was doing the race on a wing and a prayer. He had borrowed the entry fee and then, despairing at his lack of funds and the seemingly insurmountable problems before he even left Falmouth on the transatlantic feeder race, he phoned home in tears ready to quit the race. An 11th hour benefactor took him and his girlfriend Gwen home for a four course meal and a night in a proper bed, instead of his yacht's bunk. Neal was back working on the boat next afternoon with renewed vigour. 'Never having money doesn't mean you can't make your dream come true,' he said. But his troubles were far from over. He faced the toughest journey of all across the Atlantic when something as simple as a failed jubilee clip nearly cost him his yacht and his life. The discharge hose from the bilge pump was leaking back into the boat's anchor locker. Water found its way into the second watertight compartment through a leaking observation hatch. Petersen, asleep, was woken by the sluggish performance of his yacht. At one stage he estimated he had two and a half tons of water in the forward compartment. He was getting ready to abandon ship. It was blowing 35 knots and he got the sails down and the liferaft ready to go over the rail. It took him four hours to pump her dry.

'How much can a man actually do to simplify his life?' he wrote in his logbook. 'I'm down to real basics: sleep when tired, eat when hungry, cry when lonely. But it's all shaped by the wind and sea. I'm hanging in here. Harry (Mitchell) is brilliant on the radio, giving me lots of encouragement.'

After his gas regulator failed Neal couldn't cook a hot meal for more than two weeks and ate cold canned potatoes, peaches, chocolate and nuts. When the young sailor finally got to Charleston he simply said: 'Thank God for watertight bulkheads.' Those on shoestring budgets risked paying the highest price of all – their lives.

The animated and talkative South African attracted phenomenal support for his cause in Charleston. There were so many helpers that he was almost redundant on his own boat. Hours before the start it seemed as if *Protect Our Sealife* was being rebuilt. A new anchor locker hatch was being sealed into position and a hardtop GRP spray dodger was being custom built over the companionway. Also working on Neal's yacht was Bill Pinkney, the first black man to do a solo circumnavigation of the five capes in 1990-92. 'It's not luck that got me where I am today, but the fact that I never believed what I was told about my chances to succeed,' said Pinkney, who had set out to be a role model for underprivileged children. Petersen, hoping to be a role model for minorities himself, was busy fitting an old solar panel, a gift from fellow competitor Mark Gatehouse, one of several skippers who had donated equipment and skills to Neal's cause.

Gatehouse, the fourth Brit in the race, was a quiet self-deprecating man sailing *Queen Anne's Battery*. Gatehouse was really a two-handed racer. His first and last solo race had been across the Atlantic in 1992 and his longest time alone at sea to date was 22 days, but he had always wanted to do a round-the-world race. 'This is old man's sailing,' he had joked. 'You only tack once a week.' He also contended that there were two kinds of solo sailors: 'Those who are so in love with themselves they want to sail alone, and those so unpopular that they *have* to sail on their own.' Gatehouse had lightened his aluminium boat by more than a ton, reducing the number of winches from 17 to 6 and drilling holes in everything that wasn't structural. Down below the yacht looked like a cross between a spacecraft from the film *Alien* and a metallic Swiss cheese.

The British sextet was completed by Josh Hall (32) and Chaniah Vaughan (49). Josh, like Robin Davie, had completed a circumnavigation in the last BOC Challenge sailing his 50-footer *New Spirit of Ipswich*, which he had now sold to Vaughan to compete with in Class II. Josh was stepping up to Class I with the 60-footer *Gartmore Investment Managers*. It would be the yacht's fourth time

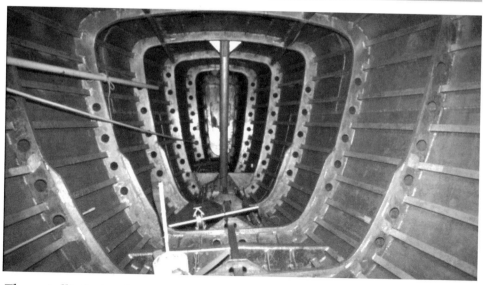

*The metallic Swiss cheese interior of Mark Gatehouse's* Queen Anne's Battery, *looking like a set from the film* Alien. PHOTO: PATRICK ROACH

around the globe. The fact that Josh's yacht was emblazoned with sponsors' names did not detract from the fact that he had struggled to make ends meet and had a considerable investment in the yacht himself. From a childhood of dinghy sailing, Josh had got his big break when he helped to build the catamaran *British Airways* and spent the next three years sailing with Robin Knox-Johnston. He was fifth in his class in the 1988 Singlehanded Transatlantic Race.

Niah Vaughan, the quiet man of the fleet, was a latecomer to sailing at the age of 35. A former professional rugby player from Cumbria, he had worked as an engineer, surveyor and diver in the oil industry in South Africa and Australia and had renamed Josh's old boat *Jimroda II* after his late parents. It would be the yacht's third time around in a BOC Challenge. The sea had featured prominently in Niah's life. His childhood was spent on the harbourside in Whitehaven, where his late father, James, was a fisherman. Two of his brothers, merchant seamen, were lost at sea.

For American Corinthian Arnet Taylor sailing the 11-year-old *Thursday's Child*, the BOC Challenge was like running a political campaign. 'You're always raising money and permanently bankrupt on any given day. There's a crisis every morning. A little more money would take some of the pressure off. I would be spending more time sailing and less time knocking on doors.' Arnet's total sponsorship from various companies was just $50,000. His boat, for which he had paid $140,000 was owned by a corporation in which he was a partner. He reckoned the race would cost him $300-500,000 even after selling the boat. 'This is probably one of the most self-indulgent exercises I have ever done. But no matter how singular this activity is, it's the result of lots of people's efforts on my behalf. Spiritually I should be in Class II. It's the way I feel.'

*Thursday's Child*, launched in 1983, was ahead of her time and bristled with so many ideas like water ballast and a pivoting rudder that other monohulls in her class had looked obsolete. Until 1989 she had held the New York-San

Francisco speed record and until 1993 the transatlantic speed record. But she had sailed 60,000 miles since the last refit. Now the hull had been stripped completely. 'We took out every piece of wiring and dropped the keel. There were 1,000 components on the shed floor,' said shore manager Merfyn Owen. The mast and boom had been replaced. Arnet already carried a 50 hour penalty having arrived in Charleston late for the start, but like the other underdogs, it was the race he was passionate about, not the result.

On Monday, five days before the start gun was fired, one competitor unexpectedly withdrew. Frenchman Yves Parlier, winner of the inaugural BOC Transatlantic Challenge dropped out with funding problems. His yacht *Cacolac D'Aquitaine* was named after a French chocolate drink manufacturer which sponsored him, but he needed one million francs ($200,000) for his BOC campaign and the money wasn't forthcoming. Now there were 20 skippers in the competition.

Meanwhile the lone woman in the race, Isabelle Autissier, who thought she had a short work list, arrived with a very long one. Sailing from Newport to Charleston, her yacht had buried its bow in a wave and the following sea had dumped a ton and a half of water in the cockpit, flooding the cabin, pinning Isabelle against the chart table and blowing all the electronics. Radios, autopilots and other equipment were destroyed. The yacht had to be rewired. 'My credit card is in the red and my crew and I have a lot of extra work,' she declared, 'but I will be ready for the start.'

Isabelle, a sailor since the age of seven, was the first woman to complete a BOC race last time around. She was hotly tipped to do well in this race with her yacht *Ecureuil Poitou-Charentes 2*. 'I can't see any reason why a woman should not do this race. I began cruising and crossed the Atlantic alone for fun. Then I began racing and thought it would be a challenge to combine the two and race alone.' Beneath her gentle manner this charming French engineer and marine science professor from La Rochelle concealed what someone once called 'a wickedly competitive determination'. With a crew of three aboard *EPC2* she had just slashed eight days off the record for the passage from New York to San Francisco around Cape Horn.

As the countdown to the start of the race got nearer that final week in Charleston the docksides reverberated to the sound of power drills, sanding machines and hammers. 'That's why they start races – so you can finally stop work on the boat!' said David Scully, a man with a million dollar machine – a radical high-tech 60ft flying saucer called *Coyote* – and a shoestring budget. The yacht had been built for America's best known solo yachtsman, Mike Plant, who had conceived her to race round the world non-stop himself. Tragically, *Coyote* had been found floating upside down in mid-Atlantic in 1992 with her bulb keel missing and no sign of Plant. Scully had chartered the yacht from Plant's former fiancée, Helen Davis, who had salvaged it and shipped it home to America to be extensively upgraded. In Indian lore the coyote, a prairie wolf, is a 'trickster who travels alone and eats sparingly'. Scully's campaign budget was certainly lean and he was hungry for success.

For all the competitors the last few days before the start of the race were exhilarating and exhausting in equal measure. Time was running out to complete work on the yachts – checking the rig for that loose shackle pin that could spell disaster in mid-ocean and ruin years of work and sacrifice – loading all their provisions for the 7,000 mile voyage to Cape Town, attending receptions and spending time with family and friends. The BOC is more than just a race, it's family and every race start, stopover and finish is a reunion. Among former competitors who were there to wish good luck were Americans David White, the founder of the race, and Tony Lush, Frenchman Philippe Jeantot, twice a BOC champion, Hungarian Nandor Fa and former Australian skippers Kanga Birtles and Don McIntyre.

Charleston, which had replaced Newport, Rhode Island, as the host city for the Challenge had made the race the centrepiece of the city's annual maritime festival and hundreds of people gathered around the marina to view the yachts. On the final night ashore before the race began people took their seats outside the marina for an open air bon voyage concert by Charleston Symphony Orchestra. With a cooling breeze offering welcome relief from a sultry night in the Deep South, each skipper was escorted on to the concert platform with the colours of his nation paraded before him as the national anthem played. Then they took their seats with wives and families as the programme of music from the competing nations was played: Vaughan Williams for Britain, Bizet for France and Rossini for Italy.

Sitting in the audience a few seats away from Harry and Diana Mitchell was sailor Deb Castellana from Florida. On her way to Charleston to see the boats she had told her husband, with a slight threat in her voice: 'Don't you even *think* of doing one of these BOC races!' Now after being in Charleston a few days she had decided that perhaps she might want to take part in the race herself one day. She had seen Harry on the docks working on his boat and now she watched him relaxing with Diana and their daughter, Marcia. Five months later, when Harry was heading for Cape Horn and his gold earring, Deb wrote to Diana: 'I must tell you what an inspiration you have been. I watched you and Harry at the concert that night. I am sure you were filled with worry, fear and concern about the trip ahead, but one couldn't see it. Your eyes were bright and twinkling and you were full of support for Harry's endeavour. It taught me so much about what it really is to be a good wife. Your strength and courage deserve an award as well as Harry's.'

The concert that night culminated in a spectacular firework display. As spectators drifted home, the French support crews were having their own party on the docks while some shore crews worked through the night in a desperate bid to tick the last job off the work schedule that had plagued them all week. There was even a Not the BOC Prizegiving. The awards included a tin of dog food for Helen Davis and *Coyote*, aspirin for Neal Petersen, 'who had been through a lot of headaches recently' and Ex-Lax for Harry Mitchell, 'who didn't give a shit'. Except that he did.

Harry, who estimated he had eaten 50 oysters and drunk too much champagne, was sleeping on *Henry Hornblower* on his last night in America 'so I can stow a few things on the boat myself and know where to find them when the excitement's all over ... '

One yacht would remain tied up to the dock after all the others had left for the start line next morning. Floyd Romack, the 66-year-old New Jersey restaurant owner, who had named his 50ft boat *Cardiac 88*, after his heart attack of that year, delayed his start for a week so that he could attend his daughter's wedding.

For years Floyd had wanted to sail around the world. 'The heart attack just accelerated my schedule,' he said. One day in May 1988 he was in his Cape May restaurant, Ocean Deck, talking to a friend when he felt pressure in his chest. Within an hour he was in hospital hooked up to machines pumping in a drug that dissolved blood clots. 'At one point my heart stopped and they gave me two shots of adrenaline and it brought me back to life. There was a nurse there who had worked for me as a waitress a few years back. I said, "How ya' doing?" and she said "A lot better than you!".'

Floyd had already tasted a different kind of adrenaline, sailing his yacht solo across the Atlantic and back for a second time to compete in the BOC Transatlantic Challenge. On the Charleston dockside he was a popular figure. 'When you have a heart attack or cancer, it's like a fraternity,' he said. 'People say I'm really boosting their day.'

His doctor told him: 'Floyd, I can't recommend that you should sail around the world, but I can't recommend anyone sailing round the world, so good luck!' Floyd had taken out a second mortgage to finance his dream.

'I've been a single parent since my divorce 20 years ago and I'm very close to my daughter. I'm happy with my decision to postpone. If I missed her wedding I wouldn't be able to race with a clear conscience. I know it will be difficult to catch up, but I have two goals. One to get around the world, the other to beat Harry Mitchell.'

For reigning BOC champion Christophe Auguin, competing in his flying saucer *Sceta Calberson*, one of the yachts using third millennium technology and steering by a joystick, the goal was different: 'At the end of the race I would like to speak better English than Giovanni!'

## *Charleston, South Carolina to Cape Town, South Africa (6,865 miles)*

# *2 · 27,000 Miles to Go*

A t noon on Saturday 17 September, under overcast skies and a 15 knot southerly breeze, the fleet of nineteen boats from seven nations jockeyed for position in an area ironically called 'the safety zone'. The start line was four miles offshore and the multitude of spectator craft threatened to swamp some of the competitors. There were close misses and heart-stopping moments.

Harry Mitchell on *Henry Hornblower* was blowing his brass foghorn as he cast off from the dockside thronged with cheering spectators. On board Harry's yacht was the 20th BOC skipper, Floyd Romack, who should have been sailing his own boat across the start line, but had been given permission to postpone his start for a week so he could attend his daughter's wedding. Also aboard were Harry's Charleston host, Eugene Fallaw, Jack Cowie, from IBM, and myself.

Soon after we'd cast off the tow line in the starting area, the wind died away and we found ourselves being swept perilously close to the 270ft US Coast Guard cutter *Northland* marking one end of the startline. Commander Rodney Raines admitted the incident 'raised his blood pressure a bit'. As we helplessly drifted to within 10ft of the wall of steel, the cutter went into astern and Floyd hailed a passing motorboat to throw us a tow line. With seconds to spare *Henry Hornblower* was plucked from danger. Harry, taking the drama in his stride, gave another encore on his foghorn for the spectators. Time was running out and his scratch crew bade him farewell and tumbled into transfer boats. Harry was alone.

Watching from the *Northland* was Mary Plant, for whom the race start was an especially poignant moment. Her son Mike had competed in both the 1986 and 1990 BOC Challenges. But in 1992 he was lost at sea on the maiden voyage of *Coyote*, which capsized when the yacht's keel fell off. It was refitted for the BOC Challenge and was now being sailed to Cape Town by David Scully. 'The boat is a tribute to Mike. To see the boat out there, and David Scully on his own, I said to myself "Mike, please take care of David'," said Plant's mother.

Choosing opposite ends of the start line, the two 50ft favourites in Class II led

*Anything to keep the boat lightweight. David Adams took his toilet off for leg one, but put it back for the southern ocean.* PHOTO: BILLY BLACK

the fleet when the start gun fired, with Australian David Adams' *True Blue* edging ahead of Italian Giovanni Soldini's *Kodak* by a boatlength. Not far behind was American Steve Pettengill on *Hunter's Child*. Defending French BOC champion, Christophe Auguin, sailing *Sceta Calberson*, was the only Class I competitor to start with a reefed mainsail.

As *Coyote*'s slim bow quickly accelerated to hull speed, skipper David Scully was adjusting the autopilot and doing a little sail trimming and tweaking. Then, deciding everything was just as it should be, he sat down on the weather rail, legs dangling, arms resting on the lifelines, and enjoyed the spectacle in which he was a leading player. Looking aft, he saw a chase boat full of spectators and a loud cheer carried across the water from those on board. Scully hoisted his arm and, with a broad smile on his face, acknowledged their good wishes. He looked calm, even relieved. Like other skippers, after years of determined preparation, Scully, a Paris-dwelling US expatriate married to a Frenchwoman, was finally alone, sailing his dream. He was a man with a million dollar yacht, which he had chartered, and a shoestring budget. Lack of funding was his Achilles' heel. 'It means you spend most of the time preparing your boat, instead of preparing yourself. You start the race tired and financing is a constant concern. That's a weakness and one I'm going to have to overcome to be competitive.'

The first emergency alert of this fourth BOC Challenge round the world race came just two hours after the start. A distress signal was picked up from the EPIRB (Emergency Position Indicating Radio Beacon) aboard Giovanni's yacht *Kodak*. Each yacht in the race carried at least two EPIRBS, devices that transmit an SOS signal, via a satellite, to agencies around the world, giving the yacht's

*Having trimmed and tweaked his sails, David Scully enjoys the spectacle of the Charleston start from the weather rail of* Coyote. PHOTO: PATRICK ROACH

name and position. EPIRBS could be activated either by the skipper or, on many yachts a unit was mounted on the yacht's stern rail, and would be deployed automatically if the boat sank and the skipper had to abandon ship. In this instance, Race co-ordinator Peter Dunning breathed a sigh of relief when the young Italian sent a message that his unit had been accidentally triggered. All was well aboard *Kodak.*

The same could not be said aboard *Newcastle Australia.* Skipper Alan Nebauer was working down below on his yacht some four hours into the race when he heard a huge thump underneath the boat. 'I was making 10 knots and it stopped the boat cold,' Nebauer said. Dashing on deck, he saw that he'd hit what looked like an abandoned raft. There was lots of flotsam scattered in the gulf stream – a legacy from the exodus of Cuban refugees fleeing to America. Alan had collided with a big wooden pallet, about eight feet wide, with flotation drums lashed on. It took him two hours to dislodge the various timber pieces and a length of rope caught around his keel. It would be another 5,000 miles, in totally unexpected circumstances, before the full extent of the damage became apparent.

Alan, who had dreamed of sailing round the world since he was eight, was sponsored by the city of Newcastle. He and his wife, Cindy, both committed Christians had cruised and lived aboard their 25ft sloop for five years and sailed 10,000 miles from Australia to Canada (via Tahiti and Hawaii) to study at Bible college. Down below Biblical quotes on yellow stickies surrounded the chart table. The bow of his yacht bore the legend: 'Seek the Lord while he may be found'.

Three hours after the start of the race, Arnet Taylor on *Thursday's Child* had Steve Pettengill in sight and was reaching along at 15 knots. He jumped down below for a snack bar and a drink of water when bam! the boat was flung over on its side. 'I flew up on deck and realised we'd gybed. The water ballast was on the wrong side, the rudder was sticking up in the air and alarms were going off all over the boat. I disengaged the autopilot and grabbed the helm. No response. It was jammed.' He had to heave to for five hours to try to fix things. By that first night everybody, including Harry Mitchell, had disappeared over the horizon.

As the boat rolled in 25 knots of wind and ten foot seas, Arnet battled to solve the problem with his jammed steering quadrant and autopilot. He knew then that leg one was going to be a game of catch-up. 'I spent more time fixing the boat than sailing it over the next few days. I thought of returning to Charleston, but gambled I could fix things underway.'

Conditions for the fleet's first night at sea were nearly perfect: a full moon and a fresh southerly breeze. As the rest of the fleet ploughed on through the night, one skipper did turn his yacht back to Charleston. Three hours after midnight, Italian Simone Bianchetti, at 25 the youngest skipper in the race, tied *Town of Cervia* up at Charleston docks to make repairs to his electronic autopilot. Arnet, his closest competitor, stayed in contact with him on VHF radio that night as he headed back. 'I wanted to encourage him to make the decision to press on, as I had, but realised that the nature of this race requires support for decisions already made, so I encouraged him to make the best of it. He was very upset.'

While the BOC skippers were busy trimming sails and charting a course to Cape Town, Floyd Romack, restaurateur and one-time pharmacist, was heading for Charleston International Airport to catch a flight to Philadelphia and then drive to his home in Cape May, New Jersey, to get ready to give away his only child, Adrianne, at her wedding later that week. 'It was sad watching everyone go without me, but I'll catch up,' he vowed.

At dusk towards the back of the fleet, Romack's close friend Harry Mitchell was enjoying his traditional happy hour gin and tonic, standing in the companionway of *Henry Hornblower*. Scanning the empty horizon, he had mixed feelings of loneliness and contentment. He was finally underway on his third attempt to complete a BOC Challenge. Eight years ago, in the 1986-87 BOC Challenge, Harry had sailed another 40-footer, *Double Cross*, halfway round the globe when disaster struck on the third leg of the race. After leaving Australia, his yacht was badly damaged in a gale and he was forced to alter course for the south east coast of New Zealand, to make repairs. With no charts of the area and disorientated in the darkness, he sailed his yacht onto a sand bar east of Bluff, ending up high and dry on a beach. After three days the yacht was salvaged, but Harry was compelled to retire from the race. Devastated by his bad luck, he sold the boat in New Zealand and flew home.

Time passed by and Harry bought a new boat, *Mitak*, which he renamed *We Are Lovers*, and entered the 1990-91 BOC Challenge. He set off in the summer of 1990 from the River Hamble in England to cross the Atlantic for the start of the race in Newport, Rhode Island. But 100 miles west of the Scilly Islands on his second night at sea fate struck again. It was a clear, moonlit night and the yacht

*Harry's yacht,* We Are Lovers, *after she gave him a 'bloody nose'.*

was sailing at five knots in a light south westerly wind. Harry was down below clearing up after his evening meal when there was a sickening thump and the boat started to shake. He looked up through the window and saw a massive dark shape, like a cliff, racing by. Dashing up on deck he screamed: 'This must be a dream. Wake up!'

'I was never so angry,' he recalled afterwards. He had collided with a cargo ship which dragged the yacht along its side until there was a twang as the cap shroud and a running backstay, supporting the mast, parted and the yacht suddenly lurched free. The ship steamed on, disappearing over the horizon leaving the yacht floundering in its wake with an enraged Harry surveying the damage on deck in disbelief.

With the unstayed mast twisting and bending he quickly dropped all sails and set up spare halyards to support the rig. With a scrap of foresail to keep headway he had to wait for daylight to see the extent of the damage.

The yacht had run into the side of the bulk carrier. Fortunately its foam sandwich construction had absorbed some of the impact. Apart from a crushed bow section and shrouds, Harry had got off relatively lightly. He jury rigged a mast support and winched it up as tight as he could. He tried to climb the mast to replace the shroud, but it took him the rest of the day to pull himself up as far as the first spreader. 'It shows how old and weak I was,' he joked.

For five days he continued sailing towards the Azores, staying on one tack to avoid straining the damaged rig. But when the wind veered he was pushed too far south and when he changed tack he realised he might lose the mast. Reluctantly, he admitted defeat and turned the yacht around to head back to Plymouth. For a second time, Harry's dreams of sailing around Cape Horn had been dashed, this time before he had even started in earnest.

Disheartened, but not defeated, Harry had his boat hauled out for major repairs and flew to Newport for the BOC start to wish fellow competitors the luck he hadn't enjoyed himself on the third Challenge.

As a young lad in the Sea Scouts, Harry had once travelled all the way from his South Coast home to Liverpool to sign on as a deckhand on one of the last square riggers bound around Cape Horn. But he arrived too late after the ship had sailed.

'Never say die', was Harry's motto. It's never too late. Here he was, four years later, and less than 100 miles from Charleston, hoping it was going to be third time lucky. He was in this race to cross the finish line which he had just left behind him. That would make Harry a winner as far as he was concerned. Between then and now lay 27,000 miles, eight months and a world of uncertainties.

Streaking away well to the south and leading the front of the fleet was Isabelle Autissier, who was in the race to win and leave the opposition in her wake. In the first 22 hours she had sailed 298 miles at an average speed of just over 13 knots. Isabelle's love of the sea began with dinghy sailing during holidays in Brittany as a child. Then she started cruising with her father, an architect now aged 71, in his 30ft aluminium yacht sailing to Spain and Ireland. At the age of 26 she built her own yacht *Parole* and sailed with friends from France to Brazil and the Caribbean. From there she set sail alone on the return crossing to France. That was when the seed was planted which grew into singlehanding.

Her fellow countryman, defending BOC champion Christophe Auguin, was ten miles behind her, while David Adams on *True Blue*, held a slim five mile lead over his Italian rival on *Kodak*. As Adams left the start line, he handed reporters another of his off-the-cuff tailor-made quotes: 'I'm hoping that out of the next 130 days at least ten of them will be fun.'

'When the first guys did this race,' said Adams, 'it was an adventure. Now, to me, it's a yacht race. Everything we have is in this race and we don't even own the boat. We sold the house, the car and our own boat so we could borrow a boat for the last race (the 60ft *Innkeeper*). It still took two years to pay back the bills.' Money was still Adams' biggest worry. This time he was on loans from some of the same companies that sponsored him last time. Having given up the lucrative dual-income-no-kids lifestyle with his lawyer wife, Caroline, he was adamant that this would be his last race. 'I look at my bank account and there is nothing in it. It's time I earned some money after this …'

In the bid to keep boats lightweight, some skippers knew no extremes. David Adams had replaced his yacht's toilet with a bucket to save weight. Another had changed to plastic cutlery.

Mark Gatehouse sailing the ketch *Queen Anne's Battery*, noted that the new 60 foot boats were 'rocket ships'. They just ease along about 10 per cent faster than us "cruising boats".'

Luckless Simone Bianchetti was back at Charleston dockside for a second time two days after the start, having discovered water leaking into his boat around the keel. His fellow Class II competitor, South African Neal Petersen, also had troubles and was on deck in the moonlight on his third night at sea examining a slack forestay. He suspected it was broken. Using a spare halyard to secure things, he rolled up his foresail and changed course downwind under staysail until he could assess the situation in daylight. A few hours later he notified Race HQ that he was heading for Bermuda, three days away, to make repairs.

For Harry Mitchell the first three days had seen excellent progress, with nearly 200 miles on the third day. 'I thought "I've got it now, I'm not going to be last," I'm beating Robin and Neal, my closest rivals.' And then for the next few days, Harry ran into a series of windless zones. It was a chance for him to have a computer teach-in over the radio with Niah Vaughan, skipper of *Jimroda II*.

Harry was one of the old school and sat at his chart table confronting his new fangled IBM laptop computer while Niah coached him in the finer arts of word processing. Harry was computer illiterate. His wife Diana admitted that he had hardly even used an automatic bank card.

'Remember the "On" switch at the back,' instructed Niah. 'You can adjust the brightness with the slide at the top of the keyboard. Now try Create-Edit and enter.'

'What's "enter"?' asked Harry.

'Try typing your name and the boat's name,' said Niah. Fifteen minutes passed by and silence reigned over the airwaves.

Niah called back. 'Are you still there Harry?'

'Yes I'm just finishing typing my name... ' came the impatient reply.

'When you've typed the boat name, call me back,' said Niah. 'Meanwhile, I'll cook dinner, eat and wash up ... '

It was going to require a long teach-in to get Harry up to speed with the state of the art satellite communications on the BOC Challenge.

Steve Pettengill (43), America's best sponsored entrant in the race, backed by a million dollar budget from boatbuilder Hunter Marine, was sailing well with *Hunter's Child*, and had taken the lead. But he wasn't feeling so well himself. Fighting off a flu bug caught before he started the race, he was taking lots of vitamins and drinking liquids. 'I've only cooked one meal since the start, nor had much sleep at all,' he reported after three days of fast sailing.

*Hunter's Child* was a floating laboratory for Hunter Marine as well as an evolution of *Thursday's Child*. Before a line was drawn it was a mathematically calculated hull shape with half the wave-making drag of *Thursday's Child*. A taller, lighter rig had been added and Pettengill was constantly trying to find that extra bit of speed. A methodical man with meticulous attention to detail, he knew his boat inside out and was able to fix anything. This was the first time he had raced round the world. His longest solo time at sea before was in the 1988 solo Transatlantic when he took 21 days. His last visit to the Southern Ocean was when he capsized in the 60ft trimaran *Great American* 200 miles from Cape Horn. Pettengill, a businessman as well as a professional sailor, had worked with Mike Plant on *Coyote* and had been invited to sail with Plant on his fatal Atlantic crossing when the boat capsized. But he had flown instead to France to assist Nigel Burgess. Both died at sea within days of each other. 'There's always room for more caution,' said Pettengill. 'I'm sure I'll wear my harness more, though the deaths of Mike and Nigel were not related to wearing a harness.'

By now many in the fleet had stalled in a high pressure region of light and variable winds. Arnet Taylor *(Thursday's Child)* and Nigel Rowe *(Sky Catcher)* were doing a miserable three knots. Harry Mitchell, 50 miles behind, was managing 5 knots. David Adams summed it up succinctly: 'Very hot and more wind in an empty balloon.'

Harry's biggest problem, he discovered, apart from lack of wind, was lack of water. He'd forgotten to top up his water tanks in Charleston. Luckily it rained the first three days out and he managed to save six gallons in a bucket hanging under the mainsail. He even filled his ice cooler. But there would be very little rain on this leg.

Isabelle Autissier's pre-race strategy of heading east before turning on a southerly slant paid off as she found consistent winds and re-took the lead. JJ Provoyeur, heading in the same direction, sailed through the fleet and found himself alone in second place, averaging 9 knots with Isabelle. JJ's *Ben Vio* was an old Rodger Martin design which had been sailed non-stop round the world in the 1989 Vendée Globe Challenge by South African Bertie Reed, as well as campaigned in the previous BOC Challenge under the name *Grinaker*. Provoyeur, a 43-year-old native South African, owned the Cape Town boatyard at the Royal Cape Yacht Club where *Grinaker* was built. He finally got his chance to compete in the race when the boat became available and he had spent four months working 24 hours a day to get her ready with no time to seek sponsors. He removed a ton of weight from the yacht and kept her painted white, ready for a sponsor's name with a familar sign on the hull in Charleston: 'Sponsor Wanted'.

Neither JJ nor the yacht were considered a contender by close race observers. Undaunted, JJ declared: 'Other boats may be faster, but I've got a racing mentality.' The only self-sponsored competitor in Class I he said: 'I'll have to work for a couple of years after the race just to pay back loans.' But by Cape Town he had found his sponsor and renamed his yacht.

A few hours after gaining second place, his progress slowed as he recovered from a frightening accident when his neck got caught in the mainsheet during an accidental gybe. In a message to Race HQ he reported: 'My neck is badly bruised as well as my throat inside. I have great difficulty in swallowing and I have an area on my upper lip where the skin is removed. The lips are swollen, but the cut is not deep. I will find it hard to push the boat for the next few days.'

Race co-ordinator Peter Dunning requested regular updates on his condition. Giovanni, the 28-year-old Italian skipper of *Kodak*, was in radio contact with JJ and expressed his concern in a telex written in his own remarkable phonetic English: 'Ciao. Everytync well. I sipic every 4 auar wit Ben Vio. He hav an acxident. I dont knoo hao big. Maibi is good if the doctor ken kontakt im via telex. I dont wont ask for the doctor, bat I tink is better. Ciao Giovanni.' Race HQ, the 24-hour nerve centre of the race, had to decipher, evaluate and act upon all manner of communications received every hour over the next eight months.

Towards the end of the first week, Giovanni was 80 miles ahead of his arch Australian rival David Adams. Even though his yacht *Kodak* was 10ft shorter than the Class I boats, Giovanni had overtaken them to arrive in second place behind Autissier.

His yacht was a direct descendant of the Class II winner of the last BOC Challenge, *Servant IV*, which he had bought and then lost in the Atlantic while competing in the Quebec-St Malo race. Undaunted, he commissioned a new

*Only a picture alas – Giovanni surveys his painted bathroom aboard the spartan* Kodak. PHOTO: PATRICK ROACH

boat, *Kodak*, a light, simple 50-footer with spartan accommodation, minimal headroom below decks and a towering sail plan. Giovanni had all his food in big plastic watertight bins which could be moved about as movable ballast. His only luxury was a 'bathroom' – a mural of a Victorian bathtub complete with brass faucets and a postcard sized harbour scene painted by his girlfriend, Elena, an interior designer, on a wall of the cabin. Soldini, gregarious and full of laughter ashore, enjoyed the company of music aboard, 'anything from Jimmy Hendrix to Mozart, but mainly Mozart.' The yacht sported the sticker 'TOXIC BOATS'. The irrepressible Milano resident had convinced the head of a drug rehabilitation clinic to allow his patients to help build *Kodak* as a therapeutic aid to their recovery. The recovering drug addicts wore T-shirts emblazoned 'Toxic Boatyard'. While this Italian's best efforts were paying dividends, his compatriot, Simone Bianchetti, set off on his third attempt to rejoin the race to Cape Town.

Niah Vaughan, meanwhile, had a mid-ocean encounter of a strange kind with Josh Hall's *Gartmore*, which appeared over the horizon ahead of him on a collision course. As the gap between the two yachts closed, *Gartmore's* sails seemed to be flapping, then the yacht suddenly altered course and went across his path, heading into a dark thunder cloud. 'I'm not following him in there,' thought Vaughan, who tried calling up *Gartmore* on the radio without success. Concerned that Josh's boat was behaving erratically, Niah sent a message to Race HQ requesting them to make contact with *Gartmore*. For a moment he wondered if the yacht was under autopilot and Hall had gone over the side. Then *Gartmore* re-appeared from the thundercloud and began pulling away as Josh came on the radio to explain he had been having problems with his jib and he didn't feel like speaking to anyone.

Back in Charleston, having attended his daughter's wedding in Philadelphia, Floyd Romack set out a week behind the fleet to begin his race to Cape Town. His red yacht *Cardiac 88*, was towed out of the city marina and down Ashley River to the ocean. The yacht's hull boasted a picture of a heart covered with a zig-zag of lines representing a bad ECG. On board, a local reporter noted, were Floyd's beta blockers, diuretics and other medicines. Floyd's heart attack, instead of delaying his schedule to sail around the world one day, had accelerated it.

'Good luck to you, I've had one (a heart attack) too!' said an elderly man on the dock. 'If your heart's going to stop, it might as well stop while you're doing something exciting!'

Floyd, who had taken out a second mortgage on his home to fund the trip, did not enjoy the good sailing conditions experienced by his fellow competitors a week earlier. In his first 18 hours at sea he covered just 57 miles. He reckoned his expenses for the BOC would be well over $100,000. 'I don't want to know how much it's going to cost me. Otherwise the boat would probably have to be renamed *Cardiac 94!*'

Robin Davie's *Cornwall*, the only boat to have sailed north of Bermuda, was enjoying good sailing and a sunny day for the first time. At the end of his first week at sea Robin had sailed 1,049 miles, while his computer told him that he had closed the distance to Cape Town by only 658 miles. On his first night at sea a 30 knot rain squall had flattened the boat, shearing the autopilot off at its deck fitting and jamming the furling headsail. It had taken him two hours to restore normal service.

Later he was to admit that in going north of Bermuda he had committed his biggest error of the leg. 'I went north-east to try and get around a calm. It was bloody death,' he lamented.

Next day a calm had descended. 'There is not a cloud to be seen as the sun rises on a windless day in paradise. The airs aren't even light anymore. I've been going nowhere for eight hours. The odd cat's paw creeps my way for a minute or two before pushing off to wherever cat's paws go ... '

The calm gave him a chance to do some repairs. Otherwise, Robin squatted in his companionway with the Autohelm remote control in hand, steering the boat to every wind shift to maintain speed. 'I wrap the sleeping bag about me at night, setting the fire bell alarm for 15 minute intervals. This way I don't sleep for long and I keep the boat moving. I've been here for 36 hours now ... ' Eventually the wind reached 4 knots and steadied up so he could get his head down. 'It's been a hard day's night!' Davie signed off his message to Race HQ.

Josh Hall, ahead, reported 'it was good practice for the doldrums'. An indication of how calm it was during these first weeks was that Josh was able to complete a tax return, spending the day with invoices and receipts strewn around the cabin before filing it back home via satellite telex. Ernst & Young, his project accountants would be impressed.

Nigel Rowe aboard *Sky Catcher* announced his own important new discovery. 'Robin, Harry and I have agreed to name a new area out here north of Nares Abyssal Plain and south of Bermuda. It will be called "Nigel's Windless Plain". I was the first to discover it and have spent by far the most time exploring it ...'

Frustrations sometimes got the better of skippers. One windless afternoon

Nigel stood in the cockpit, clenched fists in the air, and screamed at the top of his voice 'GIIIVE MEEEEE MOOORE WIIIND!' He stamped his feet, thumped the spray dodger with his fists till they hurt and then did it all over again before slumping in the cockpit feeling both better and worse. 'Better because I had given vent to my feelings. Worse for the same reason. It had been a childish tantrum, and I gave myself a severe talking to a bit later in the day.'

By the ninth day of the race, tales of the horse latitudes came from much of the fleet caught in the light wind belt. The region, between 20 and 30 degrees north in this area of the Atlantic, is notorious for frustrating, shifting breezes. It earned its name because here in the last century trading ships dumped their cargo of livestock over the side to conserve precious supplies of drinking water.

After 60 hours in Bermuda making repairs to his yacht, and fitting a new forestay, Neal Petersen untied his tow line outside the reef and sailed into the night to rejoin the race. 'If I'd allowed the residents more time, they would have built me a new boat while I waited. I didn't have to do a thing, but rest, eat well and enjoy myself,' he said. 'When I tried to make arrangements for payment, they would hear nothing of it. A supermarket invited me in to fill a trolley of fresh supplies.' Petersen, eager to share his adventure and repay his debt, volunteered to give a talk to fifty primary school pupils. 'Hopefully the next land this vessel and I see is Cape Town's Table Mountain. Must go now and eat the ice cream before it melts on me.'

Hours after Petersen left Bermuda on race day eight there came the shock announcement from Mark Gatehouse on *QAB* that he was withdrawing for 'strictly personal reasons'. In a fax to Race HQ, Gatehouse announced his retirement from the BOC Challenge. 'We plan everything to the smallest detail when we undertake these races. What we can't plan are overtaking events in our business and private lives. I had great difficulty concentrating on the race (at the beginning), but hoped that as the race progressed and I started to do well, my mind would drop on the case in hand. Sadly, even moving up among the star boats didn't help.'

Gatehouse, Britain's best prospect in the race, retired at the top of his game. After a slow start, he sailed steadily through the fleet and was second in class when he altered course for the Azores. He was just 58 miles behind Autissier and sailing 2.5 knots faster.

Robin Davie was minding his own business at dusk that evening when a 100,000 ton red tanker hove over the horizon. The English captain introduced his ship as the *Red Seagull* from Galveston, Texas, bound for Suez. They chatted for a while as the tanker passed a mile off Davie's stern. Then a voice came up on the radio asking 'Is that you Robin, talking to that big red tanker just in front of me?' It was Harry Mitchell, a small speck on the horizon behind Davie with all sail set and poled out. Last week Robin had been 30 miles behind Harry after his sail around Bermuda. With night falling, the two yachts resumed their separate ways so they would not meet up with a bump in the middle of the night.

The gap between the front runners in the race and those towards the back of the fleet had already opened up to 1,000 miles-plus. Tailenders Robin and Harry, as well as Nigel Rowe, Neal Petersen and Arnet Taylor were 5,500 miles from Cape Town. Robin reported 'the slowest day so far' in Nigel's windless zone – 70 miles from noon to noon. Harry, drifting along at 1.8 knots, had been on the

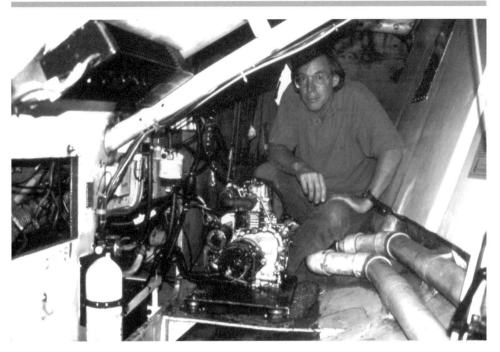

*The cause of all Arnet's problems on leg one was the failed generator that left him cut off from communications with the rest of the fleet.* PHOTO: PAUL GELDER

radio telling Neal the true story of the tortoise and the hare, but with a new twist. Compared to a sea turtle, Harry's yacht was certainly a hare, but while becalmed Harry had just looked over the side and watched a turtle swim by and overtake him. Robin was down to 2.8 knots. 'Progress is snail pace. This is beginning to look like a very, very slow first leg for some of us,' he reported prophetically. It was the slowest sailing he had done in his 11 years with the yacht. The big black and gold *Cornwall* spinnaker had flown most of the week. 'An eye-catching sight, but not many eyes out here to catch it,' he sighed. With no cooling breeze, *Cornwall's* black hull felt like an oven down below and Robin's daily drinking allowance of half a gallon of water was supplemented by fruit juices. For Floyd Romack on *Cardiac 88*, things were even more frustrating. He was nearly 2,000 miles behind the leaders.

The yachts were now seeking the narrowest crossing band possible through the wind-starved doldrums, where lack of air leaves sails slatting and nerves rattled. Isabelle Autissier, sailing a tactically flawless race, was the first to cross the Equator, puncturing the doldrums at their narrowest point, 20° west.

JJ Provoyeur in fourth place conceded: 'She really did get her weather right. She had only one day of slow going while everyone else had four or five.' JJ had earlier sent the message: 'I can't, in my wildest dreams, imagine wind as fluky as this has been. In the time it has taken me to type this little note, I've already been on deck three times to make fairly large sail trim adjustments.'

Arnet Taylor in 12th place in the fleet continued to have a fraught passage. Steering problems at the start of the race had now been replaced with power problems. He had lost the use of his alternator, the heart of his onboard electrical charging system, which had parted company from the diesel generator when the aluminium bracket broke off. Using hose clamps, wire and wedges to jam it back in place, he could run the generator for only 15 minutes before it over-heated. 'Between handsteering and using power from the solar panels and wind generator I can make progress at a reduced pace,' he reported, but radio communications would have to be rationed.

Arnet had also been shaken by a close encounter 1,000 miles north of the equator with a passing ship just before midnight. *Thursday's Child* had been sailing along at 14 knots in 35 knots of wind and Arnet had been on deck ten minutes earlier. The horizon was clear, but because of bad visibility that night he was using some of his precious battery power for a radar scan on the 15 mile range. Sitting in the cuddy, stretching out his lean six-foot plus frame, he looked upwards through the glass bubble above his head and saw a dark shape looming alongside. Leaping to his feet he jabbed the autopilot, bringing his yacht up into the wind. Whatever it was he'd missed it by just a boat length. 'I was going so fast and the seas were so big that he'd disappeared on the four mile radar range when I looked him up. I don't think he ever saw me. The ship was about 150ft long and may have been a Japanese fishing vessel. If I'd hit the guy it would have been my fault. There is no debate about that.'

Race day 22 was the 70th birthday of Race communications co-ordinator Peter Dunning. Congratulations came from fellow septuagenarian Harry Mitchell: 'Welcome to the More Mature Senior Citizen's Club, signed Harry Full of Wind Hornblower.'

There was little to celebrate for some of the skippers. Nigel Rowe was counting the cost of an encounter with a squadron of kamikaze flying fish that had smashed his wind generators. 'For someone whose electrical talents are stretched at home with the need to change a fuse or light bulb, I am keeping my fingers crossed,' he said after cannibalising one unit to mend another. 'I'll need more wind to know if I've made a good job or botch of it.' *Sky Catcher* also had rigging problems. 'I wonder what's next? I'm having to fix these problems as best I can, but this is not playing to my strengths at the moment.'

Japan's Minoru Saito, meanwhile, was waging war on a persistent leak on *Shuten-Dohji II* in the daggerboard housing. Minoru was another shoestring sailor who, like Robin Davie, was doing the race for the second time in his old yacht. He reckoned it was the fourth largest sailing boat in Japan after the three America's Cup boats. 'In Japan to have a boat this size is worse than having a golf course,' he joked. 'They think you're Rockefeller or Ted Turner.' Minoru's sponsors were from Australia or New Zealand, with the exception of ten people in Japan who each donated $1,000 to his campaign and had their names on a bronze plaque mounted on the bridgedeck. Minoru's leak was the legacy of a Japanese typhoon that had damaged his yacht three years previously, leaving a three inch crack at the back of the centreboard case. Somehow the crack repair had failed. For the last two or three days Minoru had been hand pumping. Now, having repaired his electric pumps and re-engaged his diesel engine, he was still taking up to 20 gallons of water an hour. He had no charts for Brazil and every few hours Nigel Rowe was calling him to check how he was coping with the leak.

For David Adams, who had crossed the Equator into the southern hemisphere, things were better. 'The sun is shining ... pretty little clouds and the wind is here and for once it's where it should be. It's times like these that make you think they invented the northern hemisphere so us southerners know what hell is like,' he reported.

Adams was trying his level best to get past Giovanni. 'I'm going to have to try something. I'm going due south. It's nip and tuck whether we'll get around the corner of Brazil. But as I'm behind, I have to take the risks.' Later Adams was 'getting knocked into Recife Brazil, hardly clearing the beach' and was heading east again making good speed.

Day 23 was the slowest collective day for the fleet since the race began, with several skippers, including David Scully, Josh Hall, Niah Vaughan and Nigel Rowe failing to pass the 40 mile mark on their 24-hour runs. In an attempt to whistle up some wind Niah had a miniature toy bird, a farewell gift from an admirer in Charleston, whose chirping was activated by vibration. In the calms, he put the bird on the radio chat hour.

'Being out here is like being lost in the country,' reported Scully. 'There are no signs. No one to ask. And even the features that are supposed to be easily identifiable, like the doldrums or the Trades, are a lot less obvious than one would like. There is just no frame of reference.'

Robin Davie on *Cornwall* was into his eighth day of calms and had forgotten where the bunk was as he continued to catnap on deck. Could this be the promised wind, he wondered as *Cornwall* started to heel a degree or two. He trod carefully around the deck fearful of upsetting the wind gods. There was a swish and gurgle of water flowing past the hull as the breeze stayed and the yacht slipped along at 6 knots over an almost flat sea. 'It felt as good as doing 200 mph at Indianapolis,' said Robin. In celebration, he cooked a beef, vegetable and potato stew, which he ate at the chart table. For once he wasn't called to the cockpit to trim the sails. He set his alarm timer for 40 minutes and turned into his bunk for the first time in nine days.

The sleep was pure luxury. After 40 minutes he awoke to find the wind still steady and *Cornwall* on course. He grabbed another 40 minutes. In this way, he had 10 hours sleep that night and a few more the following day.

On *Henry Hornblower*, Harry had discovered that boxes of freshly laid eggs he had bought in Charleston were infested with maggots. 'As I lifted one box a great cloud of flies flew out,' he said. From 72 eggs, he managed to save 12. He hadn't provisioned with any bread, so every day he made flapjacks out of water and flour and fried them, rationing himself when he started to run out of flour. Lunch was usually a cup of powdered soup, or a can of sardines or tuna. Supper was a stew, followed by canned fruit. He still had a leg of dried Cumbria ham hanging in the cabin. It could be eaten raw, or cooked. Harry never did discover the exact curing process for these hams, but someone had read in a book that hams had been cured by burying them for some time in manure. In this case, that process was unlikely. The hams, a gift from Niah, were from Richard Woodhams who had the Royal Warrant.

A thousand miles ahead on *Jimroda II* Niah Vaughan tempted fate by sending a message home: 'Boat in good shape. We have not had many breakages so far.' Up to this point his main concern had been leaks in the bow and stern areas from water coming over the decks while crashing to windward. He had been bailing out 15 to 20 buckets of water daily. Two whales had also come close to the boat two days earlier, one flipping its tail yards away giving him a further soaking. A few hours after his 'boat-in-good-shape' fax, Niah was resting below in the early hours of the morning when a bang on deck roused him into action. He dashed topside to find the roller furling foresail had broken free. The shackle securing the drum to the deck had sheared in half. He attempted to secure the flailing sail by getting a rope around it, but in 25 knots of wind it was difficult to tame. He went below to fire up his laptop computer and send a cautionary message to Race HQ telling them what was happening – just in case he had an accident. 'I have an emergency on board at the moment. My heavy No 1 genoa roller furler shackle at deck level has sheared. The sail was out when it snapped. I have it lashed behind the main. Hopefully the wind will die so I can effect repairs. Slight damage to the boat and myself.'

The drum was tangled in the guardrail and although Niah took down the guardrail, two rolls of the sail had somehow wrapped around the foil, preventing it from being lowered. Eventually, he spotted that the flogging sail had worked the rolls out and, seeing his chance, dived for the halyard and got it down. It slipped over the side of the yacht into the water and he spent another hour before managing to drag it back into the cockpit. It took him four hours to clear things up. But during the whole time he kept sailing under mainsail and staysail rather than hove-to. 'I wasn't going to stop and let someone get past me,' he said. 'But when I rolled out of my bunk this morning it felt as though I had gone ten rounds with Joe Frazier!'

Niah was making 200 miles a day, but he wasn't pushing the boat for that extra 20-30 miles. Next day he crossed the equator into the Southern Hemisphere. 'Seventh time for the old girl. Quite a record eh!' he said, signing off with his familiar 'Y'all have a good day.'

By now, race leader Isabelle Autissier was defying conventional wisdom and making a risky manoeuvre, edging east towards South Africa several hundred miles to the north of the established route. The danger was in cutting the corner of the South Atlantic High too closely and stalling in the predominantly light breezes. Again her strategy paid off as she set a scorching pace, extending her lead to nearly 600 miles.

More than 2,000 miles behind her, Neal recorded: 'The more I am at sea, the more I fear those ashore will forget me. Life ashore goes on as normal. Now and again we are remembered. But out here, we never forget those ashore.'

By day 26 Minoru Saito was making arrangements to divert to Brazil to fix his persistent leak. Robin Davie had made contact with a US radio ham net and advised Saito to call into the Brazilian seaside village of Cabedelo where there was a contact on a cruising yacht from the previous BOC Challenge race. This would be worth its weight in gold to Minoru, who had no charts of the Brazilian coast, spoke poor English and had lost the use of his engine.

Bianchetti too was having problems with a leak of up to 500 litres a day. His yacht had been left standing on her keel in Charleston and it was thought that the pressure may have started the problems. The pounding the boat had been taking also revealed another weak spot: the hull was delaminating over an area half a metre long, forward of the mast, and some 30 centimetres above the water-line. Soon Simone, too, would be forced to make an unscheduled stop in

Cabadelo, where repair time would cost the Italian four days out of the race.

Robin Davie, literally in the doldrums, was experiencing torrential rain squalls with 20 knot gusts in between calms and light airs. He gave a graphic description of the frustrations. 'It's midnight with a full moon over an oily calm sea. Three knots of breeze pushes *Cornwall* along at two knots. I'm tired and I slip below and put the kettle on the stove to make a mug of cocoa. I hear the sails flapping. It's like a game of cat and mouse. The instant my back is turned the wind changes. Quickly, I'm back up in the cockpit to alter course and trim the sails.

'I set the fire bell alarm for 15 minutes and, wrapped in my sleeping bag, doze in the hatchway. A flapping sail or the bell will wake me. This goes on for three hours. Then I'm woken by more wind. I notice it's much darker because the moon has vanished behind a cloud. The boat suddenly heels through 10, 15 and then 20 degrees as the rush of wind rises to 24 knots and a torrential downpour of rain hits the yacht. Bang! within seconds *Cornwall* is on her beam ends. I release the genoa sheet and reduce sail, turning the boat downwind. She comes upright and within two minutes the wind drops and the rain has stopped. I'm soaked to the skin as we resume our course to Cape Town, back to a two knot drift again.

'This rain squall will be repeated many times each day and night as great cloud pillars build to several thousand feet and develop their own wind systems. The calms in between try the patience of Job.

'A grey dawn reveals the horizon dotted with massive cloud banks, each one a potential five minute gale that will take me a little further south towards the equator. It's time for a check around the deck, a bit like a farmer checking his estate, except mine is only 40ft by 12ft and a good look round takes five minutes. A good cup of tea first thing is a necessity.

'The wind is fairly steady at six knots, so I grab several 30 minute sleeps in the bunk, taking me up to noon. Time to send the daily message to Charleston Race HQ and join the radio chat hour to talk with other competitors.

'By mid afternoon the calms and squalls are back with a vengeance. But at least my water supply is rapidly being replenished. I only carry 30 gallons of fresh water, allowing four pints a day for 60 days. A bucket strategically placed under the boom catches water running off the sail. In this way I collect 15 gallons for showers and shampoos.

'Most of the time I use baby wipes to keep the skin clean. That's okay, except you end up smelling like a baby's bottom. So it's a great pleasure to get out on deck and enjoy my first wash, shave and shampoo of the trip. But I won't claim it made me feel like a new man!

'I usually play my old 1950s and 60s music cassettes (Buddy Holly, Elvis, Chuck Berry) most of the day. The evening radio chat hour at 2000 GMT gives me a chance to catch up on fleet gossip. By then it's dusk and time to charge the batteries and cook the evening meal (tonight a tin of American smoked ham, beans, fried eggs and potatoes).

'The moon has risen and the squalls have given way to a steady seven to nine knots of wind. I'll catch some 40 minute sleep tonight, catching up on what I've missed over the last three nights as we head towards the Equator looking for the steady south-east Trade winds. Welcome to the doldrums!'

Despite being overtaken by Simone Bianchetti, one of the youngest BOC competitors, veteran Harry Mitchell showed he still had the right stuff with a noon-to-noon run of 143 miles. But the gap between the tortoise and the hare had stretched over many horizons. While Harry's narrow-beamed ten-year-old cutter was still 4,000 miles from Cape Town, Isabelle's 60ft flying saucer, with its radical 15ft canting keel and massive sail-carrying power, had just 1,400 miles to go to the finish line in Table Bay.

# 3 · Welcome Aboard Mate!

As the fleet settled into the start of its fifth week at sea, defending BOC champion Christophe Auguin faced a critical shortage of electrical power. His main and back-up generators had failed, leaving him with limited use of his autopilots and forcing him to hand steer for up to 20 hours a day. Harry Mitchell and Neal Petersen had arrived at the outer fringes of the doldrums, while Minoru Saito celebrated crossing the Equator with saki and a small dried sardine. Nigel Rowe offered Neptune the three things he would not like to sail without – an onion, champagne and garlic.

Some 700 miles south of the Equator, Josh Hall had been in the south-east trades for about five days and was going great guns under full sail. The seas off this section of Brazil's coast had been unsettled, with bands of current kicking up some nasty, confused seas and Josh was hand steering to stop the boat slamming over the backs of the waves. Dusk was coming up with the wind blowing mostly over 22 knots true as *Gartmore* powered upwind at 10 knots. She came off the back of a wave, like many others that had threatened to loosen the fillings in the skipper's teeth. Josh nudged the wheel, expecting a soft landing, but was thrown up against it as the boat staggered to a standstill.

'It was the most horrendous landing you could imagine. The boat reared up and there was the most incredible rending sound as the bow came down. I realised something really bad had happened. It was almost as if we'd run aground,' he said.

As the yacht picked herself up again and started sailing, Josh rushed below, punching the Autohelm 7000 self-steering into action as he went.

BOC yachts have exceptional safety features, including a forward collision bulkhead designed to cope with just this sort of emergency. Already a huge amount of water had flooded the yacht through a 10ft-long gash. Water was halfway up the inspection and access hatch of the forward watertight bulkhead. Worse than that, the bulkhead itself had been fractured by the impact, allowing water to pour into the main part of the hull.

'My heart went to my stomach. It seemed as though it was happening to somebody else ... as if I was watching a bad movie. I had never felt so panicked or scared in all my time at sea. The fear came in waves. I didn't know what to do first. The real danger is paralysis of fear, not fear itself. In my mind I just knew I had to prioritise things. In a panic situation you try to quell the panic. I thought "Is this it?"

'My adventure aboard this superb racing machine had turned into a nightmare. To get hold of myself, I was walking up and down very quickly in the cabin thinking "What do I do first? What do I do?" Suddenly there was so much to do that a full crew would be stretched to its limits.'

His first priority was to send off a Mayday signal. He rushed to the chart table and hit the two red distress buttons on the Trimble Galaxy INMARSAT-C telex modem. He had to stop for a few seconds and read the instructions. Within minutes UK Coastguard officials in Falmouth alerted Charleston Race HQ that Josh was in trouble. It was 1950 GMT. At the same time he threw the breaker on the INMARSAT-M satellite telephone, which would take about ten minutes to warm up. *Gartmore* was one of only three yachts in the race equipped to telephone direct to anywhere in the world.

Next he did his best to shore up the damaged area with floorboards and sail-bags as water gushed in. Because she was holed in such a structurally strong area, Josh felt that *Gartmore* had struck the corner of something hard, like a shipping container. He switched on the big electric bilge pump forward of the watertight bulkhead and led another hose into the damaged area from a take-off on his water ballast pump. With all his pumps going he was shifting the best part of 5,000 gallons (19,000 litres) of water an hour. Despite this, there were two or three feet of water throughout the yacht and it was rising.

He picked up the telephone to call Race HQ and let them know what was happening. Peter Dunning, an old friend, was on duty. As the co-ordinator of every BOC Challenge, Dunning has been through every crisis in the race and was typically calm and reassuring. He agreed that Alan Nebauer on *Newcastle Australia*, 90 miles to the north west, was Josh's nearest competitor. Charleston would try to raise Alan by radio or Standard-C to divert him to the rescue.

It was agreed that Josh would leave his SSB radio on the usual 4MHz frequency that skippers chatted on every eight or twelve hours, and he would wait for Alan to call. As a back-up rescue aid Josh agreed to activate his 406MHz EPIRB (satellite distress beacon). Finally, he would talk to Race HQ on the phone every hour to update the situation.

Outside, it was getting dark and Josh needed to get the mainsail down to stop the yacht burying her bow under water. He also needed to turn around and start heading towards Alan, instead of away from him. With half the staysail up, *Gartmore* was jogging along at some 3 knots with the whole foredeck awash. Josh hoped that slowing her down would stem the flood of water inside. The fact that the bows were down with the weight of water up forward helped to keep the batteries and engine dry at the back of the boat. Josh desperately needed them to maintain power to his bilge pumps and communications. He used pieces of floorboard to make a dam at the main bulkhead around the galley to stop water flooding the batteries.

'Once I got started, the effort and involvement removed the panic. What helped was having dealt with other situations. I've been involved with dismastings, broken booms and personal injury and it all stood me in good stead. But my biggest asset, communications-wise, was the telephone COMSAT had sponsored me with.'

Some 20 minutes after Josh's Mayday, Charleston made contact with Alan Nebauer who responded to their urgency message. At first Alan wondered if something had happened back home. Then, when he heard Josh was in trouble,

he worked with communications co-ordinator Larry Brumbach to plot an intercept point for the two yachts. *Newcastle* proceeded on a southerly heading at 7 knots, while *Gartmore* set a course to the west at 4 knots. This gave an average combined closing speed of 11 knots and put Alan some seven hours away.

Nigel Rowe on *Sky Catcher*, also equipped with a satellite phone, worked with Race HQ to provide a communications safety net between Josh and Charleston, aided by Arnet Taylor (*Thursday's Child*), Robin Davie (*Cornwall*) and Niah Vaughan (*Jimroda II*).

By now Josh was coming to terms with the fact that *Gartmore* was fatally stricken. For a time he had thought he might be able to shore up the damage, stem the influx of water and limp somewhere. But the nearest land was 500 miles away. He accepted that his yacht was just going to be an island for him before rescue came. He would be lucky if she remained afloat. The creaking and groaning of the watertight bulkhead was frightening. If it burst open, the torrent of water into the yacht would be unstoppable. *Gartmore's* satellite phone was ringing every half hour as Josh dealt with 15-20 calls over the next few hours before Alan arrived.

Falmouth Coastguard, who were officially co-ordinating the rescue, called every hour and the Brazilian Coastguard on standby called four or five times. They were searching for ships nearby, but were unable to locate any. The Brazilian's English was undoubtedly better than Josh's Portuguese, but the language problems prompted some bizarre exchanges. As Josh failed in his polite attempts to explain that he didn't have time to answer bureaucratic inquiries about the yacht's registration papers, he was forced to hang up on them saying, 'Sorry, I'm too busy!' He knew the rescue was being organised at Falmouth and Charleston.

He also wanted to speak to Laura, his wife, back home in Ipswich. He didn't want to scare her, but was concerned that she might have received a clinical call from an official who had registered his EPIRB alert. He wanted to reassure her. He also needed to hear her voice. A few days earlier she had called him to say that she was expecting their second child. Now it was his turn to break the news that their yacht and life savings were sinking under his feet.

Back home in Suffolk it was 10 o'clock in the evening when Laura picked up the phone. She had already spoken to Peter Dunning, who had spelled things out very well, so Josh didn't have to go through it all. But it was a very emotional phone call.

'I broke down a bit at that point ... we were a bit teary. I remember saying "I just want to be at home." Laura was very good. She's very solid and strong and I guess she'd had time to deal with the situation. Peter had assured her help was on its way to me. I phoned three times throughout the whole night's drama to let her know how it was going and also just to hear her voice. My parents drove over and spent the night with Laura. When my younger brother rang me a few minutes later for a chat I don't think he believed me when I told him the yacht was sinking and I was about to get into the liferaft.'

Time ceased to have much meaning for Josh as he pumped and prayed. He had first made radio contact with Alan some two hours after the fatal collision. 'I can

Opposite: *Josh Hall's yacht, powering upwind at 10 knots off Charleston in conditions similar to those off the Brazilian coast when his race came to a sickening end.*
PHOTO: PATRICK ROACH

remember the relief that he was on his way. He asked me if it was bad and I said "Yes, get here as soon as you can." But I didn't want to panic him because I knew he'd be sailing as fast as he could. At the same time, I wanted to impress on him the urgency of my situation. We agreed to speak on the radio every half hour.'

In an attempt to defuse the tension in the midst of Josh's crisis, Alan Nebauer tried cracking a joke over the radio.

'What?' said Josh, failing to see the humour.

'Don't worry it's just my Aussie humour trying to cheer you up,' said Alan.

A few hours later, Alan had his own sense of humour failure when he lost contact with Josh for more than an hour. With two bilge pumps, the engine running and water slopping around, it was so noisy down below in *Gartmore*, that Josh, who was forward trying to shore up the damaged hull, failed to hear Alan calling him on the radio. Ninety minutes passed by before he remembered his radio schedule. Alan, meanwhile, had been 'freaking out' having called constantly and received no reply.

Down below on *Gartmore* it was a depressing scene with the water level still rising. Josh, up to his hips in water, had put on his survival suit. By now his concerns were concentrated on the integrity of his watertight bulkhead. If it gave way, or the pumps packed up, things would escalate rapidly. He decided to put his liferaft over the side, as an insurance.

'It was a six-man liferaft and I remember how heavy it was. I could only just pick it up ashore. But a frightened man has the strength of ten... it went over easily and I tethered it alongside and inflated it so it was ready if I needed it. I was sponsored for all my safety equipment by a local company back home – Suffolk Sailing. When I left Shotley Marina to head to the start of the race the boss, Graham Gardiner, came down to wish me well and I'll always remember him saying: "Unlike all your all other sponsors, I hope you never have to use what I've given you!" I was going to seriously disappoint him. There I was using *everything* he'd given me.'

In one of their radio calls Alan encouraged Josh: 'Try to save as much kit as you can.' In the drama and panic of the situation it was something that hadn't even occurred to Josh. Each hour from then on he spent about ten minutes between pumping trying to grab bags which were already packed and throw them into the liferaft.

'I'd borrowed a couple of laptop computers and put them in the liferaft, but they got swamped. I grabbed family photos of Laura and Sam (his son aged two-and-a-half) which were stuck above the chart table. What do you take? My whole world was in that boat. You look at all the bits and pieces of gear that you accumulate over the years ... I felt we were one of the best equipped and prepared boats. I had to abandon all my navigation books and the sight reduction tables given to me by Robin Knox-Johnston. But I managed to grab my sextant. If I'd only managed to grab one thing it would have been the sextant.

'Alan was being updated on my position constantly by Race HQ who were polling my GPS by INMARSAT-C. He picked up the signal from my radar transponder from ten miles away. We agreed that to confirm my position I'd send up a red parachute flare, so I went on deck and fired one off. My masthead lights operated on a 24-volt system and were very powerful. He'd seen us.

'We were also fortunate that when Alan closed on my position there was almost a full moon at 0300 in the morning. Eventually Alan came up on the radio and said "Can you see me?" I went up on deck and there he was in the moonlight, 200 yards away. He rolled up his headsail and we went over to talking on our waterproof handheld VHFs.'

As Alan Nebauer looked across to *Gartmore*, illuminated by her cabin and deck lights, he realised she was going down. She was a sad sight. 'If you love boats you just hate seeing them in those situations. I'd hoped maybe we could put a collision mat under the hole and sail to Brazil, but it was obviously not possible. *Gartmore* was very low in the water.'

Conditions had improved as far as the sea state was concerned, but it was still too dangerous for Alan to come alongside. The pitching in the swell could have damaged *Newcastle*'s hull. It was agreed that Josh would transfer to *Newcastle* in the liferaft. His final act before he abandoned *Gartmore* and his dreams was to turn off the bilge pumps and open up all her seacocks, thus ensuring that his prized yacht would sink for miles to the bottom and not pose a danger to any of the following yachts in the BOC fleet.

He found his longest line to hand, the mainsheet, tied it to the liferaft and jumped in. 'I thought it was important to stay attached to something at all times. But as it turned out it was a mistake.' The liferaft drifted 60-70yds downwind, and as *Gartmore* surged on the ten foot waves the mainsheet snatched the liferaft, causing it to be swamped.

Alan passed close by under reefed main and threw a line to Josh, but just as he went to grab it the liferaft was violently jerked by its line to *Gartmore*. Letting go of Alan's line, Josh grabbed his knife and cut the umbilical cord to *Gartmore*. Severing this last link to cut himself adrift seemed a final symbolic gesture.

'I was on my own for the next ten minutes as Alan did another circuit round the liferaft. It was the loneliest I've felt at sea. Sad and scared, even though he was close by, and these were all fairly alien emotions to me. It felt strange to be bobbing around not tied to anything. *Gartmore* was such a tragic sight in the moonlight. The number of times I've pulled away from the yacht in the dinghy leaving it on a mooring... but from the liferaft it was awful to see her as she laboured hull down.

'Alan's seamanship was superb as he rounded up on the raft for a second time. I tied on his line and he dragged the liferaft up to *Newcastle*'s wide open transom. I scrambled on board, safe at last.'

'Welcome aboard mate,' said Alan.

'Thank you!' said Josh, in the understatement of the race.

'We were both very emotional,' said Josh. 'I stood for about an hour at the back of Alan's boat totally stunned by it all while he got organised to get underway.'

As Alan stowed Josh's bags down below, *Newcastle* jogged around under mainsail. It must have been over an hour before Josh got his survival suit off. They had to get rid of the liferaft, and since it was impractical to bring it aboard they cut it up with a knife and let it sink.

Eventually they got underway as dawn came up. 'Neither of us wanted to stay around to see *Gartmore* sink. When we left, the light of the radar transponder in the rigging was still flashing just under the spreader. The decks were awash.'

Not long after Alan picked him up, Josh sent a message to Peter Dunning at Race HQ: 'Safely aboard *Newcastle*, thank heavens... I'm scared, tired and dazed, but okay. I guess I'll be accompanying my best ever friend here to Cape Town, unless I can be landed on terra firma by a passing chopper. When we left the scene it was still dark, but *Gartmore*'s decks were almost awash. Tell Laura I'll call her when Alan's batteries have recharged. Thanks for all your help mate, Josh.'

Later still: 'Thanks again for being there for me last night. *Newcastle* was an angel that appeared from a very gloomy night. Can you let me know if you have lost *Gartmore*'s signals yet? I would like to know ... '

Josh hadn't eaten since lunchtime the day before and within an hour of getting onboard, Alan had a pot of stew on the boil, but Josh didn't feel much like eating. It would be two days before exhaustion took over and he could sleep.

As Josh sat below at *Newcastle*'s chart table, still dazed and shocked by the sudden end to his adventure, Alan got the boat sailing again. Given the conditions, she should have being sailing at nearly 10 knots, but Josh could hear Alan up on deck ranting and raving because the boat would only do 4 knots. In the midst of Josh's crisis, Alan had been facing his own emergency. 'I hate to tell you this, but I've got a problem with my keel,' he eventually blurted out to Josh.

*Newcastle* had felt sluggish as he had been sailing to the rescue. 'I thought I was trying too hard,' Alan said later. But below the waterline the keel fairing, which had been damaged in collision with the Cuban refugee raft on day one of the race, had opened up like a big wing. The damage wasn't structural, but the movement had caused some leaking at the keel housing. So two hours after he'd boarded his rescue vessel, Josh was bailing out Alan's bilges with a bucket and sponge. It took a while for Josh to be able to laugh at the irony.

Having Josh aboard certainly put Alan's keel problem into perspective. 'I'm a bit of a whinger. There I am, moaning about a few drops leaking from the ballast tank and he's lost his yacht!' said Alan.

An hour or so later, in daylight, they both looked over the side and could see the broken keel fairing acting like a drogue as the two foil pieces moved like wing flaps on a plane. They knew the fairing had to break off before they could make any progress and discussed the options of going into the water and trying to rip it off or diverting to Brazil for repairs.

They needed to fill the water ballast tank, but with the scoop behind the keel it wasn't working, so they tried sailing the boat backwards to fill the tank. After four or five gybes and tacks there was a rumbling as the fairing broke away and sank. *Newcastle* was free from her sea anchor, but would still prove to be about 30 per cent slower.

Later that day Alan sent a message to Race HQ. 'You may have noticed our erratic course. I've been breaking in my new crew.' He went on to tell Peter Dunning, 'My fibreglass keel fairing has separated from the structural keel blade. We are now sailing on the raw steel keel beam. There is no structural damage and all is well onboard. It's slow going. We can only manage 5 knots in 20 knots of breeze.' Alan's passenger offered another explanation: 'They just don't build these Australian yachts with enough wind around them ...'

For Alan the race had suddenly stopped. He'd had a good run until David

Opposite: *A graphic illustration of the gap between the tail-end Charlies and Isabelle Autissier's rocket ship* EPC2, *soon to arrive in Cape Town after 35 days. Bringing up the rear is* Cardiac 88 *which set out a week late, while* Henry Hornblower *still has 3,397 miles to go.* BY COURTESY OF COMSAT MOBILE COMMUNICATIONS AND COMPUSERVE

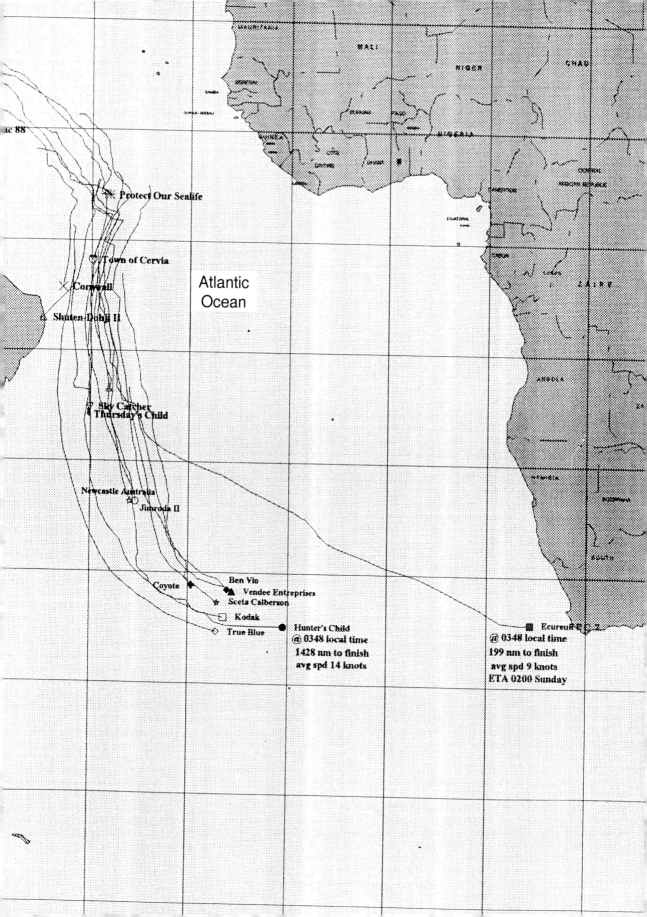

ac 88

Protect Our Sealife

Atlantic
Ocean

Town of Cervia

Cornwall

Shuten-Dohji II

Sky Catcher
Thursday's Child

Newcastle Australia
Jimroda II

Coyote

Ben Vio
Vendee Entreprises
Sceta Calberson
Kodak
True Blue

Hunter's Child
@ 0348 local time
1428 nm to finish
avg spd 14 knots

Ecureuil P.O.Z.
@ 0348 local time
199 nm to finish
avg spd 9 knots
ETA 0200 Sunday

Adams passed him near the Equator. Now, with the damaged keel, he knew that he'd blown his chances on the first leg. And when Josh came aboard, his attempt on a true solo circumnavigation was also at an end. The nature of the adventure had changed for him. The solo sailor had been robbed of his solitude. 'It wasn't the same any more, even though I didn't mind having him there,' said Alan. 'We got on really well.'

In the first BOC Challenge, Francis Stokes had rescued Tony Lush from the sinking *Lady Pepperell* and remarked: 'Having someone on board with you changed the character of the race in that there is someone there with you to share the anxieties and frustrations. You gain in companionship but lose the pleasure of solitude. I believe the net result is to detract slightly from the racing effort.'

For the rest of the fleet, the sinking of *Gartmore* had been an unsettling experience, to say the least. Nigel Rowe remarked on 'the apparent randomness with which fate can single you out of a crowd and deal such a savage blow.'

Arnet Taylor was not the only skipper who double-checked his panic bag and survival suit that night. 'You don't imagine this sort of thing is going to happen while sailing in the tropics. You think it's going to be in the Southern Ocean with icebergs and horrendous weather conditions. It drove home how vulnerable we are at any time or place.' With his shoestring budget, Arnet couldn't help thinking 'of all those lovely sails of Josh's going down with the boat – if only he could have thrown his asymmetric spinnaker over the side attached to a couple of floats … ' In Cape Town Arnet was to buy one of Josh's old foresails from his shipping container.

Messages of support for Josh flooded over the radio and satcom system from fellow skippers and people watching the race all over the world.

The drama of Hall's tragedy overshadowed the triumph of Isabelle Autissier, who celebrated her 38th birthday that day, stretching her overall lead to 1,223 miles.

Like horses coming from the outside into the final stretch, the race for second place in Class I was a near dead heat as Jean Luc Van den Heede, JJ Provoyeur and Steve Pettengill closed to within 12 miles of one another. Minoru Saito, meanwhile, was towed into Jacare Shipyard in Cabadelo, Brazil, to repair the steady leak in the daggerboard trunk of his 50-footer. Every few hours for eleven days Minoru had been pumping an estimated 200 litres of water from his boat. He was to spend three days in Brazil before temporary repairs were complete. Two of those days were spent trying to find the right person to do the repairs and careening the yacht to apply underwater epoxy. There were no lifting or haul-out facilities. A few days after he left Cabadelo, Minoru's yacht was still taking in five to ten litres an hour, but it was a big improvement. Before he had been pumping 12 hours a day. By the time he arrived in Cape Town it was down to three or four hours a day.

In a radio call to Race HQ from his new berth on *Newcastle Australia*, Josh Hall reported that, having succeeded in transferring food stores from his sinking yacht, the travelling gourmands had shared a coq au vin dinner. As solo sailors used to solitary confinement and now sharing a small space it took a few days before Josh and Alan adjusted to one another's company. 'We both talk a lot and there was a lot to talk about during our first week together,' said Josh. 'He was trying to keep my spirits up and I was trying bolster him up with his keel problems.

In fact, we both lost our voices after two days because we weren't used to talking that much! The circumstances of our being together were extraordinary enough for us not to think about it too much. We both enjoyed having someone else do the dishes, that's for sure.'

By now Niah Vaughan had overtaken Alan and Josh, moving into third place in Class II. With less than 2,000 miles to sail to the finish, David Adams was continuing to make inroads into the vanishing lead of Giovanni on *Kodak* as the two skippers continued to wage a private duel for first place.

Five weeks to the day after the race start in South Carolina, flowers began arriving on Saturday morning at the grounds of the Royal Cape Yacht Club as Isabelle Autissier was poised to sail into the history books as the first woman to win a leg of any BOC Challenge race. She was set to smash the 37d 11h record for leg one set by Alain Gautier on *Generali Concorde* in the 1990-91 BOC Challenge.

Some 130 miles from the finish line, Isabelle radioed race officials and apologised that she was going to keep them up all night. 'There was a full moon and this huge mountain was lit up like something in Hollywood. I could see it from 30 miles,' she said. Next she saw the lights of the spectator boats, first one or two then hundreds. At 0252 local time on Sunday, on the last blast of a fading southeasterly breeze, the 38-year-old engineer and marine science professor from La Rochelle crossed the line in Table Bay with an elapsed time of 35d 8h 52m, leaving the men 1,200 miles astern battling in her wake for second place.

It was a remarkable achievement by any standards. No major ocean race has ever seen a lead like it, said *The Sunday Times* correspondent, Keith Wheatley. Isabelle herself saw no significance whatsoever in her position as the first woman BOC victor. 'I'm just happy to be the winner. That's enough,' she said. 'Maybe for other people that's important, but not for me.'

Her time knocked 2d 2h 20m off the record. And the Charleston to Cape Town leg (6,865 miles) had been 127 miles longer than its host port predecessor of Newport.

Despite the hour, several hundred well wishers gathered at Cape Town's Victoria & Alfred Waterfront to greet the French heroine who responded by lighting a flare and waving to the crowd from the foredeck of her yacht. 'It's incredible. Even now I don't think I totally realise what has happened,' she said. Later at a press conference she said her weather forecasting ability had played an important role in her triumph. 'There were two or three things I did better than the others with regard to the weather.'

At the back of the fleet that night Floyd Romack, who had started a week behind the fleet, had 4,238 miles between him and Cape Town. Even Harry Mitchell had 3,397 miles to go, while Neal, 19 miles from Harry, was clearly envious. 'She'll be having breakfast on the terrace in the morning, and I'm not even in the same hemisphere!'

For Harry Mitchell cooking in his galley one night, the safety 'bumstrap' that he clipped on to the cooker and around his waist to brace himself against the motion of the yacht suddenly broke. The webbing was rotten and he fell backwards, striking the corner of the chart table. He lay on the cabin floor in excruciating pain gasping for breath for several seconds. It took him an hour to get off the floor. Harry only had one kidney, having damaged the other one playing rugby for his Hampshire team. The blow against the chart table had struck in the region of his surviving kidney.

'I was crawling around for two or three days. I couldn't cough or sneeze. The pain lasted nearly a month,' he said on arrival in Cape Town. 'A hot water bottle was my saviour. I used it to ease the pain.'

Giovanni Soldini, meanwhile, was experiencing rudder problems after a collision with a whale the previous week. The rudder had begun to delaminate and he had 'gone swimming' to cut off the trailing edge. Fellow Italian, Simone Bianchetti had arrived in Cabadelo to start repairs on the leaks that had plagued him since the start of the race, as well as hull delamination problems. There was only 2mm of skin left on parts of the affected hull just above the waterline near the bow.

On the morning of race day 37 Neal and Harry were the last of the fleet to cross the Equator, excepting Floyd. Harry had two teabags hanging on the guardrail of *Henry Hornblower*, 'so that Neptune could come aboard and have a cuppa with me.' The truth was he'd thrown them overboard, but they'd caught on the rails and stayed there until Cape Town. Neal had saved his Crossing the Line celebration for the afternoon when he cut up a melon, the last of his fruit. He found he had another reason to celebrate a few hours later when he saw Harry Mitchell's yacht on the horizon. They had been on the look out for each other since sunset the previous night, when they were nine miles apart and spoke on VHF radio. 'Harry and I spent the entire night in sight of each other. We shared the watchkeeping. He kept watch over me till midnight, so we didn't collide. I took the midnight to 0400 shift. Then he sailed away from me. I can't keep up with him,' admitted the young pretender.

That morning it was Steve Pettengill's turn to cross the finish line, sailing into second place with a time of 40d 16h 08m, but he was trailing Isabelle by more than five days. A highly experienced sailor, Pettengill had over 150,000 sailing miles to his credit. His 1989 record from New York to San Francisco in the 60ft trimaran *Great American 2* had been broken earlier that year by Isabelle.

With another five sailors from four nations scheduled to arrive in Table Bay, it was going to be one of the most eventful weekends in the history of the BOC Challenge. Late on Saturday night, defending BOC champion Christophe Auguin crossed the line in third place with a time of 42d 04h 58m. If he was disappointed in his showing, almost a week behind Isabelle, the pre-race favourite didn't show it, nor did he make excuses. 'I had over 30 days to get used to the idea that Isabelle might be a week ahead of me. I am just happy it is finished,' he said. 'I have only two litres of water left. My timing is perfect!'

Bearded and smiling, Auguin, who had been plagued by electrical problems, explained that his failed main and back-up generators had left him with limited use of his autopilots, forcing him to hand steer for up to 20 hours a day. 'It is not a big handicap,' he said modestly. 'It's more a stress situation. Normally I spend five to ten hours a day watching the weather and navigation. I am losing about one day altogether because of the generator problem.' In the last 10 days he had enough sun on his six 50 watt solar panels to power up the Autohelm. And during the last week, he had sought medical advice from his physician in France for treatment to a deep gash above his knee which he injured in a fall. 'The next leg will be a new race for me now,' he said.

Less than five hours later, at 0350 on Sunday morning, Australian David Adams took Class II honours in *True Blue* and broke the previous record set by Yves Dupasquier in the last BOC by more than two days and five hours. Adams, who had taken sixth place in the last BOC Challenge racing the 60ft *Innkeeper*, tipped his hat to winner Isabelle: 'She hit every waypoint spot on and turned the fan off as she went by!'

At one point, Adams trailed rival Giovanni Soldini (*Kodak*) by a demoralising 452 miles, but he clawed his way back into contention by sailing an extreme westerly course as the boats crossed into the South Atlantic. Comparing the first leg of this BOC Challenge with the previous one Adams said: 'This one was a bloody nightmare. The wind wasn't where it was supposed to be. It was light and frustrating. You just couldn't get a run on. It was just really bloody hard. I tore four spinnakers in the last four days into Cape Town and spent five hours hand-sewing one and patching the others with tape as soon as a hole appeared.'

Shortly after daybreak, with billowing cloud laying the famous tablecloth over the Table Mountain, BOC veteran Jean-Luc Van den Heede, hove in to view to finish with a time 42d 13h 54m. The three-times solo circumnavigator, a former maths teacher who had packed wine and foie gras for the voyage, was also confounded by the racing conditions. 'There were no tradewinds,' he said. 'The doldrums were very strange. Many of us were stopped by a big high pressure in the South Atlantic.' Van den Heede summed up the leg 'C'est la vie...'

Later on Sunday afternoon under beautiful summery blue skies local favourite JJ Provoyeur closed the coast with his huge masthead spinnaker pulling him homeward. He crossed the line in company with dozens of local yachts giving him an emotional welcome home. The South African had not been expected to press the leaders in his 1989 built yacht. 'They didn't consider me and in the end they had to. Except for Isabelle, they only finished a day ahead.' His time of 42d 22h 04m put him fifth in Class I.

Just after midnight, Giovanni Soldini steered *Kodak* across the line with a time of 43d 06h 22m and was still able to break the former Class II record by over a day. The wild weekend was finally over.

Back out at sea and still a week away from the finish line, Josh Hall was busy messaging Race HQ from Alan Nebauer's yacht announcing that the breakfast menu of chocolate chip pancakes had been reduced by his 'abysmal culinary skills' to chocolate chip fried porridge. Prophetically, he told Peter Dunning: 'If you need a teaboy for the winter months give me a shout!'

On Monday afternoon, coasting along smoothly on a favourable inshore breeze, David Scully in *Coyote* finished leg one and reckoned he'd 'probably covered more distance than any other yacht in the race.' He had found the wind on the nose for three quarters of the race and was disappointed that *Coyote* had sailed poorly to windward. His time was 43d 19h 34m.

Tail-end Charlie, Floyd Romack, with 3,500 miles to go, reported frustrating conditions. 'I want to go east, winds push me south or north. I want to go south, they push me east or west. Calms, light and contrary winds ... I've had more than my share. It's a nightmare! Across the Equator is supposed to be better. Can't wait. If you want the exact location of the doldrums just note my position. They have been with me for the past two weeks.' The lament was signed, 'Frustrated Floyd'.

Robin Davie celebrated his 43rd birthday on day 46 by surpassing remaining

Class II competitors with a best day's run of 177 miles. He had 2,000 miles to go. The sunny days and balmy breezes of the tropics were now a thing of the past. 'A tracksuit topped by oilskins is dress of the day,' reported Davie. 'Last apple being eaten. Onions are the only fresh veg left on board. Hard tack and ship's biscuits the rest of the way, plus two eggs for breakfast every day.'

Harry Mitchell and Neal Petersen were having a match race against each other as well as the restart clock as Neal slipped past Harry this time. Sixteen years ago, as a boy growing up in Wynberg, outside Cape Town, Neal had read the books by Francis Chichester and Alec Rose sitting in a tree house in his back garden. 'I remember being so inspired by those two circumnavigators, that I converted my tree house into an imaginary boat. With ropes from the branches and two long poles lashed, I was able to row my make-believe vessel and fantasised being on the high seas.' His dream had come to life during the first BOC Challenge in 1982 when he met competitor Richard Broadhead as the yachts arrived in Cape Town.

'I had been sailing a couple of years and followed the race with awe. I was an admirer of these adventurers and when the boats set sail I vowed to myself that one day I would sail with the fleet.' Neal had tried for four years to find sponsorship for a 50-footer, designed by Cape Town naval architect Phil Southwell. When it was too late to build the boat he looked at chartering or buying a secondhand yacht. It didn't work, and with less than a year to the start, he was left with no choice but to lengthen by two feet his own home-built yacht, *Stella-R*, which he had sailed in the singlehanded Transatlantic Race and the two-handed Round Britain and Ireland Races. He lived on the boat in a shed in Ireland with Gwen his Irish girlfriend while they poured every penny they could get into the cost of preparing the boat, renamed *Protect Our Sealife*.

'Several times the easiest thing would have been to give up the dream. There were many times when Gwen and I ate cereal for days at a time because there was no money for proper food. A week before the Charleston start I saw a ray of hope. ALTECH, an American company, committed themselves for a small sponsorship, and a South African brandy manufacturer, 100 Reserve, gave me some sails. Here I am now, with 2,500 miles left of this leg, looking back and happy. My boat might not be fast, but the dream is materialising. Some day I will sail in the BOC and Globe Challenge races aboard a purpose-built 60-footer.'

Meanwhile, in Table Bay, Niah Vaughan, the fourth Brit left in the race after the retirements of Mark Gatehouse and Josh Hall, became the first Brit to cross the finish line at noon local time, with a third place in Class II and a time of 48d 18h 01m. *Jimroda II*, Vaughan's 50ft yacht was on its third BOC Challenge. In the 1986-87 race it snatched first place in Class II as *Airco Distributor*, with Mike Plant at the helm. In the last race, renamed *New Spirit of Ipswich*, it came third with Josh Hall at the helm.

'She's a great old boat,' Vaughan said. 'She's twice as heavy as *True Blue*, *Kodak* and *Newcastle Australia*, but they're all twice as prone to something going wrong or breaking. The old girl was strongly made and she's going great.'

Back home in Niah's hometown of Whitehaven, Cumbria, four flagpoles were erected – one for each port of call during the race. As he arrived in Cape Town, *Jimroda*'s racing pennant was hoisted below the South African flag. Soon the whole town would know Niah had arrived.

Nine yachts in the BOC fleet still had to finish. Neal Petersen, three weeks

(*Above*) Eve of race fireworks display at the BOC Marina in downtown Charleston, South Carolina.
PHOTO: BILLY BLACK

(*Right*) Harry Mitchell is held aloft by fellow skippers at the prizegiving after the BOC Transatlantic Challenge feeder race from Falmouth to Charleston. Left to right: Nigel Rowe, Yves Parlier (winner), Jean-Luc Van den Heede, Neal Petersen, Niah Vaughan and Carl Brinkmann. PHOTO: BILLY BLACK

*Opposite page*) Isabelle Autissier streaks away in *EPC2* to a decisive win in the first leg. The new 60ft BOC yachts are rocket ships compared to us 'cruising boats",' said Mark Gatehouse. PHOTO: PATRICK ROACH

*Right*) Leading edge technology on display in the navigation station of Isabelle Autissier's yacht *EPC2*. PHOTO: PATRICK ROACH

*Below*) Low-tech disorder aboard *Henry Hornblower* as Harry Mitchell reorganises stowage in the cabin of his 40ft yacht. PHOTO: MARK PEPPER

America's best sponsored entrant in the race, Steve Pettengill. His state-of the-art yacht, *Hunter's Child*, had a million dollar budget. PHOTO: PATRICK ROACH

South Africa's Neal Petersen built his own boat, *Protect Our Sealife*, and borrowed the entry fee for the BOC Challenge. At 27 he was the youngest skipper in the race. PHOTO: BILLY BLACK

(*Opposite page*) On top of the world: David Barnaby checks the rig of *Hunter's Child* for that loose shackle that could spell disaster. PHOTO: BILLY BLACK

(*Inset*) The array of lin on *Hunter's Child*. Th speed indicator bears a sign 'Fun Factor'. PHOTO: PATRICK ROACH

*Top left*) Josh Hall helms his pride and joy, the 60ft sloop *Gartmore Investment Managers*, which sank four miles to the bottom of the Atlantic on race day 29 of leg one. PHOTO: GARY JOHN NORMAN

*Bottom left*) The minimal galley. Italian Giovanni Soldini's unconventional swinging galley arrangement aboard the spartan Class II *Kodak*. PHOTO: PATRICK ROACH

*Above*) Neal Petersen, the first black South African to compete in the BOC Challenge, arrives to a hero's welcome in Cape Town. PHOTO: CEDRIC ROBERTSON/PPL

*Right*) Blowing his brass foghorn as he cast off from the Charleston dockside at the start of his 27,000 mile adventure, Harry Mitchell on *Henry Hornblower*. PHOTO: PAUL GELDER

(*Above*) Home safely: rescued sailor Josh Hall arrives in Cape Town 22 days after his yacht sank, a passenger in the yacht of 'my best ever friend' Alan Nebauer's *Newcastle Australia*. PHOTO: BILLY BLACK

(*Right*) Involvement with hundreds of school pupils all over the world following the race was one of the spin-offs through the Ocean Watch education programme. Here Steve Pettengill enjoys a session aboard *Hunter's Child*. PHOTO: BILLY BLACK

*The smile says it all for shipwrecked mariner Josh Hall, reunited with his wife and son.*
PHOTO: BILLY BLACK

away from finishing, was singing the praises of modern satellite communications and INMARSAT-C linked to his latptop computer which 'keeps me in contact with the ones I love and miss. During the night that magic light flashed to indicate incoming mail. A few minutes later a message from Gwen in Ireland was delivered to me here in the middle of nowhere. Tomorrow she will be in Cape Town awaiting my arrival.'

Robin Davie recorded a personal best of 204 miles in 24 hours in *Cornwall*. 'Nothing to write home about when the 60-footers manage 320 miles, perhaps, but in the 11 years and 65,000 miles that *Cornwall* and I have sailed together we have never quite managed the elusive 200. *Cornwall* and I had grins like Cheshire cats.' For Robin 190 miles a day was a good day; anything under 120 miles a poor day and less than 100 a bad day. In the last 10 days, running before westerlies into Cape Town, he topped 200 miles on four days.

Floyd became the final vessel in the fleet to slip over the Equator, offering Neptune a tea bag, cookie, cracker, trail mix and Vodka. 'He welcomed me into the Order of Equator Crossers and I made him an honorary member of the Old Farts Club.'

Robin Davie, who had offered the milk of a coconut when he crossed the line three weeks earlier, offered his congratulations to 'Pink Floyd', Romack's nickname among some BOC sailors. 'Well done on joining the rest of the hooligans in the southern hemisphere.'

As the nearest competitor to Minoru Saito, Robin's progress towards Cape Town was interrupted in the middle of the night with an urgent satellite message. Saito's EPIRB (distress beacon) had begun to transmit its emergency signal to land stations and Robin was requested to divert to Minoru's current position

130 miles south-west as a precaution. False alarms were nothing new with EPIRBS. For Nigel Rowe, the next closest competitor to Minoru, who had just finished supper and was finishing his last bottle of champagne listening to some gentle Mozart, the call to arms was about as welcome as a cough in a concert hall. He wondered if it was an exercise.

In gale force winds, Robin put three reefs in his mainsail and turned *Cornwall* into the wind and seas to head towards his Japanese friend. After four hours, Race HQ correctly guessed that since Minoru's boat was continuing in the right direction at the right speed, the EPIRB had been accidentally activated or washed overboard. On the morning radio schedule it was confirmed that Minoru's beacon alarm was, indeed, a false one.

The incident underlined the uncertainties of rescue. Josh had been saved within a few hours by a fellow competitor sailing towards him in favourable winds. It would have taken Robin many hours beating against headwinds to reach Minoru. A long spell in a cold liferaft was a stark reality. Checking safety equipment was vital. 'Another skipper will always be the best hope of rescue,' reflected Robin.

A few days away from Cape Town, Nigel Rowe decided to have a matinee entertainment with his tea. He had shipped aboard *Sky Catcher* some cassette tapes of books and plays. His library included Jules Verne's *Around the World in 80 Days*, Daphne du Maurier's *Frenchman's Creek*, and John Le Carre's *Tinker, Tailor, Soldier, Spy*. 'I found the sudden exposure to everyday sounds of life ashore – walking on gravel, a London taxi, the clatter and conversation in a restaurant – a little disturbing. I had forgotten all about them. How familiar, comforting, yet wholly inaccessible they seemed.' Like others, Nigel felt deprived by his solitary confinement and the dismembered voices over the long range radio were no substitute for human contact.

For Arnet Taylor the ordeal was over as he crossed the finish line last in Class I with a time of 51d 15h 29m. 'I was out of it competitively from day one,' he admitted. 'My steering and autopilot problems took a few days to get sorted out and really cost me. There was more damage control than I would have wanted. But it was a very thorough sea trial.' Taylor had sailed 8,300 miles and his feet had not touched terra firma for more than eight out of the last 100 days. He had left Portsmouth, New Hampshire, to sail his BOC qualifier in August, spending just 36 hours ashore in the Azores before sailing to the Charleston start. There he had five days ashore before the race for Cape Town.

Later the same evening Alan Nebauer crossed the line with Josh Hall his passenger of the last 22 days. Alan wanted to sail across the finish line at top speed. He turned to Josh and said, 'Grab the wheel while I go below to get a few things', thinking of his light headsail.

'We made a big mistake,' said Josh. 'All the paparazzi were there snapping away with their cameras with me on the helm. It turned into a bit of an issue about whether the rules had been broken. We were just glad to be there.' Alan, given the opportunity for Josh to be taken off his boat before he crossed the line, insisted Josh stayed on board. It was a gesture much appreciated by the shipwrecked mariner.

Traditionally, each finishing yacht gets a magnum of champagne, but Alan was a non-drinker and Josh didn't feel as though he had anything to celebrate. 'It seemed really wrong. They wanted us to get excited about opening a bottle of champagne, but we couldn't,' said Josh. 'We just wanted to see our families. Alan

*Choking back the emotion at the Cape Town press conference; Josh Hall, Alan Nebauer and sons.* PHOTO BILLY BLACK

was re-united with Cindy, daughter Annie and Vance. I managed to sneak off while Alan was being interviewed and found Laura, Sam and my parents.'

On every BOC Challenge a skipper in distress has been rescued by another competitor. But there is nothing specific in race rules about the situation. 'There probably should be,' said Josh. 'It's very important psychologically for the rescued skipper to have some sort of active role on board. It's like getting back on a horse after falling off. You need to get your confidence back.

'After I'd been rescued, the last thing I wanted to do was go off singlehanded on a yacht, but by the time I arrived in Cape Town I was in a lot better shape to deal with what happened to me, having spent 22 days with Alan, than if I had just been flown straight ashore. I was also in better shape not to feel frightened of going to sea again. If I'd been flown straight ashore, I don't know, but part of me feels that maybe I would never have gone to sea again. It's hard to believe, but it's what I felt at the time.'

The dilemma is where you draw the line between finding a 'therapeutic' role for the rescued skipper, without offering an unfair advantage to the other skipper. 'We didn't suddenly turn it into a two-handed boat, but it was impossible to avoid discussing things,' admitted Josh. 'If I happened to be on deck and saw a squall coming I wasn't going to just stand there and watch it happen. I'd go and tell Alan "You've got a problem on your boat!" Basically I would be up all day and I would sleep all night. Alan would be catnapping and running the boat. We shared the cooking. I wasn't standing up there handsteering, but we talked weather and tactics. The whole thing might have been more of an issue if Alan hadn't had a keel problem which put him so far behind.' Alan's time of 52d 01h 11m gave him fourth place in Class II.

With *Newcastle*'s arrival in Cape Town, the media were eager to quiz Josh and Alan about the mid-ocean rescue drama at a packed press conference at the

Alfred & Victoria waterfront. Both sailors sat with their young sons on their knees. Josh was surprised at how emotional he was. 'I'd had three weeks to deal with it mentally and I thought I'd pretty much come to terms with it all. I started to give an account of what happened and just broke down in tears. I hadn't actually cried about the loss of the boat until then. It suddenly all came home to me.'

For Josh the race was over and while it was difficult to stay in Cape Town it was equally difficult to contemplate getting on a plane and flying home. For the last eight years, life had revolved around the BOC Challenge and while it would be hard to watch preparations and see the start of the next leg, Josh believed in facing problems and not running away.

Now that his own project in the race was over, he turned his energies to helping the man who had rescued him and worked on the refit of *Newcastle Australia* for the Southern Ocean. Better to go home feeling something positive than negative, he thought.

But he still found he couldn't attend a lot of the BOC Challenge functions. 'I was a part of it, yet I wasn't a part of it. I wasn't a skipper anymore. Nobody quite knew where to put me and I felt really awkward. It was difficult for all the other skippers. They didn't quite know what to say. I didn't want what happened to me to overshadow them. It was their race now.' Happily, as a result of staying on in Cape Town, opportunities came up for Josh to remain with the race until the end. He was invited to Charleston by Race Director Mark Schrader to join Peter Dunning's communications team, and he and Laura were flown to Sydney by *Newcastle Australia*'s sponsors to help in Alan's publicity drive.

While work began on the damage to *Newcastle* from hitting the raft, Alan estimated that the keel problem had cost him a week's time. 'So I'm really looking forward to leg two and proving a point.'

Back at sea, the danger of UFOs (Unidentified Floating Objects) came home to Robin Davie while he was on the foredeck changing headsails. He sensed a shape over his shoulder and looked round to see a huge harbour bell buoy floating along. 'If I'd been 15ft the other way I would have hit it. It was just pure luck that I happened to be up on deck. There was quite a sea running.' Days later Neal Petersen encountered another UFO when he hit a six foot long wooden sleeper on his port side. 'I was below when the thud came and charged on deck to see it drifting in my wake. Luckily, it was a glancing blow.'

In Table Bay Nigel Rowe became the 12th yachtsman to cross the finish line with a time of 52d 21h 04m. His passage had been a marathon of anxiety, disappointment, exhilaration, and new discoveries about his mixed skills as a single-hander. 'For someone whose working life has been spent in busy offices, crowded airplanes, and comfortable hotels, with other people to take care of the things I didn't want to deal with, two months at sea alone has seemed at times like the trials of Hercules.' He related a litany of troubles he had faced on *Sky Catcher*: a ruined headsail, a failed mast compression strut and boom vang, and both wind generators smashed by kamikaze flying fish. His impressions of the trip? 'I liked the first three days and the last five, where I had the best sailing. The bit in the middle was a little miserable...'

Life was no less miserable for Neal Petersen, who felt he 'could be the last person left on earth. It's incredibly quiet out here. No planes flying past, no ships to talk to, no whales and dolphins, not even birds. I'm glad I'm not a drinker. It would be easy to drown one's sorrows out here.' Neal had ten cookies left and only two cups of his favourite drinking chocolate. He had grown used to living at a 30 degree angle of heel, sitting on a sail bag, never sleeping more than 75 minutes at a time and having no one to talk to.

'It's worse than life in prison, and having lectured in five maximum security prisons in Ireland, I know! I can identify with the prisoners on several things: lack of freedom to walk around, poor food, endless time on your hands and cramped quarters. But at least prisoners get visitation rights and don't have to deal with bad weather and damp bunks. But I won't swap my lifestyle for theirs since I've found a type of freedom you find only in your mind and soul. Sailing single-handed, I know myself in a way that I doubt I would have discovered ashore.'

A thousand miles ahead of Neal, just 14 miles separated Robin Davie in *Cornwall* and Minoru Saito in *Shuten-Dohji II* in their duel for sixth place in Class II. Robin was counting out the last two gallons of diesel, three gallons of water, three Mars bars, four tea bags and ten onions. His last eight eggs from a batch of 120 from the hens at Mepkin Abbey monastery near Charleston, had lasted him 56-plus days and not a bad one among them. As he was powering towards Table Bay in a rip-roaring westerly breeze he placed his regular order to be sent out with Mark Schrader and the welcoming boat: 'Four pints of fresh milk, a tub of coffee ice cream and two packets of low tar cigarettes. I don't think many shops will be open when I get in.'

Neal and Harry, who had been holding each other's hands since the Equator, continued their match race as Harry overtook Neal this time. For the second time since the Equator they were in sight of one another. 'I closed the gap during the night,' said Neal. 'At dawn I spied Harry on my starboard bow and hoisted an asymmetrical spinnaker, knowing Harry can't carry one at this angle. I am slowly but surely catching him up.'

In the early hours of day 58, Robin Davie found himself virtually becalmed nine miles from the finish line. The city was lit up before his eyes as he drifted slowly into Table Bay on gentle zephyrs of wind. Two lifeboats came out to meet him with spotlights glaring. As he was towed to the Royal Cape Yacht Club at three in the morning, the obligatory bottle of champagne was thrust into his hand, but Robin was more interested in the coffee ice cream and several pints of fresh milk.

He was the 13th competitor to finish leg one. His passage (58d 08h 45m) had taken only 12 hours longer than leg one in his last BOC race. 'I had good winds right through. It was a helluva good run. I was just six days through the doldrums this time, where it took 12 in the last race. But I'll never do this leg again in a 40-footer.' Of course, he had said that last time, too.

Twelve hours later Robin was followed by Minoru Saito. The 60-year-old Japanese veteran arrived in Cape Town flying a storm trysail instead of his working mainsail which had been badly damaged in the storm 12 days earlier. His repair to a leak in his daggerboard trunk had only slowed the flow of water. 'I had to pump out five to ten litres an hour every hour for the last 15 days,' Saito said, 'but it was better than before when I was pumping 150 litres an hour!' The verdict on leg one from Minoru was: 'Too much work. Too much worry.'

Four Class II sailors remained in the race: Neal Petersen, 1,200 miles from Table Bay, was leading the quartet, followed by Harry Mitchell 18 miles astern,

Simone Bianchetti and Floyd Romack. All four were racing against the clock and the thirty day rule which stipulated that yachts must finish within 30 days of the arrival of the first boat in their (respective) class. Since David Adams had established a new Class II record the deadline was only 13 days away. The restart for leg two to Sydney was ten days away. Floyd Romack with 2,500 miles to sail was clearly in jeopardy of disqualification.

Over the next two days Harry slipped back badly, but he found time and the battery power to respond to a message via Race HQ from a dietician working on a research project on solo sailors and wanting to know about the first meal he was mentally planning in Cape Town. It was his longest message of leg one. 'Peter: received your fax: chest 37 and half inches; waist 35; hips 38. My head is very small. If I arrive in the morning: a breakfast of three eggs, bacon, tomatoes, mushrooms, coffee, toast and marmalade. If I arrive in the afternoon a large fillet mignon steak and French fries, mushrooms, fruit dessert, coffee. If it's evening: roast beef, potatoes, Yorkshire pudding, fresh asparagus and a good woman. Amen, Henry Hornblower.'

By day 65 Race HQ were concerned that Harry had dropped back 100-plus miles on Neal and appeared to be stalled. They sent the following message: 'Good morning Harry. Is everything okay on board? Your progress at half a knot is a bit disconcerting. Have you run out of wind? Please let us know what is happening. We await your reply with bated breath. Pete and Larry.'

Harry replied: 'You two guys with bated breaths, promise not to tell, my boat needs wind, and I ain't had none since dawn, while *Sealife* and *Town of Cervia* forge ahead with 10 knots. Everything else OK and thanks for your concern. Happy Horny Henry Hornblower.'

Harry had now fallen into a hole and was 200-plus miles behind. 'Neal, myself and Simone were all rushing in together and I was slowly catching up when I fell into a windless hole and lost two days while they rushed on. I'd been close to Neal twice and I was encouraging him because he was very despondent about arriving late in Cape Town and missing all the people he wanted to talk to about sponsorship. He was really chuffed when he flew away from me while I sat there wallowing in light airs. I had one day when I went backwards 15 miles! The worst thing in sailing is lack of wind. I know I can beat Robin Davie. I was ahead of him the first two weeks, but then he did the right thing and I got caught in calms. I'd rather have storms than soul-destroying calms. The last two days I was literally in tears. I had the same thing in 1986 on the second leg to Sydney through the Bass Straits when I covered just 100 miles in four days,' said Harry.

'The worst moment is sitting with absolutely nothing happening whatsoever. No books to read. Not enough power to put the radio on, because the solar panel is down. I didn't like to run the engine very much because I didn't have much diesel. It's like sitting in jail with nothing to do all day. You're not tired enough to go to sleep. Everything around you is flat calm, like glass. I had a bucket bath every 15 minutes.'

For Neal these were the longest hours of the race. 'So many years of dreaming and planning. So many years of struggling. I cannot believe that I am now counting down the final stretch in hours. There was a time when I was counting down the time to this day in years.' The Cape Doctor gusted at up to 30 knots to welcome Neal home and he could see the loom of his hometown lights reflected in the

*Having run out of wind, Harry resorts to a bucket bath every 15 minutes to keep his cool.*

clouds as he crossed his outward track. In the last four years he had sailed *Protect Our Sealife* some 30,000 miles solo, including crossing the Atlantic five times.

Neal sighted Table Mountain at midnight in the moonlight from 15 miles out. The gale force winds had abated and he was doing about 5 knots, but the breeze was still dying. He had already been passed by his rival, the 25-year-old Italian.

It was, as Media Relations Manager Herb McCormick said, 'a morning for mothers to reunite with sons who are living their dreams.' Three and a half hours after midnight, Simone Bianchetti cried, 'Mama!' as his mother Maria climbed aboard *Town of Cervia* to embrace her son after he'd crossed the line. He lit a flare to celebrate as he was towed into the docks. Bianchetti's time was 67d 9h 33m. 'I was not very lucky with my boat, or the weather,' said the former Italian Coastguard in a masterpiece of understatement.

Petersen's raucous mid-morning welcome was in stark contrast to the Italian's almost anonymous pre-dawn arrival. Neal's 71-year-old mother, Stella, greeted her son with a shout, 'Now you are home!' from one of the spectator boats. Fireboats described long arcs of spray as *Protect Our Sealife* (formerly named *Stella-R*, after his mother) was taken under tow. Petersen basked in the attention of being the first black South African to compete in the race. His time was 67d 16h 59m. 'It was a long tiring voyage and it's great coming home. I spent many of my boyhood days dreaming of this race. I watched the very first BOC leave this very Bay and I said to myself "I want to be there!" And now I am.'

In the new South Africa of President Nelson Mandela there were no longer any

*They'd been 'holding each other's hands since the equator': Neal greets Harry on his arrival at Cape Town.* PHOTO: DIANA MITCHELL

racial barriers at the Royal Cape Yacht Club. But most of the bartenders in white mess jackets were black. When Neal tied his red yacht up at the club pontoon after competing in an elite world-class sailing event and kissed his white girlfriend, Gwen, on the dockside 'it was a scene that was virtually inconceivable when the race last visited here in 1990,' said *Sunday Times* journalist Keith Wheatley.

While the young guns celebrated, the 'Old Men of the Sea', sailed on. For Harry there were 240 miles to go. Floyd faced 1,500-plus miles. Harry's target for Cape Town had been 55 days, but it took him 69d 21h 54m, three days more than he had taken in his previous yacht, *Double Cross*, in 1986. His timing was perfect – arriving in Table Bay as the rest of the BOC fleet appeared over the horizon on their way to Sydney for the second leg.

'It was quite a sight... the first time I've been coming in as they were leaving!' said Harry. 'I called up on the radio and someone suggested I might as well carry on .. except I only had three days food left! It was the biggest welcome of my life. Everyone followed me in from the start. They were all throwing beers at me. It was worth coming in late just for that! I felt like Robin Knox-Johnston being welcomed back from a circumnavigation.'

Harry's wife, Diana, was on *Rescue 3*, one of the South African lifeboats, which diverted to his yacht as soon as the start was over. *Rescue 3* was also towing David Scully's *Coyote* back to the yacht club with its mainsail damaged.

Harry radioed in to report his own time across the finish line, informing the timekeeper it was 'six minutes before 1400 Zulu.' 'In this country we don't call it Zulu time!' Mark Schrader reminded him later at the dockside.

Harry was towed past the banner welcoming BOC competitors on Cape

Town's dock pierhead. The port manager had told journalists at a press briefing that morning that when he asked his workers for suggestions, one had, in all innocence, come up with the slogan: 'Hello sailor! Have a great time between legs!' Another suggestion, 'It's great to get a leg over', had actually been accepted and displayed before being hastily removed. By the time Harry arrived it simply said 'Welcome to Cape Town'.

Tied up on the same pontoon he had been on in the 1986 race, Harry reflected on his fortunes. Leg one had been much tougher than eight years ago. 'I don't know if it's me or the boat. I can't remember sailing into so many calms before. Only Floyd had it as bad.' Sheer determination kept him going. 'Think young!' said the veteran, who looked as if he'd been out for a daysail in the Solent. 'You have to forget you've got one kidney and arthritis in one knee! Each person has a separate horizon and on that score you make the best of what you see on that horizon. I listened to the World Service. I kept busy with a sail repair that took two days. I mended a pair of glasses and repaired an old alarm clock that Floyd had thrown out. Those are the kind of things you occupy yourself with time on your hands. It's like a fella in a marathon race. It goes on and on, and you just want to get to the end. But 70 days was getting a bit much for me!'

If the BOC Challenge is the longest, loneliest race, Harry had experienced it to the limits. He had been at sea longer and, to conserve his limited battery power, had made minimal use of his radio to keep in contact with others in the fleet. Neal had been his only contact most of the time. 'Concern about the power drain by the INMARSAT-C (relaying the yacht's position to Race HQ) spoiled my whole voyage. It had to be switched on the whole time,' he said.

Harry boasted to well-wishers that he had 'the brownest bum in Cape Town! I didn't wear any clothes for five weeks, except when I went to bed at night and put on a T-shirt.' He had missed all the parties, including the prizegiving the previous night. When told he was booked into a room at the Breakwater Lodge, a former prison now converted into a three star hotel, Harry exclaimed: 'From one prison to another...'

But while other high-tech yachts had faced long repair lists, Harry's repairs for *Henry Hornblower* were minor: a damaged foresail and some work on the mainsail and windvane. 'He wasn't going fast enough to break anything!' joked Diana. Dan McConnell, BOC Media Operations Director, came to shake his hand and said: 'I can't wait to get to 70 and be as popular as you Harry, with people swarming all over my boat!'

Asked by reporters what he had been looking forward to most of all when he arrived, Harry replied: 'Meeting Diana, my wife. We've been married for 42 years.'

The last skipper to arrive in Cape Town, American Floyd Romack, turned up 12 days later after everyone else had disappeared over the horizon bound for Australia. It was 82 days after the Charleston start and he was ten days outside the 30 day rule. The rule was designed to discourage stragglers and keep the fleet together for safety reasons. In the lonely wastes of the Southern Ocean, where the best chance of rescue was by the nearest fellow competitor, the rule was especially relevant. No exceptions could be made and Floyd was disqualified.

# 4 · Race Against the Clock

Stopovers on a round the world yacht race can prove an impediment to, as well as an interlude from, the rigours of singlehanded sailing. Sleep patterns and bio-rhythms, which sailors have taken days to adapt to, are suddenly disrupted and will have to be re-established all over again. Against the emotional pleasures of being reunited with loved ones has to be offset against the impending turmoil of another farewell.

For the smaller yachts in the race, the Cape Town stopover was a difficult one. Mentally and physically the first leg, a long haul with fickle weather, means less time in port to prepare for the next. The most graphic illustration of this was the arrival at Cape Town of Harry Mitchell as everyone else left – the leaders having enjoyed a four week layover. 'I'm always in exceptionally good shape from the time the start gun goes until I cross the finish line,' said Robin Davie. 'The problems start at stopovers. Finding the money and the time to get the boat in shape is a race against the clock as well as the odds. It would be nice if stopovers could be a more relaxed, enjoyable experience.' Cut off from the downtown tourists at the Royal Cape Yacht Club, Robin was trying to sell T-shirts and sweatshirts. If he could raise enough money he could replace some more halyards. A timely grant from the Foundation for the Sports and the Arts helped towards the cost of buying a replacement long range radio and new sails. On the first leg Robin had used an old mizzen donated by Mark Gatehouse. South West Sails in Falmouth sent him two new sails in Cape Town.

For David Scully a low budget in Cape Town meant he could have only one shore crew, his brother-in-law, and though they worked double-time, *Coyote* wasn't ready for the start. In this race there's no time for what ifs and regrets; competitors must make the best of their boats and the miles still to go. 'I just want to get going and let the boat do its thing, and I hope nothing breaks to slow me down,' Scully said, tempting fate.

Arnet Taylor's shore support team were learning fast that every adventure has its price. *Thursday's Child* needed $40,000 before leaving for Sydney, which meant more furious fund raising by Katie Paine. Her mother, Nancy White-Thompson, a former editor at *Harpers Bazaar* magazine, offered a $5,000 antique tea set for auction at Sotheby's New York. 'We've got a guy out there on the thinnest shoestring budget of the bunch who's come up with bubble gum repairs to stay in the race,' said one supporter.

*Alan Nebauer disconsolately surveys the remains of his keel, smashed by a Cuban liferaft. All that is left is the main beam structure with some of the ballast attached.* PHOTO: CEDRIC ROBERTSON/PPL

Harry Mitchell, Neal Petersen and Robin Davie would argue about who had the thinnest shoestring, but if Arnet was short of cash he had something better than shoestring. One of his sponsors, the shoe-maker Timberland, had given him shoes; he bartered with a pair for $200 work on the yacht.

Arnet's shore team had put together something called 'The "Need" (as opposed to "Wish") List', which added up to $25,000 worth of necessities, like a survival suit, a heater, and rig repairs. A couple of extra sails were added, courtesy of Josh Hall and Steve Pettengill, and *Thursday's Child* eventually left Cape Town in excellent shape.

Back on home territory, JJ Provoyeur, who had given $1 guided tours of his yacht in Charleston, had written 800 letters to potential sponsors while his wife, Christine, was giving scores of presentations. He had given himself two weeks in Cape Town to find a sponsor. He was writing his resignation speech before he tied up a £100,000 sponsorship deal with a computer software company and changed the name of his yacht from *Ben Vio* to *Novell South Africa*.

David Adams believed in keeping things simple, but despite his anxiety over adding weight to the boat he installed a 'luxury' for the next two Southern Ocean legs – a toilet. Others, more weight conscious, including Isabelle Autissier, declined such comfort. Arnet Taylor joked that his shore manager, Merfyn Owen (a lightweight multihull designer) was barely talking to him because he was fitting a heater aboard *Thursday's Child*. 'Merf weighs things that come aboard by the gramme,' he said. Adams was taking a heater, too. He had a toe that was still numb from sailing in the Southern Ocean in the last BOC Challenge. 'It was so cold you couldn't get to sleep. Hot water bottles only lasted 20 minutes.' Nigel Rowe had left it too late to buy a heater and was searching Cape Town for hot water bottles – a scarce commodity in Africa.

Leg one of the fourth BOC Challenge had proved an unpredictable start to the adventure of a lifetime. In leg two the skippers faced unrelenting low pressure systems bearing gale-force westerly winds and mammoth seas in the Roaring Forties and Furious Fifties. 'The second leg of the race is the most physically challenging,' said Robin, who knew. 'It's spring in the Southern Ocean, but you've still got cold weather coming from the Antarctic, together with the potential for big storms. In the third leg, even if the weather is bad, you know what to expect. You've got a lot of Southern Ocean miles under your keel and a lot of experience in handling the boat, ready for rounding Cape Horn.'

## Cape Town
## to Sydney, Australia
## (6,698 miles)

# 5 · Sea Dark, Sky Crying

Fourteen of the remaining BOC Challenge fleet of 18 yachts sailed across the Cape Town start line for the 7,000 mile voyage through the treacherous waters of the Southern Ocean to Sydney. The most poignant figure to wave them off was Josh Hall, who busied himself by doing the race commentary for some 300 BOC AFROX guests on one of the South African Navy ships. He hadn't been keen to do it, but he knew it was going to be a difficult day and it kept his mind occupied.

Of the four who didn't make the 26 November re-start, two, Neal Petersen and Simone Bianchetti, had postponed to complete repairs and preparations to their yachts. With impeccable timing, Harry Mitchell, a few miles off the Cape, was threatening to make the start line into a finish line. Late starter Floyd Romack still had more than 1,000 miles to sail to Cape Town.

An hour before the high noon start Arnet Taylor's *Thursday's Child* was still tied up to the dockside of the Royal Cape Yacht Club, as he busied himself putting the finishing touches to the installation of a new weather fax machine. In true BOC spirit, fellow competitor David Scully, who had the same model weather fax aboard *Coyote*, hopped aboard to give Arnet the fastest lesson ever in how-to-use-a-weather fax. Ironically, it was Scully who became the first casualty of leg two before the start gun was even fired. He blew his mainsail and was forced to return to the Royal Cape Yacht Club as the rest of the fleet jostled for best position on the line.

Under clear blue skies with a 15 knot south westerly breeze, an armada of spectator craft dotted Table Bay to wish the fleet bon voyage. Sixteen South African Airforce Harvard jets flew over the bay in a diamond-shaped formation followed by three helicopters trailing the South African flag. Red and blue balloons were released from tugs. In the excitement Steve Pettengill suffered a severe gash to his scalp during pre-start manoeuvres when he hit his head on the top of the companionway hatch as he scrambled on deck just before the gun went off.

Niah Vaughan on *Jimroda II*, one of the oldest boats in the race, stole the limelight and provided further evidence of his competitive streak as he sneaked over

*Even sailing cautiously at the start to avoid a collision, Isabelle's* EPC2 *made a spectacular sight in Table Bay.* PHOTO: PAUL GELDER

the line to lead the fleet away from the Tavern of the Seas. He was followed by the red ketch of Jean-Luc Van den Heede.

Close behind, David Adams had set himself a target of 28 days to reach Sydney. The incentive was to get to Australia before Boxing Day and the start of the fully crewed Sydney-Hobart yacht race. 'The sight of hundreds of bloody maniacs coming down the east coast of Australia is not something I am looking forward to,' said Adams. 'This leg is an important one for me and Alan because we are going home.'

Isabelle, who was starting out with a five and a half day lead on her fellow competitors, chose a cautious start to avoid disaster in the scramble. But she immediately held spectators spellbound with her speed as she got underway.

'I will not have to take risks,' she said. 'Maybe some of the others will. It's quite cold and dangerous if you have to take risks in the Southern Ocean, so I'm glad I won't have to do that.' By nightfall Isabelle was in a tacking duel for first place with Van den Heede.

To reduce the odds of danger from collisions with icebergs drifting northwards from Antarctica, race organisers had established a waypoint at 53° south and 72° east, which skippers had to leave to starboard. Anyone sailing south of the waypoint, monitored by the satellite communications system, faced disqualification. Nobody was complaining.

Back at the Royal Cape Yacht Club, Scully was examining his severely damaged mainsail with his support crew. The high-tech composite fabric had failed, either as a result of delamination or deterioration through exposure to UV radiation. 'It's what happens when you use leading edge technology. You're a proving ground for gear and sometimes you're proved wrong.' The man with a million dollar boat and a shoestring budget walked up the dock and admitted 'The shoestring's getting shorter these days.'

Downcast, but not out, Scully was lucky to be able to borrow a secondhand mainsail from former Cape Town BOC competitor Bertie Reed. It had already been around the world in the last BOC race on *Grinaker* and at full hoist was the equivalent of his original sail with one reef tied in. But given the strength of winds in the Southern Ocean its smaller size was, perhaps, academic. There, reefed sails are a way of life. It would have to do. Choice was not a luxury he could afford to indulge. 'This is like trying to do a Formula One race on one set of tyres,' he said. 'You get a bit more behind with each circuit.'

Scully set off in the early hours of the next morning, only to be jinxed again. This time he had to turn back to deal with problems on the electrical circuit board of his autopilot. As Scully finally rejoined the fleet for a third time at mid-morning on Sunday, Alan Nebauer, having rounded the Cape of Good Hope, diverted to the Navy port of Simonstown to repair a faulty alternator. When Alan set off later the same evening, he had lost several hours on the fleet and reckoned it put him in a different weather pattern, costing him several hundred miles.

Arnet Taylor had faced up to a multitude of equipment failures on the first leg, but he hadn't expected the gremlins to creep back aboard *Thursday's Child* quite so soon on leg two. His long-range SSB radio packed up after broadcasting for ten seconds, his IBM laptop computer acquired 'a stellar virus', the newly installed heater went out after two delightful 'glowing evenings' and a generator fuel fitting dumped a gallon of smelly diesel fuel in the aft compartment.

But the biggest blow came in the early hours of the morning after the race start. While beating into strong winds near the fleet leaders his big foresail, a Kevlar genoa, exploded spectacularly as he was rolling it in, leaving 20ft ribbons streaming through the rig. 'This had the same effect as removing third gear from our 12-year-old car,' he reported. He was now reduced to a staysail for upwind work. In light conditions his performance took a nose dive.

'Nobody to blame but myself. I knew the sail was tired, but I was up near the front and gaining, so I pushed it too hard and for too long.' Arnet was paying the price of a low budget and old gear. 'The first and the last weeks of these passages are pretty demanding,' he reflected. 'Just getting adjusted to sorting out minor issues, watching for shipping and, of course, sailing the boat ...' Before long, *Thursday's Child*'s gremlins would return with a vengeance.

Meanwhile, the gallic trio of Isabelle Autissier, Jean-Luc Van den Heede and Christophe Auguin were first across the 36th parallel, moving into battle for an early lead. Once more, Isabelle and David Adams were at the top of their respective classes.

Robin Davie on *Cornwall* had experienced a slow start and was feeling distinctly under the weather, suffering from a flu-type bug, sore throat, headache and hot and cold sweats. He'd taken to his bunk, keeping his humour intact as he sent a message: 'We're cracked off in 15-20 knots easterly and heading south for paradise.'

The first week had barely begun before it was apparent that purgatory, rather than paradise, was where the BOC yachts were headed. A 50-knot south easterly gale ripped through the fleet, leaving what Herb McCormick called 'a sailmakers' bonanza of savaged mains and jibs'. Jean-Luc's *Vendée Enterprises* had a torn mainsail, forcing him to carry on under three reefs. Christophe's yacht had a ripped headsail which became fouled in the rig, forcing him to wait for conditions to moderate before he could free it. As Harry Mitchell and Neal Petersen set off from Cape Town in a fresh westerly breeze to rejoin the race on the afternoon of day five, after a quick turnaround, the worst was yet to come that evening. Before he left, Harry was quite relaxed and enjoyed a pot of tea with Diana, served by the Royal Cape Yacht Club.

'Harry and I will be talking on the radio this evening,' said Neal. 'There are no secrets between us. We have a fantastic relationship. We're important for each other's morale. We keep each other going.' On their first night at sea, the two skippers glimpsed their last sight of civilisation – the shaft of light sweeping the horizon from the Cape of Good Hope lighthouse, perched spectacularly on its rocky precipice at Cape Point, a granite finger at the foot of Africa. Here the waters of the Atlantic and Indian Oceans merged in a maelstrom which had claimed the bones of many a ship and sailor. With 20 knots of wind blowing, this solitary sentinel of the Southern Ocean soon vanished in the blackness of that first night of December.

More than one thousand miles ahead, Isabelle Autissier's was the southernmost boat in the fleet, speeding along under staysail and reefed mainsail at more than 13 knots. The wind was freshening to 25 knots with gusts up to 30. It took just a split second and an unavoidable slam on the portside for her dreams to suddenly come toppling down around her. A rigging screw on the yacht's main port shroud failed and the mast collapsed over the starboard side, snapped at the base.

'I felt like I had been hit in the stomach. I thought "No. Not this. Not here." It was already over for me. But what was the use of yelling, shouting and crying in the southern mist for a victory that was completely lost?' Isabelle asked herself. She sent a tantalizingly brief message to Race HQ in Charleston: 'Dismasted. No danger immediately.' Her approximate position was 1,200 miles from Cape Town, 48° 52m south 38° 46m east.

Then there was no time to waste. A mast can become a horrific hammer of carbon fibre threatening to puncture the hull of a yacht. The winch at the foot of the mast was already starting to smash a hole in the deck.

With hacksaw, pliers and a knife, Isabelle scrabbled about on her knees cutting away the rig as the yacht rolled helplessly. The water temperature was just three degrees and water was flying everywhere. She tried to save the boom, but then that, too, broke, dragged down by the weight of the mainsail.

Ninety minutes later, the entire rig had been cut away and thrown overboard. Isabelle stood on the bare deck of her yacht which bore the scars of disaster. She had one complete spinnaker pole and half of a broken one. 'There are 5,000 miles left to Sydney. I feel so much like crying for my lost hopes. But this is the way racing goes. Great happiness in Cape Town. Great sorrow here.'

David Adams, 65 miles away, who had been the first in the fleet to cross into the northern limit of the Roaring Forties, was notified of Isabelle's dismasting and immediately diverted to her position, sailing at 11 knots in storm force winds.

All day long in rough sea conditions and strengthening winds, Isabelle worked to set up a replacement rig. The work was exhausting and intricate. In an eloquent

*Using a storm jib as a mainsail and a small upside down jib as a genoa, Isabelle's jury-rigged EPC2 managed 100–160 miles a day.*

message to her supporters in France, she described her plight: 'Thirty knots of wind, sea dark, sky crying. I'm working to clear off the deck and see what I can do. There is almost nothing left on deck. Nothing left of my dream. But I won't think about that now. I am safe … ' By evening she had managed to put the small pole at the mast foot, ready to use it as a support for raising the main nine metre pole as her replacement mast the next day.

Out of the mist and the darkness that night the ghostly silhouette of David Adams' *True Blue* suddenly appeared and swept past riding the ocean swell under three reefs. Adams had been Isabelle's ex-crewman on *EPC2* in the New York to San Francisco record-breaking attempt the previous winter. He was a close friend. More than anyone else in the race he would understand the emotional turmoil Isabelle was suffering.

As Adams passed to leeward again Isabelle could see his silhouette on deck. His arrival was reassuring. 'How are you Isa? Can I help?' he shouted at the shadowy figure on deck waving a torch. The mastless boat was, in Adams' words, 'rolling her guts out'.

'No Dave, just think about me. It's just so good to see you that's all. Good luck. Have a good race, see you in Sydney,' she called back.

Adams stayed on station for a while. Words seemed inadequate. And in the conditions conversation was impossible. They could only talk in bursts of shouting. Then they switched to 'talking' for a while on their laptop computers, via the satellite.

'There was nothing I could do. There was no way Isabelle was going to get off and no point in my hanging around. If you accept outside help you are disqualified,' said Adams afterwards. Soon his blue hull faded away in the darkness. But he was deeply affected. 'Isabelle didn't need my help so I carried on. But for two days I couldn't get anything together. The sight of her alone on deck with that grotty little spinnaker pole up in the air was just too much, especially since I couldn't help. I was surprised by how much it affected me.'

For Isabelle, too, it was hard to keep up her spirits. 'Everything tastes like ashes and I am physically and morally exhausted. What is the point in continuing a race already lost? But I already know I will carry on because one cannot quit like that. I am in the race until I cross the finishing line, no matter what it takes.'

As she slept that night it was blowing 40 knots and *EPC2* was drifting due south of two remote island outposts: Marion Island and Prince Edward Island. Coastguard officials in South Africa had been notified and had an aircraft on standby alert.

'Perhaps the Indian Ocean doesn't want me,' thought Isabelle as she lay in her bunk. She had suffered a dismasting four years ago on this same leg of the BOC Challenge, but nearer Sydney, off Tasmania. On that occasion the mast had broken at the first spreader and she had successfully fashioned a jury rig and sailed into Sydney Harbour to step a new mast. Once again the only woman in the race, she gained many admirers by going on to complete her circumnavigation.

At the crack of dawn next day, Isabelle began work afresh on erecting an emergency mast. Using her small five metre broken spinnaker pole, with a halyard rigged from the top, she raised the nine-metre pole. 'It sounds easy, but in the bad weather it took me 24 hours crawling on my hands and knees and after many trials,' she said. 'I am forgetting about the second leg. My goal is to arrive in Sydney with enough time to make preparations to start leg three with the others.'

Under two tiny headsails, Isabelle set course for Kerguelen Island, a remote French outpost some 1,200 miles away that was home to weather and scientific research stations. Two days later, when the sun was out, she worked to reinforce the base of her new mast with epoxy glue and carbon fibre. She wound a length of small diameter rope around the mast and glued it together to add thickness at the foot. In the damp conditions, to help it dry, she made a tent around the mast and used her small emergency generator inside to add warmth.

*EPC2* was averaging 4 knots and was expected to arrive at Kerguelen Island in 13 days. Sources in France confirmed that a replacement mast for her yacht had been found on Reunion Island and was being shipped to Kerguelen on a French cargo vessel. But at 13 metres it was much shorter.

While Isabelle nursed her yacht towards a safe haven, Arnet Taylor had picked up one of her radio calls requesting help in relaying communications. His understanding of French was fragmentary, but he noticed that there was 'no panic or tears in her tone, just a friendly competence in dealing, intrepidly, with a very dangerous situation. She had become a friend and I was glad that she was alright, and unharmed. And, yes, I was inspired.'

Arnet, meanwhile, at the end of his first week at sea, faced the return of more gremlins on *Thursday's Child*. Having retired to his bunk for his midnight siesta, he woke suddenly when the boat gybed. The water ballast was on the wrong side and he realised that the yacht was out of control. He arrived on deck feeling groggy and hit the autopilot to swing the boat downwind before sorting out the tangle of sheets, guys, poles and sails on the sloping deck. He then tried to get control of the helm. But when he grabbed the tiller there was no response. He looked over the stern and saw that the rudder had been torn off its lower attachment. It was hanging by a few shards of fibreglass. He didn't know if the damage had been caused by the sea, or if the yacht had collided with something. Fortunately, there was no apparent damage to the hull. By the time he had squared away the chaos on deck the rudder had totally disappeared. He alerted Race HQ to his emergency and Niah (*Jimroda II*) and Nigel (*Sky Catcher*) kept a listening watch on the radio in case their assistance was needed.

One unique feature of *Thursday's Child* is a small skeg, or dagger board, on the stern to help the yacht track in heavy weather. The skeg had a short shaft and a couple of bearings at the top, and was conceived as an emergency rudder when fully pushed down and pinned in place. Arnet was dubious about its long range merits, but by the next day it was pressed into action. It gave the yacht more stability and allowed him to hold a course more effectively. But he wasn't taking any chances. He altered course northwards, heading for calmer latitudes to nurse *Thursday's Child* out of the Roaring Forties and towards Australia at slower speeds. Returning to Africa against prevailing winds was not an option.

A second skipper who altered course to the north-east under small headsail to attempt repairs was Steve Pettengill, who had rigging problems on *Hunter's Child*. In 15ft seas he climbed the mast to replace a broken rigging rod with a double strand of rope that he winched up tight from the cockpit. Later, after multiple trips up the mast in 15ft seas, he made a more substantial repair and was back underway preparing his yacht for gales packing winds of 50 knots, expected to strike the fleet within 24 hours. He felt sick about Isabelle's dismasting. 'I wish we could have spoken, but I found myself putting out fires of my own. I'm sure that her seamanship will get her to Sydney and I'm looking forward to getting our match race going again.'

Eight days after the restart two yachts were still in Cape Town waiting to start the second leg of the BOC Challenge. *Town of Cervia*, skippered by Simone Bianchetti, had left once, returning a few hours later reporting continuing leaks in the hull. Floyd Romack, 300 miles from Cape Town, felt he had been at sea 'forever'. He had missed the deadline to restart and was due to discuss his future in the race with officials on arrival.

On *Jimroda II*, Niah Vaughan was busy putting a radio call through to his home town of Whitehaven, in Cumbria. His contact 6,000 miles away was Jim Gregg, who was immensely proud of the 'local lad who had sailed into Table Bay third behind the fast boys' and who'd had a flying start, first across the line for the second leg.

'We live and breathe salt water in this part of the world. Ask them in the local hospital,' said Jim. 'When they stick a knife in you, it's not blood that comes out, it's salt water!' Jim would soon know. He had been on the waiting list for an operation for two years and as Niah's call was put through by the operator from the South Atlantic an ambulance had pulled up outside his house to take him to hospital. 'You'll have to be quick,' Jim told Niah when he picked up the phone.

Later, as Jim was being wheeled, still conscious, into the operating theatre, the anaesthetist leaned over and asked him: 'Are you the Jim Gregg who's supporting Niah Vaughan? How's he doing?' 'Even then they were more interested in Niah than my treatment!' said Jim.

After the operation, a young surgeon came to see Jim next day. 'How are things going?' he asked. Jim told him he was a little bit sore, but otherwise not bad. The doctor replied: 'I didn't mean you, I meant how's Niah getting on?' This was the extent of Whitehaven's consuming interest in Niah's place in the BOC race.

As the fleet braced itself for storm force winds, Christophe Auguin had opened up his lead over second-placed Jean-Luc. The deadly rivals in the 50ft class, David Adams and Giovanni Soldini, were separated by a mere nine miles. It was snowing at the front of the fleet as they started to enter the Furious Fifties. Sub-zero temperatures made deck work difficult. Isabelle was still making slow progress towards the Kerguelen Islands.

On day nine, the morning edition of the fleet's satellite newsletter *The Trailer Gazette*, the newspaper read by more singlehanders over their morning coffee than any other, reported that Harry Mitchell was 'doing yeoman's work by positioning himself so that no one can attack the fleet from the rear.' Mitchell, some 1,500 miles back at 39° south, responded with a letter to the Editor: 'Hey you radio bums, what gives with this Gazette? First, who is the chief editor? Who is the reporter? And, most important, who is the office tea boy? Second, we would rather hear what a success Clinton is having or what's happened to Mickey Mouse, not the crazy things happening to nutcases out here! Congratulations, Henry the Blower.'

After nine days of racing, Robin Davie on *Cornwall* found himself deep in the Roaring Forties at 48° south, 800 miles west of Kerguelen Island. He had been raiding his medical supplies to keep his flu-type symptoms at bay. His friend Minoru Saito, coping with yet another leak on *Shuten-Dohji II* from a deck fitting over the galley, announced on the radio how 'boring, boring' it was with no gales, no big seas, no hail and no snow, all of which they had experienced four years ago. The contrast couldn't be sharper, agreed Robin, who remembered only too well how bitterly cold it had been with 30-40 knot winds coming off the Antarctic ice mass.

'Being of a wimpish disposition towards the cold, I feel I could be bored all the way to Sydney!' thought Robin, who was now experiencing constant, clammy, cold fog. It was just like being off the Grand Banks of Nova Scotia, or off the Dodman in Cornwall in a winter mist.

Neal Petersen was recording his fastest average speed in the race with 10 knots over a six hour period between position reports. He had sent a brief message back to Race HQ: 'Hi guys, it's blowing 30-plus out here. I feel scared, small and a little lonely. It's getting cold. Already looking forward to Sydney and missing Gwen.'

Neal snuggled down into his bunk for a snooze. He woke, literally hitting the roof, and landed back in his bunk, tearing out some of the cabin's electrical wiring as he grabbed wildly for a hold on something in his upside-down nightmare. At 0945 GMT on day ten of the race Neal became the second yachtsman to be dismasted in 40-45 knot winds. It was just five days since he had rejoined the race with Harry.

Neal was 300 miles south of Port Elizabeth when *Protect Our Sealife* was rolled by a breaking wave and suffered a knockdown that broke the yacht's mast between the first and second spreaders. The EPIRB, mounted on the stern rail, was washed overboard and activated. It was Floyd Romack, still underway on leg one, who relayed Neal's initial distress call to the South African authorities and stayed in contact.

Waves washed over Neal's boat and the top section of the mast hung from the rigging, poised precariously to fall and possibly puncture a hole through the deck. Neal looked up anxiously. Over the next six hours it was a waiting game as he watched for metal fatigue, in case the mast top 'spear' fell before the weather abated and he could secure things. His cooker was out of action, with pieces of it scattered around the cabin. A leak over his bunk made things even more uncomfortable as he got wet with every wave that swept the deck. He tried to get some rest and dry his boat while his thoughts raced with various plans to fashion a jury rig and sail his yacht back to port.

As Neal drifted helplessly Harry Mitchell, 90 miles north-east and his closest competitor, was ploughing on at 6 knots having himself survived a knockdown in the storm. There were half a dozen eggs in the toilet bowl, loaves of bread in the clothes locker and the charts were all over the saloon. It took days to find things. The glass in his gimballed brass *Gypsy Moth* oil lamp over the galley had been smashed in the violent motion.

In his last BOC Challenge Harry had never had a knockdown. Now he estimated the waves were as high as his mast. As *Henry Hornblower* staggered to the top of a wave it was like looking down into a valley in the Lake District, thought Harry. He didn't linger long in the cockpit. His biggest worry was broaching or gybing while running before breaking seas. 'Your ears are tuned to listen for every creak and knock,' he said.

When Harry heard of Neal's dismasting it upset him badly. He and Neal were competing in their third singlehanded race together, after the OSTAR and the BOC Transatlantic Challenge. They had spent most of leg one sailing in company, or at least staying in radio contact. Now Harry faced the long trek across the terrible expanse of the Southern Ocean alone at the back of the fleet. Most of the time he would be more than 1,000 miles from his nearest competitor. He hadn't looked forward to this leg of the race. Now the spectre of loneliness loomed even larger.

Neal eventually managed to get his heater going and was warming up. He was drying his sleeping bag and planning a night in his bunk resting before starting on erecting his jury rig at daybreak. Neal was aided throughout the early hours of his ordeal by regular radio contact with Robin Davie, who relayed advice and encouragement. Davie reported back to Race HQ: 'Neal is optimistic about his chances of making it back to Cape Town. I suspect that Port Elizabeth, London or Durban might be the achievable result.'

With the top section of his broken mast secured alongside, Neal had rigged a block and line to stop the remaining bottom section from wobbling around. The sideways thrust when the mast broke had caused the base of the spar to sheer off the mast step inside the yacht. Neal had lashings down below to try to secure the gyration and motion of the bottom of the mast.

On day 12 Robin continued to update Race HQ on Neal's progress: 'He's having a difficult time ... with the wind in the north the best course he can make is a little south of east. He needs more favourable winds to be able to close the coast.' Soon Robin himself was expecting to feel the force of the depression that had blown Neal out of the race. French forecasters were predicting 50-60 knot winds at 48° south in the next couple of days. The options for Robin were to keep going, as he was, heading eastwards, or to pull up to the north, hoping for lighter winds. 'It's a case of man or mouse, and I suspect that the squeaking will be audible if you go to the top of St Agnes Beacon (in Cornwall) and listen,' he said.

As Neal battled to save his boat, Simone Bianchetti sent off a distress message on *Town of Cervia* which scrambled rescue services worldwide. The signal from his INMARSAT-C unit was relayed to a rescue control centre in Greece, who in turn contacted Race HQ in Charleston. But as the National Sea Rescue Institute (NSRI) crews set off in their lifeboat from Cape Town, Bianchetti called off the operation, altering course under his own power to Cape Town. So far Bianchetti had returned to port more than any other yachtsman in the race. Questions would be asked about his suitability to continue in the race.

Bianchetti's Italian compatriot Giovanni Soldini was, meanwhile, skilfully and relentlessly driving his state-of-the-art downwind flyer in a continuing private duel with David Adams as the two yachtsmen dipped below the 51st parallel. The duo, setting a frenetic pace in their match race for Class II honours, were lying fourth and fifth in overall fleet standings, ahead of four of the larger, and theoretically much faster, 60-footers.

Adams was keeping a close eye on the low pressure system that had wreaked havoc with Neal and Harry and was now tracking towards them.

'That front is going to catch us soon,' said Adams. 'In a race like this you can expect at least one decent storm and this is probably it ...'

David Scully, on his first Southern Ocean adventure, was having problems generating power aboard *Coyote* and wondering if anyone had a recipe for penguin? 'I am forced to drive much of the time and sing to keep warm. I would be happy to take requests and dedications from fellow competitors. Expect heavy demand for Buddy Holly's *Every Day (It's Getting Closer)*, *Blue Skies*, and, for those south of 50° south, *Radar Love.*'

For Scully the worst part of the voyage had been at the beginning when the grub screws holding his roller furling gear had started to come loose. He'd had to climb the forestay foil twice and finally managed by stringing spinnaker poles together to give himself something to hang on to. 'I hope Loctite isn't poisonous, because I swallowed a lot of it,' he said. Later on his water ballast tank burst, filling the cabin with 300 gallons of swirling water.

Day 13 of leg two was unlucky for Simone Bianchetti and Floyd Romack, who saw their hopes for completing a solo circumnavigation dashed for separate reasons. Bianchetti, back in Cape Town to repair his yacht, finally withdrew. Keel problems and safety concerns were cited as the main reason for his resignation. Floyd Romack finally arrived after a long and lonely epic 82-day voyage from Charleston, only to be disqualified under race rules for failing to complete the leg within 30 days of class leader Adams' finish. As a consolation, Race Director Mark Schrader invited Floyd to rejoin the fleet in Punta del Este and sail the final leg home in an unofficial capacity. It was an offer which Floyd, tired and disappointed, seemed likely to accept.

In the last few months Floyd had sailed across the Atlantic twice and sailed from America to South Africa. It was more than many yachtsmen do in a lifetime, never mind at the age of 66. 'He's done it with exceptionally good humour and he's had a lot worse weather than we had to contend with. I take my hat off to him,' said Robin Davie.

Neal Petersen, some six days away from Port Elizabeth under jury rig, conceded in an eloquent message to Cape Town that he would not be able to continue in the race. He estimated that repairs would take so long he had no chance of reaching Sydney in time for the start of leg three.

'I have asked more of my boat than I had built her to give. She has given me 99 per cent of my requests. Most important, she has kept me alive in troubled waters. I hang up my sea boots for now. I have not failed. I have not succeeded. It is time to regroup my resources and strengths and in 1998 I will have a campaign to finish what I have started. I'll be back in four years, come hell or high water.'

Already, the defiant Petersen was planning his next BOC Challenge, but for now his dreams of being the first black South African to circumnavigate the globe were put to rest. After a 10 day passage under jury rig he was finally taken under tow to Port Elizabeth. He, too, was hoping that after repairs to his yacht he would be able to sail to Punta del Este and join the fleet, unofficially, for the final leg back to Charleston.

The BOC fleet was now reduced from 20 yachts to 15.

After eight days under jury rig and still four days away from Kerguelen Island, Isabelle Autissier was able to report emphatically that 'sailing with a jury rig is not fun!' even though she was managing between 100 and 160 miles a day.'When the weather is good (under 25 knots of wind) I can use the storm jib as a mainsail and the small upside down jib as a genoa. The boat is doing between four and eight and a half knots (my best speed).'

Another competitor considering a diversion to Kerguelen was Minoru Saito, who had suffered a failure of both electronic autopilots as well as a broken windvane. He was having to hand steer or lash the wheel. An autopilot will steer a better course 90 per cent of the time than 90 per cent of helmsmen. As American solo sailor Phil Weld once observed: 'You can get too dependent on your autopilot. Then when it fails, you're like the mother with three kids under six when the imported English nanny quits. Back to gulped meals, snatched naps and no time for pondering the weather map.' Minoru was about to face 4,000 miles of the world's worst ocean without his nanny.

# 6 · 'A Great Place for the Mother-in-Law'

Robin Davie on *Cornwall* had sailed 1,200 miles in the last seven days. Good progress in view of the light weather. As the threatened 50 knot storm blew through to the south of him, Robin reported that 'the lion didn't roar and the mouse didn't squeak.' But south-east of Kerguelen Island it was cold, with days of thick fog as well as some pleasant sunny days. At 51° south, Robin was no further south than Bude in Cornwall is on a northerly latitude. And strangely it was only seven days to midsummer's day in the nearly freezing Southern Ocean.

Along with the fog and the cold everything was damp. The deckhead and bulkheads were wringing wet and dripping, the chart table navigation instruments were beaded with condensation. Even his bedding was cold and damp and would never dry out until *Cornwall* sailed northwards into warmer Australian waters in another 15-17 days.

Robin was well geared up for the cold with Polar Bear suits and leather lined sea boots, donated by Cornwall College. He kept the cabin hatchway open to the elements all the time so the boat temperature inside was the same as the outside. This helped to keep the condensation level down. By dressing warmly he could move between the two without getting hot or cold.

'The only really warm and comfortable place on *Cornwall* is the bunk, better known as Sleepy Hollow. Once I climb inside my sleeping bag, with two more bags on top as quilts and a hot water bottle, it soon warms up from its cold, damp state. Sleepy Hollow is a warm haven, but every hour the firebell rings and the reality of getting out of a warm bunk into a cold cabin and climbing into cold damp foul weather gear is most unpleasant ... The warmth of Cape Town and heat of the tropics is a distant memory. I suspect *Cornwall* the yacht has a better chance of a white Christmas than Cornwall the place.'

While Robin had escaped the fierce low pressure system, on the third weekend of leg two, the leaders found themselves battered by 60 knot gusts and lethal cross winds. The skippers of seven yachts faced survival rather than racing conditions. David Adams, who had soared ahead into second place overall, was 143 miles behind Christophe Auguin whose mainsail was stuck at the second reef. Forced to leave the sail up all night, it was no wonder the French flyer packed in some miles on the rest of the fleet. The Frenchman was celebrating his 36th birthday on 10 December and suffered two knockdowns in dangerous cross seas. 'My birthday was like being in a shaker ... the sea was like champagne,' he reported. After the knockdowns he had to scrape his breakfast off the ceiling of his cabin. 'The seas were very dangerous. In a six hour stretch the waves arrived from all directions.' Despite the ordeal of the worst storm he had sailed in, Auguin said: 'I feel good and the boat does, too. My best speed has been 30 knots as recorded on the GPS, but it was faster on the sea.' His best 24 hour run to date had been between 330 and 340 miles.

Having grabbed four hours sleep, David Adams reported it was 'blowing like stink, about 50 knots. We're bucking around all over the joint. Four knockdowns, no wind instruments, snow instead of rain. Great place for the mother-in-law.' Adams' sassy sense of humour played down the real hazards of the vicious storm that was overtaking him and other skippers. Calling home on his satellite phone during his 40th hour of battling the storm, Adams told his wife, Caroline: 'I'm absolutely stuffed. I've been 24 hours at the wheel in 40-60 knots. It's just survival out here. Not racing. I've just got the jib up and the top of the main to keep ahead of the seas. These are the worst seas I've been in. The boat is half full of water. My bunk is soaking and the stove won't work. I've broken four stanchions, but otherwise the boat is holding up well.'

At one point in the cockpit he had looked behind him and swore he wouldn't do that again. The sight was awesome. Later he described conditions as 'bloody terrifying, especially the seas which were gigantic. I was thinking, we're not going to get out of this. I was knocked down four times and almost pitchpoled. I went over the side and was swimming at the end of my safety harness. It was survival conditions and I hand-steered for 48 hours.' Adams was exhausted and running out of ideas on how to survive. 'When control is taken away from you, things get very unpleasant,' he said later. But on the position reports it was obvious that Adams was gaining an advantage in these atrocious conditions. Adams' friend and adversary, Giovanni Soldini, crouched in the spartan cabin of *Kodak* tapped out a message on his laptop computer to Christophe Auguin posing the almost rhetorical question: 'Should I dare risk going outside to make my boat sail faster?' Christophe sent back the advice: 'Don't be crazy. Don't go outside. Stay in bed!' Soldini gave one of his infectious laughs as he read the message and sent another to his shoreside support team describing Adams as 'a crazy man' hand steering through the storm. At the same time it rankled that Adams was gaining an advantage of some 200 miles during the three day storm.

The Australian's antics certainly had a kamikaze flavour for some shoreside spectators. But the truth of the situation was revealed by Adams later. The only reason he was hand-steering was because the autopilot had no sense of fear. 'It doesn't know which waves to catch and which waves to avoid. At one stage I did activate the autopilot and went below for a cup of coffee. The next minute it was pitchpole time. The autopilot had got the yacht to the top of a monster wave, went YEEHAA! and steered us straight down the face of the wave, almost vertically. As the bow buried itself, the stern was directly above. Somehow the yacht popped out by broaching and falling sideways. We were knocked flat instead of going all the way over.'

What David Adams didn't reveal to Race HQ was that during the storm he had broken his boom and all the mainsail battens. He kept his secret for 11 days because he didn't want Giovanni to find out 'and really put his foot down'.

The carbon fibre boom, fashioned from the spinnaker pole of a Whitbread 60 yacht, had broken three feet from the gooseneck, its attachment point on the mast. The mainsheet had slipped off a self-tailing winch during one of the knock-downs at the height of the storm and the boom slammed into the shrouds and broke. 'That's all it was, as simple as that. I'm so disappointed,' Adams told his wife as he headed north a bit to get out of the bad weather. It would be another week before the bad weather eased enough to allow Adams to repair his boom. It tapered at the break so he could slot the broken ends together and fasten the joint with screws. But he needed warmth from the sun to allow the epoxy repair bandage to take effect. 'It wasn't glamorous, but at least it was up. I hope it stays together until Sydney,' he told his shore team.

For Giovanni, operating on a limited budget and having his boat built by inmates at a drug rehabilitation centre, the cost of an expensive equipment failure could mean the end of the race. He admitted to journalist Ivor Wilkins that, 'I have end-for-ended my halyards so many times they must be giddy by now!' The Italian's entire campaign budget was US $300,000 with $45,000 of that going on sails.

Another skipper who suffered a broken boom was JJ Provoyeur on his renamed 60-footer, *Novell South Africa*. JJ had four reefs in the main in 45 knots of wind when she gybed twice, snapping the heavy aluminium boom section. 'I should have had the mainsail down. The boat is safer and more manageable in those conditions,' cursed JJ as he lashed the pieces in one place and proceeded under headsail. 'No assistance required,' he told Race HQ.

The demolition derby of leg two continued as Alan Nebauer's best day's noon-to-noon run of 270 miles ended in calamity when *Newcastle Australia* dipped her boom in the water, ripping the mainsail vertically at the third reef point. 'What a bumma! I hope to be able to fix it the next couple of days when it settles down a bit,' reported Alan. There was a five foot tear in the sail. In a message to Race HQ he added: 'I've just had a weak transmission from Steve Pettengill. He sounded okay but he has suffered a knockdown. He's lost his main radio antenna and is using a spare.'

Josh Hall had picked a busy and anxious time for his coaching in Race HQ communications. And the damage reports were still coming in from the Southern Ocean. Jean-Luc Van den Heede had been hampered by electrical problems after the inside of his yacht, nicknamed 'The Red Bullet', was flooded in the storm. The bearded former maths teacher on his fourth solo circumnavigation had also suffered a chest injury during a fall. 'I have a problem with one of my ribs when I winch in the sails, but Australia is not so far away now,' he declared, 1,800 miles from Sydney.

Nigel Rowe described how 'the giant of the Southern Ocean woke up yesterday... 45 knots, cold, dark, miserable. Tossed out of my bunk, a graceless somersault across the cabin in something close to a knockdown. Made a "soft" landing on the other side... fortunately feet on the deckhead. Had a couple of other heavy knocks and one scary crash gybe.'

After nearly two weeks sailing under jury rig, Isabelle Autissier, dubbed 'Isabelle the Incredible' in the evening edition of *The Trailer Gazette*, arrived at Kerguelen Island eager to re-rig her yacht. A supply ship, *Marion Dufresne*, had arrived from Reunion Island with a replacement mast. The cargo boat, *Kerguelen de Tremarec*, carrying sails and equipment for her new rig, was due to arrive the following night. It was snowing hard and the winds were over 40 knots as *EPC2* was towed into the protected harbour by a French scientific vessel, *La Curieuse*, conducting studies in the Antarctic region. 'I am disappointed that I won't be in Sydney for Christmas, but there is a lot of work to do yet to get a mast on my boat,' said Isabelle. Repair assistance had been offered from the French scientific base at the north end of the island. At least three or four hours of calm conditions were needed to complete the installation of the replacement mast as *EPC2* lay at anchor.

'I used to count the days that separate me from the others, but now everything must be done in its time. It won't be easy. My feeling and spirit and commitment is that everything is possible before Charleston. I don't wish problems on anyone, but everything is possible,' Isabelle announced.

In the midst of the third week of leg two, Nigel Rowe was enduring his second day of severe weather with winds up to 50 knots in the midst of the Roaring Forties. 'We're getting a real pasting. The barometer fell like a stone. One real knockdown. I was in the companionway when it happened. Don't know why the boom didn't break. Water came through the companionway into the boat, but not much and I had everything well buttoned up down below, so not much mess to clear up. I managed to get at least one wave breaking over the deck on video, but I'll bet it looks like someone's thrown a bucket of water! My staysail looks like it's beginning to go at the leech. Cold and very damp down below. Sleep impossible and I haven't had any for a couple of days. Top speed this morning 19.6 knots. This is a bit on the edge for me, but I know everyone else is having it at least as bad.'

Steve Pettengill had suffered three knockdowns. His wind instruments and navigation lights were ripped off the masthead, his boom had snapped in two 18 inches behind the mast, two stanchions and one spinnaker pole were broken, and there were two rips in his mainsail. The window over the galley had also been blown off and there was two feet of water inside the boat which had left his laptop computer soaked. 'I'm black and blue all over,' he said. 'That one bruised my hip and shoulder and crunched an ear. It was as if someone had tossed this 60ft nine ton boat off a four-storey building.'

The damage forced him to alter course radically. For the next week and a half he sailed without a mainsail and had to head further north to get back into warmer conditions so that he could make fibreglass repairs to the broken boom. He made a sort of 'dry splice' to put it back together with a splint of sail battens and sections cut off the spinnaker pole. When the wind and rain allowed, he made a wet splice with GRP and resin. 'Every time I started laying glass it started sleeting and snowing,' he said. When his computer dried out many of the keys were not working so he worked out a cryptic code to his wife Patty to substitute for the missing letters in the alphabet. 'It's a good job this is a long race,' he said. 'There's never a dull moment.'

Arnet Taylor, nursing his yacht along under emergency rudder, was also caught in the big blow. 'I knew it was highly unlikely that we could sail nearly 7,000 miles in the Roaring Forties and avoid the experience altogether, but I was doing all I could to avoid it under emergency rudder. In other circumstances I would have welcomed it, just to get the looming spectre of the first heavy weather encounter over with,' he said. 'At any rate it wasn't a wild survival storm, just

*Race leader, Christophe Auguin, claimed the best ever 24 hour run in a mono-hull in his flying saucer,* Sceta Calberson. PHOTO: PATRICK ROACH

what friends from the UK would refer to as "your bog standard Southern Ocean blow". The winds were 35-40 knots, though after 18 hours they were pushing 50 knots. The seas were very steep and confused and the biggest problem aboard *Thursday's Child* was keeping the speed down so the rudder could cope.'

Later, Arnet was doing 8 knots under bare poles 'That was it for me, I squared things away on deck, jumped below and into my cosy sleeping bag for a nice two hour siesta. I could hear the seas crash over the boat, but everything felt secure. When I awoke, I saw that my "Urgent Message" light was on my Satcom-C unit linked to the computer.'

The message was from Race HQ asking him if he was alright. While Arnet had slept, one of his three EPIRBs aboard had activated, sending off a distress message. He flew up into the cockpit. The wind had moderated, but there was still a big sea running. His stern-mounted EPIRB was merrily flashing away. He quickly detached the unit, disabled it, and took it below. A sea had washed over the stern causing the unit to go off. Feeling somewhat sheepish about the incident, Arnet was thrilled to see that the system really worked

After a three day stop at Kerguelen Island, where she reported she had 'made good tourism', Isabelle had converted *EPC2* from a single-masted sloop into a double-masted yawl, using her spinnaker pole as a mizzen mast. Her new 13m main mast was from a much smaller Figaro Solo yacht and a set of sails had been donated by French yachtsmen Philippe Poupon and Pierre Follenfant. The rigging operation had been hampered by strong winds, but helped by the presence of the crane-equipped research vessel *La Curieuse*.

On the 20th day of leg two Isabelle reported: 'I'm now at sea again. Everyone has been wonderful. We worked non-stop all the time. Now I'm heading for Sydney as fast as I can.' Her new rig gave her the ability to fly 70 square metres of sail on an upwind heading and 153 square metres for reaching and running. Already her latest position reports showed she was averaging over 9 knots. On the same day, her ex-crewmate David Adams celebrated his 42nd birthday.

From the back of the fleet, Harry Mitchell, rubbing his hands together to get the circulation going, typed a message to Race HQ on his laptop computer: 'I am in the middle of a deep cold front and man it's frigid and miserable with winds at 30 knots. Oh happy Charleston days!' He added a message for his Charleston hosts, Eugene and Cheryl Fallaw: 'Tell them in no way have I forgotten them. If I make it I'll drop them a line from Sydney, signed Henry-you-know-who Hornblower.'

For Harry, the coldness was bitter. 'My fingertips were in absolute agony working with the ropes.' He had no heater for the Southern Ocean, just two hot water bottles, and one of those developed a leak. Harry planned to keep deckwork to the minimum, running with just a foresail. He had 4,000 miles still to go. The furthest south he went was 49°, and the last land he had seen through the cold mist was the faint grey outline of Kerguelen Island, some eight miles away.

By contrast, race leader Christophe Auguin had a mere 400-plus miles to sail across the Sydney finish line and was riding the favourable winds of a cold front into Bass Strait. Auguin had already claimed the best ever 24-hour monohull run by a solo sailor, a remarkable 350.9 miles sailed the previous day.

In a message home from the battlefront in Class II, Niah Vaughan admitted that he had become the fourth yachtsman to suffer a broken boom. 'I have not told anyone because I don't want the competition (Nebauer, principally!) to think I am now at a disadvantage. I want them to think I am just pacing myself!' With a 50 knot blow forecast, Niah had gone north of Kerguelen to avoid an area of shallows. But *Jimroda II* had been knocked flat in heavy seas, breaking the boom.

'We were still doing 10 knots when I lashed one of the spinnaker poles to the broken boom, using every piece of spare rope on board. We did intend to dip below 50° south on the Great Circle route to Bass Strait, but with the broken boom I decided against it. I kept further north to avoid the heavier weather. We avoided the snow, but ended up in stronger winds.' Meanwhile, Niah was still finding time to conduct a little business over his INMARSAT-C unit, with plans for a yacht club/marina and restaurant on land he was negotiating to buy back home at Whitehaven.

David Adams, having repaired his broken boom, was back to hand-steering with autopilot problems. His arch rival, Giovanni, had caught up and narrowed the gap between them to less than 90 miles, with 1,000 miles left to Sydney. Race HQ was monitoring Adams' progress via the satellite polling of his GPS, and had wondered why he had slowed down. Adams reassured them: 'Sorry to give you a worry. Crikey, the way Big Brother is watching I'm afraid to go to the loo on deck in case it's in graphic detail in downtown Charleston!'

Josh Hall at Race HQ replied: 'Big Brother here. Glad you have sorted things out. Sorry if we disturbed your fun, but it was very obvious here that for a few hours you were not on track. You can feel free to hit the dunny on deck, our software automatically trips out when a **** is in view – doesn't work too well for Isabelle though!'

Giovanni despatched another unique Anglo-Italian message: 'Hai, this is *Kodak*. Wi start to have good wedar and better temperature. Mi and the boat we fill mac better. Wi come from the metiterraneo, hot blod, wi layk the sanscain (sunshine). Ciao ciao Giovanni.'

While some were in the home stretch, others in the fleet faced a continuing uphill battle. David Scully was hand-steering *Coyote* with generator, alternator and autopilot problems. After another long night at the wheel he managed to hook up his little spare autopilot, giving him a much needed break in calm conditions. His was the only yacht in double figures, making 11.7 knots, as he faxed Race HQ: 'Please clear all obstacles out of Bass Strait. Advise traffic that a misguided missile running on fumes and digestive biscuits is headed their way.'

Minoru Saito was still labouring at the wheel of *Shuten-Dohji II* and had scratched his plans to call at Fremantle. He was now making for Albany, on the south west coast of Australia. He was suffering from severe chilling of what, in his fractured English, he called 'my footfingers', the painful big toe on his right foot. At first he thought it might be frostbite from the long hours on deck hand steering. The cockpit was sometimes turned into a freezing swimming pool as waves washed aboard. But now he thought he might be suffering from gout. The pain was mostly in the joint and he had to avoid putting weight on it.

A few days later, in sunshine and running downwind, Minoru was able to open all the deck hatches to dry out his damp yacht. He discovered that when he pressed the standby button on his autopilot it responded by displaying STANDBY on the LCD screen. He unlashed the wheel and tried engaging the pilot to AUTO. It worked. The Japanese skipper wondered if the electronics were playing 'a plactical joke' or had someone granted his wish? 'Mysterious and miraculous, I am so happy I want to go straight to Sydney in time for my birthday on January 7,' he told Race HQ. In the last BOC Challenge Minoru had spent his birthday at sea alone.

The threat of sub-zero temperatures and snow in the Southern Ocean meant that keeping the extremities warm was vital for skippers. Robin Davie had leather gloves with thermal liners for deck work, where everything you touched was either metal, and very cold, or rope and very wet. To give the cold some perspective, Davie reported that it was necessary to heat and warm up a tin of condensed milk before it would pour when he was making his cocoa. The same went for his cans of coke and Lucozade. Chewing Mars bars was like biting into a brick. 'To think that eight weeks ago I could have killed for an ice cold coke when we were in the tropics...' said Robin.

Steve Pettengill was averaging only an hour of sleep a day, having told his shore crew that he had spliced his broken boom, jury rigged his mast and rudder, rebuilt his autopilots and sewn a torn mainsail on his approach to Bass Strait. The generator was a constant problem and he had changed the fuel in its tank four times. Condensation was constantly running down inside the cabin and on to the computers and instruments. His hands were raw and swollen from gashes, from being wet and from all the glass and epoxy repair work he had done.

In front of him, David Adams, who had taken a more southerly and longer route than his rivals, hoping to pick up stronger winds, watched his lead on Giovanni dwindle to 11 miles. Adams was counting on his three years' experience working on a supply ship in the Bass Strait to be a big advantage when navigating the notoriously difficult stretch of water separating Tasmania from the Australian mainland. But soon Giovanni would be sailing so close to him that he would be able to see Adams' broken boom. Meanwhile, under her drastically shortened emergency rig, things seemed to be going better for Isabelle, as she reeled off a remarkable 24-hour run of 229 miles.

The pencil crosses on Robin Davie's South Indian Ocean chart, marking his steady progress each day at noon, showed another run of around 180 miles on day 24. With South Africa in the top left hand corner and Perth, Western Australia, in the top right hand corner, it had seemed like slow progress at times, particularly when plotting the route and speed of the 60 footers ahead of him. The first of them would be arriving in Sydney in a day or so. Robin had 2,000 miles to go to Sydney, but he was ahead of his position in the race four years ago. For him it had been another week of light winds, totally unlike the weather experienced on this leg in previous BOC Challenge races. Three nights ago the wind had come up to 40 knots-plus, and for the first time in this race the fourth deep reef went into Cornwall's mainsail, reducing it to a handkerchief-sized triangle of canvas as snow squalls blasted through.

Christophe, on his final night at sea, endured the hottest 21 December in decades, becalmed with temperatures soaring to 45°C (105°F) as he battled a strong southerly current along the final stretch. 'The wind is zero. My speed is minus two knots. My ETA is next year!' he complained. Then two hours from the finish a 40 knot southerly breeze gave him a swift, wet ride across the finish line inside Sydney Heads just before midnight. He had taken a record 24d 23h for the 7,000 mile voyage, beating John Martin's previous record by 31 hours. He had averaged 11.68 knots for the leg.

Christophe had enjoyed a week-long string of 300 mile-plus days. 'My boat is a big boat, but the Southern Ocean treated it like a very small boat during this leg,' he said. Auguin had one ambition now he was back on dry land – to go into the Australian bush and look at some trees.

Despite the litany of damage amongst the rest of the BOC fleet, Christophe had experienced few problems with Sceta Calberson, the most noticeable being his shredded roller-furling genoa headsail which had unrolled and flapped itself to pieces the third day out of Cape Town.

As Christmas approached, Nigel Rowe on Sky Catcher suffered another knockdown and crash gybe in 40 knots of wind on 23 December. This time it broke his boom vang. But even after an eight-hour stint at the helm, nursing the boat through horribly confused seas, he had not lost his sense of humour as he confessed 'a speeding offence' to Race HQ. 'It's a fair cop ... I admit it. I just wanted to do something to advance my position. I feel miserably guilty now. What got us was a breaking wave at the end of an uncontrolled surf-ride. I know, I know... I'm trying to be careful.'

Two days before Christmas, Jean-Luc Van den Heede on Vendée Enterprises was within hours of completing leg two in second place. He hadn't slept at all coming through that ship's graveyard of Bass Strait, strewn with rocks, oil fields, shipping and strong tides. After the Southern Ocean, Bass Strait is the final endurance test for tired singlehanded skippers. There is no chance of sleep here and little opportunity for rest. Exhausted after being up for three days and nights coping with adverse currents and headwinds, Van den Heede had been short-tacking *Vendée Enterprises* close to the shore to avoid the worst of the adverse current. During one tack he thought he would rest in the cockpit for five minutes. He cradled his head in his arms, leaned on a winch and drifted off into Nirvana. Thirty minutes later he woke with a jolt to find his 60ft yawl aground in the surf on a sandy beach. Van den Heede desperately pushed the tiller over to try to tack off, but it was too late. A second wave pushed the yacht further up the beach on its side. He frantically used his VHF radio to call for help, and even gave a rope to a surfer who, with the help of a gathering crowd of spectators on the beach, tried to pull the bows towards the waves, thus minimising the damage. Water washed into the cockpit and down the hatch into the cabin.

The unthinkable had happened, just 50 miles south of Sydney, and the finish line for the second leg. The nightmare of every solo yachtsman was now being lived by three-times circumnavigator Van den Heede. In the 1982-83 BOC Challenge it had happened to Desmond Hampton, who had overslept while skippering Francis Chichester's famous yacht *Gipsy Moth V*. Hampton awoke as the wooden ketch ran on to the rocks of windswept Gabo Island, where a lighthouse marked the last obstacle, Cape Howe, before the final sprint to Sydney. Hampton had lived to tell the tale, but the yacht was wrecked. Later in the same race, Richard McBride's *City of Dunedin* ran aground in the Falklands on leg three and was not refloated for 30 days. McBride and the yacht survived to complete their circumnavigation. In the 1986 BOC Challenge it happened to Harry Mitchell on South Island, New Zealand. The boat was saved, but Harry was disqualified for accepting a tow beyond the permitted limit.

Van den Heede, sensing that if his yacht was going to be saved it would be a long job, struggled into his survival suit. It was two in the afternoon and The Red Bullet had grounded inside the surf line of a forgiving sandy beach, some 10 miles south of Wollongong. The Port Kembla Water Police vessel, *Sea Hawk*, arrived at the scene after 45 minutes. The yacht was lying on its port side on a falling tide. The police wanted to take the exhausted sailor off his yacht, but Jean-Luc refused point blank.

Because the yacht was stranded 300 yards off the beach it was a risky operation to get a tow boat close enough in the surf. Jean-Luc passed a tow line to a policeman on a surfboard. The first tow attempt failed when the line parted and a 14mm stainless steel shackle bent. Jean-Luc lost track of time. The race no longer mattered; he thought only of saving his boat. His ordeal seemed to have lasted for hours. BOC race officials hurried to Wollongong beach by helicopter. The tide was coming in again and the boat was surging up and down in the waves as another attempt at towing her was tried. The line went taut and the yacht started shaking. Suddenly she was floating free and came upright in deep water.

Three hours after he awoke to his living nightmare, Jean-Luc's yacht was towed at 12 knots towards Port Kembla harbour five miles away. Words couldn't describe the sense of relief that flooded through the Frenchman.

At the port, assistance was on hand from the support crews of fellow BOC racers

*'The Red Bullet'* shows the depth of her keel, which gave Jean-Luc Van den Heede such a rude awakening on the beach near Port Kembla. PHOTO: PAUL GELDER

who had rushed to the scene. The damaged ketch was given a thorough inspection. The boat had suffered a broken mizzen boom, a torn mainsail and mizzen sails. The stanchions (which support a wire fence around the edge of the boat to help keep sails and sailor aboard) were ripped off the port side and the bow pulpit was gone completely. Divers checked below the waterline and reported no damage to the hull, keel or rudder. Water had come through hatches and was up to the bunk tops. Fortunately, the computer and electronics were on the high side, though one bank of batteries and much of the skipper's personal possessions were soaked. The water was pumped out.

While the exhausted Jean-Luc was booked into a local hotel for the night to get some rest, two car loads of shore crews from fellow BOC competitors came to the rescue from the marina in Sydney. The BOC Challenge prides itself on the closeness of competitors and shore crews. Over the next few hours, while some of their own skippers were battling to get to the finish line, the crews worked to help Jean-Luc to get underway and hold on to his second place. It was a concept totally alien to those who thought winning at any price was everything, even at the cost of a fellow yachtsman's misfortune. But this was an accident that could have happened to anybody. In the unwritten law of the sea, sailors in distress had to be helped. On that day the camaraderie of the BOC Challenge transcended its competitive spirit.

Yves 'Boux' LeBouvier and Marco, after a full day's work on *Sceta Calberson* which had just docked in Sydney, led a contingent that included Skip and Andy from *Sky Catcher*, Merfyn and Kate from *Thursday's Child*, Phil Lee from *True Blue*, and David and Anna from *Hunter's Child*. Caroline Adams, David's wife, was manning the media centre back at Pyrmont Bay Marina.

A spare mainsail for *Vendée Enterprises* was located on a French boat competing in the Sydney-Hobart race. The skipper, Lionel Pean, was a friend of Jean-Luc. The volunteers worked through the night stitching the new sail to the luff cars. Skip and Andy re-rigged lifelines and stanchions. Jean-Luc's clothes were taken to the hotel laundry. Skip climbed the mast to attach new lazyjacks and give the rig a final check.

Mark Schrader, reportedly, had misty eyes as he described the drama of dragging the boat off the beach and what a miracle it had been that the boat had run aground at that particular spot. Wollongong beach is the last bit of sand before Sydney. The next 50 miles of coast are all hard rocks and cliffs where no amount of volunteer help could have saved the yacht.

At around five in the morning Schrader appeared in Jean-Luc's hotel bedroom with a film crew to record the moment when he told a sleepy Jean-Luc: 'You're still racing. A new mainsail is coming ... get ready ... '

An hour later, after dawn on Christmas Eve, Jean-Luc and The Red Bullet were streaking towards Sydney again.

'It's unbelievable, I didn't think it was possible to save the boat,' said Van den Heede after his brush with disaster. 'It was my fault, but I had enormous luck. There are cliffs and rocks all along the shore north and south of Port Kembla. If I had landed there I would be dead.'

Some of the shore crew who had worked all night getting the yacht ready to continue to Sydney had no image of the yacht grounded on the beach. They did not see the pictures until next morning on the front page of the Sydney newspapers. There was Jean-Luc in his survival suit clutching at the boom as the waves crashed over him. They all felt a bit astounded. 'How could we have fixed that in one night? we asked ourselves,' said Kate Ford.

Sixteen hours after his BOC bid had run aground so dramatically Jean-Luc crossed the finish line some four hours later on Christmas Eve morning with a time of 27d 10h. 'I am happy to finish. But the most important thing is to save my boat. So now my red boat is the Christmas Boat,' said the beaming Frenchman

The festive spirit was upon the remaining BOC fleet still scattered at sea as Christmas greetings were exchanged over the radio. Nigel Rowe, reconciled to spending Christmas in the Southern Ocean, told his followers in a forlorn message: 'I shall be alone in a small damp room with no heating.' The weather forecast meant he would reef down, secure hatches and settle down to open his cache of presents and a bottle of champagne. Christmas dinner was 'roast beef (irradiated and foil wrapped) with peas, carrots, asparagus, onion and garlic, with a South African Cabernet Sauvignon to accompany it.' He had also stocked his yacht with a few bottles of brandy for 'when the need arises'. 'There are worse places to be on Christmas Day than in the Southern Ocean,' he reflected.

Robin Davie was getting ready to forsake 'life in the freezer for some of those character-building calms and headwinds of the Bass Strait.' Sailing the smallest yacht in the fleet (along with Harry Mitchell's *Henry Hornblower*), Robin described his Christmas aboard *Cornwall* as he sailed towards the Strait.

Christmas Day began with the service of nine lessons and carols from King's College, Cambridge, broadcast on the BBC World Service. It was four in the afternoon on Christmas Eve back in England, but 0200 on a dark Christmas morning in the Southern Ocean and blowing 40 knots of north-easterly in the squalls. The seas were rough and the violent motion occasionally rolled the yacht on to her side as breaking seas crashed on deck. After the carol service, Robin grabbed an hour's sleep before tuning into the news and sports round-up. By 0430 a bleak dawn revealed a desolate scene of grey seas, grey sky and rain, which ushered in Christmas Day. At least the wind was from the north and relatively warm compared with the snow and hail of two days ago. Robin still put on extra layers of clothing for his regular topside check of mast and sails. The staysail had daylight showing through several seams where stitching had chafed through. The sail was old and should have been changed before he left Falmouth. He took it down for the third time that week for more hand-stitched repairs, setting in its place the smaller storm jib. Then he grabbed another 45 minutes in his bunk, cursing the ear-piercing ring of the fire bell as he scrambled out of Sleepy Hollow to put the kettle on for tea and switch the radio transmitter to standby for chat hour with fellow competitors.

Robin was some 200 miles further south than Nigel, Niah and Minoru, so he could hear them faintly on the radio and eavesdropped on their Christmas greetings. He finally called Nigel, and after brief Christmas salutations, both agreed that things would be much better if the seas subsided.

With a breakfast of porridge slowly heating through on the stove, Robin tackled the first 12 inch seam that needed sewing on the staysail, then ate his porridge, with plenty of sugar and milk, straight from the pan. It was too rough to eat from a bowl, let alone contemplate the extra washing up. After cleaning the galley it was time for another couple of 45 minute sleeps, with a quick check on deck in between. The weather wasn't changing and *Cornwall* was still being thrown around all over the place.

With the midnight GMT radio schedule approaching, Robin was thinking of Christmas Eve in Cornwall – pubs closing, midnight mass and Father Christmas. Aboard *Cornwall* it was 10 am, so he busied himself cooking a scrambled egg and ham breakfast and briefly chatted to Niah on *Jimroda II*. He also sewed the remaining three split seams on the staysail, ready for rehoisting.

By midday it was still very rough and unpleasant and Robin didn't feel hungry. But at least the rain had stopped and the wind was down to 25 knots. He got himself geared up for a spell on deck where he could spend an hour or so sitting in the hatchway and feel and sense the wind and sea. 'I don't "feel" the weather changing in the way my weather maps indicate it should,' he thought.

Robin had a Christmassy hour at the chart table, opening some cards and pinning them to the bulkhead. A Christmas cassette tape played on the recorder and he ate some dried and fresh fruit, nuts and chocolate and reached out for a couple of big envelopes of cards and letters received in Cape Town from schools in America. There hadn't been time to read them before, and he had saved them as a Christmas bonus to open and read.

The boat's violent motion meant there was little prospect of getting dinner to the table, let alone cooking it. He had planned steak and kidney pie, roast potatoes and onions, with cabbage and carrots, topped off with a cheese sauce. Instead, he settled for a small Christmas pudding with two pints of custard. As the sun was setting, he took the pan full of festive feast to the chart table '... I'll need an hour or two to snooze it away afterwards ... ' he thought.

With darkness falling there seemed little change in the weather. It was still a very rough ride. The most comfortable spot was the bunk, where Robin listened to the Queen's speech on the BBC. It was three in the afternoon back home and one in the morning on Boxing Day aboard *Cornwall*, and time to catch up on some more sleep.

Robin was frequently asked if he felt sad or lonely out at sea alone at Christmas. But he had spent more Christmases at sea over the last 20 years than at home. 'I would love to be sitting down to a St Agnes Christmas dinner, but on the other hand I wouldn't be in a hurry to swap places with anyone, knowing that there will be many Christmases to sit in front of the fire, whilst the chances to sail the Southern Ocean are few and far between.'

Elsewhere on the ocean on Christmas Eve, Arnet Taylor was caught in a gale and the emergency rudder on *Thursday's Child* had delaminated and snapped off. He was 'creatively experimenting with alternative methods of steering, involving poled out headsails and any other means that come to mind.' He had the bucket ready for a brake when he hit soundings. 'My current thoughts are to aim for Melbourne and fit a rudder.' Later he announced he was altering course to Hobart, Tasmania, some 800 miles away, flying the staysail. 'I'm confident we can wander down there steering with the sails alone.'

Christmas Day in Sydney bought a quartet of BOC skippers who arrived across the finish line in rapid succession. Steve Pettengill sailed through the rain past Sydney Heads and took the finish gun and third place before the day was two hours old. His time was 28d 02h. He arrived at the dock with his wife Patty at his side to a quiet hurrah and the *Star Spangled Banner*. At the halfway point of the race, Pettengill was second on elapsed time, a day and a half behind race leader Auguin. With two more yachts arriving within the hour the champagne and press conference had to wait. Meanwhile Steve seemed pleased to have a few moments to show off the mid-ocean repair jobs he'd carried out to *Hunter's Child*.

He'd suffered several knockdowns, one of which smashed his head against the boom and left him unconscious in the cockpit. Another burst a window out of the coachroof. The boat went under so far his ears popped. 'I braced myself hoping the boat would hold together. We lay in the water a while and the window blew out. Water was coming in like a fire hose had gone off.' He had three feet of water in the cabin and the cracks in the coachroof around the smashed window were getting bigger. Pettengill began pumping out using the water ballast pump. When that blocked, he resorted to being a frightened man with a bucket. He glassed a sheet of plywood over the window hole. His work list for Sydney was impressive: snapped rigging, lost radio aerial, smashed stanchions, ripped mainsail, no navigation lights, broken spinnaker pole, soaked electronics and the broken boom and blown out cabin window.

Fifteen minutes behind *Hunter's Child*, Giovanni Soldini crossed the line in *Kodak*, shattering the Class II record for the second leg by more than two days. Giovanni had experienced few problems on his yacht, the one exception being a broken inner forestay. 'The boat is very well built,' said Soldini 'and I don't do crazy stuff. When there is too much wind in heavy weather I slow down. I attack in moderate conditions. That is where I got my lead on this leg.'

David Adams arrived two hours later in *True Blue* after a nightmarish voyage which he described as 'the worst bloody experience of my life'. He had sailed the furthest south of the fleet and admitted: 'There were days out there when I wondered if there would be a tomorrow. That storm was awesome.'

Despite the setback of a broken boom during the 72-hour gale midway through the leg, Adams still led Soldini in overall elapsed time by 18 hours. He was later awarded an additional four hours time allowance for his detour to Isabelle Autissier's dismasted yacht, which gave him first place on leg two, ahead of Soldini.

Four hours behind Adams came David Scully, sailing across the line with his borrowed mainsail which had caused him to leave Cape Town a day behind the fleet. Despite spending long hours on various repairs and mending sails he said, while drinking champagne out of a paper cup: 'This was some of the best sailing I've ever had. It was like skiing powder snow every day for a week. I was very impressed by the Southern Ocean. The boat can certainly go.'

The Christmas Day arrivals were completed by JJ Provoyeur who finished with a time of 28d 20h. JJ's rosy, clean-shaven appearance belied what, at times, had been a difficult journey. 'It's a lonely ocean out there. Lonely and at times quite scary actually. The wind is not a problem, it's the waves and the seas. They don't run in a straight line, they're confused and its the odd wave that just crunches you,' he said.

Still at sea on Christmas Day Nigel Rowe was down below and heard an enormous crash. 'A huge dead bird was hanging in my rigging. It was weird, spooky.' Perhaps the dead bird was a bad omen for the rest of the fleet at sea. The wind began to build and over the next week Rowe did not see less than 30 knots, while for 24 hours he endured sustained winds of 60-70 knots with a top recorded speed of 74 knots. 'I went out into the cockpit and it just blew me back in. I never felt the force of the wind so strongly,' he reported.

Harry Mitchell sent a Christmas 'card' to Peter Dunning and the trailer crew in Charleston: 'Has someone put the mox on me?' he asked. 'In the first leg I fell into every calm there was. On this leg I'm getting every gale there is! Right now I'm in the middle of another 40-knotter, so I'm taking it slow again, but I really don't have the time. Best wishes Henry H.'

In Portsmouth, Harry's wife Diana said a little prayer for him every night before she went to bed. Across the south coast of England severe weather warnings had been broadcast during the post-Christmas period and winds were gusting up to 70 mph.

A Christmas Day fax from Harry told Diana he was heaving to, unable to cook his Christmas dinner because of the terrible weather. Life was too short, he reflected, to be spending Christmas Day away from his family, especially in these conditions.

Astern of Harry the next big low pressure system had been brewing and was speeding eastwards. Harry's yacht was the first in the path of the big storm which was to wreak such havoc with Isabelle, Nigel, Arnet and Minoru.

# 7 · *Holding on*

It was Harry's 26th day at sea in leg two. The spray and the rain beating on his eyeballs was painful. As *Henry Hornblower* got to the top of a wave the wind was pushing his instrument dials to their stops. The dials didn't give readings beyond 60 knots. Harry closed the hatches and secured himself inside the cabin in case the yacht got rolled over. It was too dangerous to cook and he turned off the gas at the bottle and made everything as secure and tight as he could. The perspex windows were so badly crazed he couldn't see anything out of them. In these conditions he was glad the view was obscured. But it was the noise building up outside that was really frightening. 'I heard Hurricane Andrew in 1992 and that was a roar. This was like a high-pitched screaming or shrieking that went on and on and on … I thought, Oh God, I'll not survive this.'

*Henry Hornblower*, 2,900 miles from Sydney, was hove-to with just a scrap of foresail backed, enough to hold the yacht into the wind as it screamed its banshee note in the rigging. Harry was in a survival storm. His nearest fellow competitor, Minoru Saito, was more than 1,000 miles ahead, himself exhausted, hand-steering his boat in 60 knot gusts.

Of the remaining eight BOC Challenge yachts at sea, Harry the tortoise, together with Isabelle, the ex-hare of the race, were the deepest south in the Southern Ocean when the storm hit. As the fury of the storm continued, Harry wondered how long the particles of fibreglass and epoxy, from which his yacht was constructed, could withstand the hammering of the waves before they shattered. Several times an hour one of the breaking waves picked up *Henry Hornblower* and hurled her on to her side, leaving her shuddering from mast to keel. The enormous seas were grey, white and mean looking. The height of the waves, towering walls of water, was irrelevant. It was enough to say that they made a man feel insignificant.

Never one to communicate with Race HQ if he could conserve his precious battery power, Harry sent one of his rare messages of leg two back to Charleston over his laptop computer. 'I am in the centre of a severe 60 knot storm. Have lost all the blades on the wind generator. Am worried I may lose GPS antenna. The barometer is 960 millibars. The seas are unbelievable and dangerous. The conditions are the worst I have experienced ever. Hope I come through … '

Peter Dunning replied: 'Sounds horrible, hang in there. Please keep in touch and update us every three or four hours.'

Robin Davie had occasionally been in touch by long range radio with Harry, but it was very sketchy contact and he hadn't had word for five or six days. On Boxing Day he, too, was anxious to know how his friend was faring.

When the wind veered, Robin was faced with a stiff, unpleasant beat to windward. He reduced sail to his fourth reef, a pocket sized triangle of mainsail, and his storm jib. From the weather maps he could see the depression passing safely to the south of him, but the sting in the scorpion's tail was still to come. On radio schedules Robin talked with Nigel, 300 miles behind, who was still having a rough time.

Elsewhere on the storm-tossed seas Arnet was hove-to and Niah reported that *Jimroda II*, 850 miles from the finish line, was constantly awash with a metre of water as he experienced unique conditions. He had 30 knots of wind on the beam from the north west, southerly current and a three metre swell from the south west. 'We were doing 10 knots and the swell would pick the yacht up and we'd be surfing at 15 knots into the breaking crests of wind and waves.'

Some 200 miles ahead of Niah, his main rival in the race, Alan Nebauer was closing on King Island and the entrance to Bass Strait as he entered the final lap of his race. 'Entering Bass Strait was like crossing a line … suddenly clear skies, stars and moon with a favourable breeze. I don't think I've seen a star or blue skies for two weeks. It was even warm enough to start stripping away the layers of thermal clothing.'

In brutal storm conditions on the night of 27 December Nigel suffered another 'gut-wrenching knockdown'. Water was everywhere. Garbage was on the deckhead. 'Everything not tied down is now somewhere else, and one nervous skipper is holding on tight! We now have a stub where once there was a masthead wind indicator.' He described the waves as 'towering 60-80 feet high citadels of ink-black marble, with the northerly wind driving the sea across the westerly flow of the Southern Ocean. This produced some spectacularly conflicting wave patterns.'

Three hours later: 'I have an emergency on my hands. Crash gybed when the windvane self-steering unit went AWOL. Rig intact, but tiller is broken in two halfway down and the rudder is jammed under the boat. I cannot shift it at the moment. Bobbing around like a pea in a whistle.'

Later still: 'Wind 30 knots, north north west after prolonged period of 40-50 knots. Sea state hairy. Large sea, big swell, breaking waves. Have now worked rudder free, have unfurled staysail with electronic autopilot driving.'

Nigel considered the risk of going through Bass Strait with suspect steering and tried to get some sleep, while also debating the option of diverting to Hobart to lick his wounds along with Arnet Taylor. With typical *élan* in a crisis, he added 'Right now I feel like a good Martini – shaken but not stirred! My problems are small compared to others, and I'm grateful for that.'

Arnet in the rudderless *Thursday's Child* had read his forecast and was expecting to be overtaken by the storm. He had been busy battening down the hatches, and everything else. 'In these conditions,' he said, 'the seas are in charge and we practise damage control.' Arnet was less than 700 miles from Hobart in 40 knots of wind with building seas. He reported, with his usual cool understatement, that 'conditions have not been conducive to creative steering arrangements. A spinnaker pole off the stern in these conditions would have a short life expectancy.'

At the height of the storm he removed all the sails and lay a'hull, letting the boat drift in its own natural path. Nigel called him up on the radio to report close to 70 knot gusts. 'Nigel wanted to know what I had and I had to admit that as the anonometer went past 50 towards 60, I shut the instruments off and wedged myself in the bunk to keep from getting pitched around the cabin as big seas broke over us,' said Arnet. Getting more philosophical by the minute about his mounting misfortunes, Arnet later said that he felt like a case study for Adlard Coles' book, *Heavy Weather Sailing.*

Later that day, 28 December, the 32nd day of leg two, Isabelle Autissier was averaging 8 knots under bare poles in the jury-rigged *EPC2*. The wind was howling around her at 60-70 knots and the yacht had been laid over twice, creating chaos in the cabin, but things seemed to be holding up reasonably well. She tried to sleep on the cabin floor to avoid being thrown from her bunk. 'The crests of the waves were a beautiful sight, but a worrying one,' she said.

Around noon the wind eased slightly and it was time to put up the storm jib. But she was concerned about her small makeshift mast. Before she put the sail up she wanted to finish a small repair job in the yacht's aft compartment. It was a decision that probably saved her life.

The wind was gusting and had changed direction as the storm system moved on, causing the swells to combine into monstrous seas. She was at the back of the yacht in the narrow tunnel-like passage which linked the main cabin and the watertight aft compartment which contained the yacht's steering systems. 'It was then that I heard it coming … like a powerful locomotive. I instinctively crouched down. I knew it was going to flatten the boat.' A rogue monster wave crashed over the yacht, launching it through a semi-pitchpole, end-over-end. At the same time the yacht did a corkscrew rollover through 360 degrees. Isabelle was thrown on to the roof, choked by a rush of ice cold water. 'I could feel it rolling. I fell on the bulkhead, then on the ceiling, then on the other bulkhead. When I opened my eyes the boat was full of water. If I had been on deck I would have been washed away. It was very great for me that I was not there.'

The whole incident had lasted not more than 20 seconds. Isabelle crawled out of the tunnel and was speechless at what she saw. The yacht's cabin roof above the navigation station and her living quarters had disappeared. There was a gaping hole of five square metres where the carbon fibre coachroof had exploded under the water pressure. All she could see was forbidding grey sky and the sea washing in as waves continued to sweep the deck. The air pressure had plucked a lot of things out of the yacht in the rollover. The devastation was as sure as it was complete.

'I was standing in water with equipment floating around me. The batteries and generator and other electrical equipment were submerged. I was lucky. Everything that was at the navigation station was sucked out of the boat. If I had been sleeping or at the chart table, I would have been washed away…'

On deck, most of *EPC2*'s jury masts and rigging had been swept off the boat by the ocean. Isabelle's world had literally turned upside down 920 miles south south east of Adelaide. Her position was 48° south 130° east. The boat was very low in the water, almost half submerged. She had to act quickly.

'A second wave would definitely finish us,' she thought. For two hours she bailed out as much water as possible using a bucket and stretched a sail over the gaping hole in the cabin roof, using a salvaged spar as a ridgepole for her makeshift 'tent'. 'All the steering systems were gone. The tiller had come away under pressure, leaving a hole which was leaking water into the once watertight rear compartment.'

The water temperature was 3°C and the current was taking Isabelle further south, away from the nearest civilisation. The air temperature was only 5°C with the wind chill factor sending that plunging to -15°C. At first she thought she might try to go on. Her defiant optimism told her she might somehow rebuild the jury rig. But slowly the reality dawned as fatigue took over. The steering system was destroyed and she was exhausted from sailing for three weeks with a jury rig in her bid to stay in the race at all costs.

'With the state of my boat and my personal state I knew it would not be safe to try and get to Sydney. I had to save what could be saved.' Two hours after the rollover, and for the first time in her seafaring life, Isabelle took out her distress beacons, two Alden 406-EPIRBs, and as night began to fall she switched them on. 'The small lights began to flash and up there in the stars the satellite picked up my call,' she said.

Like all yachts in the BOC Race, Isabelle had at least two emergency beacons, a liferaft and survival gear in case she had to abandon her yacht in extreme conditions. 'When I switched on my EPIRBs I was quite confident of my rescue. I knew it was a good system ... I had never used it before, but I have seen it working for other people. It is an incredible organisation,' she told reporters later.

Both EPIRBs were triggered just before six in the evening Sydney time. Ashore BOC Challenge staff, alerted by a satellite ground station, immediately went into their well-rehearsed emergency procedures. An anxious message was relayed by Peter Dunning from Race HQ in Charleston: 'Isabelle, do you have problems? We have a 406-EPIRB alarm from you. Please let us know, Pete.' Search and rescue operations were co-ordinated by Australia's Maritime Rescue Co-ordination Centre in Canberra, while in France Isabelle's family were notified of the emergency situation.

The BOC Challenge has a history of fellow racers coming to the aid of competitors in distress. In this instance, Nigel Rowe, more than 250 miles away on board *Sky Catcher*, received a message from Race HQ: 'Once more we need your help. Two EPIRB alerts from Isabelle. Not responding to messages. Please be on standby. Please cease easterly progress until we sort this one out.'

Nigel, battling against survival conditions himself in the same low pressure system, was hove-to in 50-60 knots of wind with huge breaking seas. He had lashed the tiller to one side while he waited for conditions to abate so that he could make a repair to the self-steering. He replied: 'I'll stand by for news on Isabelle. Robin and I are in radio contact with each other and I will leave 4MHz open in case she tries that, although I've never heard her on the radio.'

At Royal Australian Air Force bases near Sydney and Adelaide flight crews were scrambled on long range aircraft. A military search plane was on standby to fly to the yacht's last known position at first light next day.

As darkness fell on that first long night at sea, Isabelle, realising how far from land she was, knew that no rescue bid would be attempted until the next day. The forward watertight compartment, where her sails were stowed, was the only area on her stricken yacht not submerged in water and not structurally compromised. It was there that she sought refuge.

Lots of things had disappeared in the waves. The aft compartment was full of water and she didn't know if the rudders had gone because she had to shut the watertight doors to keep the boat afloat. She gathered some clothes, food and survival gear, including a hand-operated desalinator for making drinking water, and moved into the forward compartment. After the rollover this was to be her home for the next three days. She changed into her one-piece survival suit to try to conserve body warmth in the chilling conditions and wrapped a reflective foil space blanket around her.

It was a sleepless night for BOC race officials as well as those on duty at Race HQ. All efforts to contact Isabelle by satellite messaging and long range radio had been to no avail. From the slow drift of the EPIRB signals they knew something was badly wrong, but they could only speculate. Was Isabelle still with the yacht or in her liferaft? Or had the yacht sunk, leaving only the beacons afloat to transmit their bleak alarm?

Three hundred miles to the north, Minoru Saito was placed on standby for any possible rescue bid. It was estimated it would take him three to four days to reach her position. Early next day a C-130 Hercules Aircraft left Adelaide at four in the morning on its mercy mission to find Isabelle and her yacht. The plane carried an extra passenger, Serge Viviand, head of Isabelle's shore support crew. It took the plane, equipped to drop liferafts, handheld VHF radios and other survival gear, four hours to reach the search area after a refuelling stop in Tasmania.

By dawn, Isabelle was already awake with the cold and had started work to clear the deck of broken rigging and spars ready for any rescue operation. She was tired and staggered around as the mastless yacht pitched and rolled in the heavy Southern Ocean swell. The work helped to warm her up a little, but every effort seemed slow and strenuous. She strengthened the tent frame over the smashed cabin coachroof using her metal pipe cots. Then suddenly she became aware of a different noise, a distant rumble, and looked up to see a plane flying overhead.

At around 0900 the plane had reached the search area. But sighting Isabelle was not easy. The positions given by the two distress beacons on board *EPC2* were sometimes as much as nine miles apart. And to make things even harder, from the skies above the white deck of the disabled yacht was invisible against the dramatic backdrop of hundreds of breaking wave crests. The yacht was just like a small breaking wave. It took an agonising two hours and 50 minutes before the Hercules confirmed a visual sighting of the yacht. Isabelle on deck jumped up and down and waved to the search plane to show that she was uninjured. She was reported to be 'fit and well' and 'very near the location that her distress signal had begun transmitting.' It had been an anxious 18 hours wait before the world knew that Isabelle Autissier was alive and still aboard her yacht.

'When I heard the plane it was a great moment for me,' said Isabelle. 'Communication was impossible because my radio was out of action. I sobbed with emotion.'

From the time they arrived, the Royal Australian Airforce never left Isabelle. Military aircraft relayed every few hours and remained on station, like guardian angels, keeping a watch over her and monitoring the yacht's drift. Having found their needle in a haystack, they didn't want to risk losing her again.

The rescue plane tried to establish voice contact to get details of her physical condition and the extent of onboard damage. But Isabelle's own emergency handheld radio, even in its waterproof bag, had been flooded and rendered useless. At the same time the Australian Navy frigate, *HMAS Darwin*, was despatched from Fremantle, Western Australia, on Thursday morning. It was not expected to reach Isabelle's position until late Sunday afternoon. A Seahawk helicopter was despatched from Albany to rendezvous with the frigate and join the rescue mission.

With only frustrating visual contact possible with Isabelle, the Hercules plane, flying low over the water at 200km per hour, made precision drops of liferafts and supply canisters loaded with survival items, including flares, water and a handheld VHF radio.

Knowing that Isabelle was unable to manoeuvre the yacht, the pilots and crew invented a new system. They dropped two plastic canisters strung together with a floating line. The plan was that the canisters, dropped upwind of *EPC2*, would drift down towards the yacht and float either side of the hull with the line snagging on the yacht's keel to stop them drifting past. The first drop missed the yacht. On the second the rope broke and the canisters were lost in the heavy swell and gusting winds. Eventually, Serge Viviand, on the same Hercules that had spotted *EPC2*, reported back to the BOC Challenge that an 11-person liferaft containing a handheld VHF radio had been successfully dropped in the 50 knot winds and gigantic seas. Isabelle had managed to secure it alongside the yacht which was flicking back and forth like a wild fairground ride. The liferaft was inflated and 'the yacht was bobbing around like cork,' said Viviand. 'Both *EPC2*'s masts were down, though a portion of the main spar was secured on deck.'

'The pilots' skills were amazing,' said Isabelle. 'What they could do dropping me things at high speeds just above me was incredible … through a large hole at the rear of the plane I could see small figures moving.' Frustratingly for the rescue crew, Isabelle did not realise that the liferaft contained a radio for her to make contact with the plane's crew.

By now the rescuers and Isabelle had worked out a kind of system for communicating. If they wanted her to come on deck they would pass over very low 'making one hell of a noise!' If they wanted to drop equipment they would first drop smoke markers to calculate the drift and wind direction. The crew of the Orion aircraft tried signalling by Morse and hand to tell Isabelle that the liferaft that had been dropped to her contained a radio. The second afternoon after being sighted, Isabelle located the radio in the liferaft and finally made voice contact with the crew of the Orion. For the first time she learned that the Navy missile ship *HMAS Darwin* was en route to her position, having recalled its sailors from their Christmas holidays. She was also told of plans to lift her off her yacht by *Darwin*'s on-board helicopter in two days time.

Canberra Maritime Rescue Centre co-ordinator Rick Burleigh said that Isabelle had told the rescue plane that the rear compartment of *EPC2* was flooded and she had lost all steering capability. She added that she had plenty of food and water in her stores. The RAAF Orion PC3 aircraft crew arranged a regular radio schedule with Isabelle.

Minoru Saito, relieved of his duties to divert to Isabelle, headed towards Hobart for repairs to his self-steering.

While Isabelle faced a wait of some 40 hours, she also started to come to terms with the impending separation from her yacht which had become such a part of her life after three years of work and thousands of miles. They seemed inseparable.

Harry Mitchell, 1,400 miles behind Isabelle, expressed his consternation and concern at events in a message to Josh Hall at Race HQ: 'Good grief the attrition rate gets worse. Was she hit by the same storm that hit me? The worst I have ever been through? I AM ONLY JUST HOLDING ON. The weather is still mean. What has she been through. Keep me informed. Henry.'

Several hundred miles north east of Isabelle, Robin Davie was approaching the final 600 miles to the Sydney finish line. Four years ago his progress up the Australian coast had been tortuously slow and it had taken him six and a half days. This time luck was on his side. Strong westerlies blew him at full speed through the 300-mile Bass Strait in 35 hours. At dawn on New Year's Eve, he was approaching Gabo Island to turn the corner north up the coast to Sydney.

Robin had extracted every last ounce of performance from his old battlehorse of the previous BOC race. By any standards it was a remarkable performance. As the sun rose on a new day with not a cloud in the sky, the 40ft *Cornwall* closed right into the coast to within a quarter of a mile of the beach, keeping out of the southerly current that would slow them down. Robin was still wearing most of his thermals and foul weather gear from the cold of the Southern Ocean, but suddenly it was like entering a greenhouse. The temperature rose into the 80s and it was time for shorts and T-shirt. It was bliss to be warm again and to feel a hot sun. 'I always forget something when I do the shopping for each leg, this time I had forgotten nothing, until the obligatory swarm of Aussie flies invaded *Cornwall*. Then I remembered ... fly spray!'

The wind died to a virtual calm as he drifted along at 2 knots close to the beach, but he stayed very alert as he remembered Jean-Luc's rude awakening in the pounding surf. This was the only way to keep out of the current that was pushing him backwards.

Dolphins scooted around *Cornwall* throughout the day. As night fell the wind came around to the north, dead ahead, and started to increase. Robin was now tacking into the wind with 20 minutes between tacks as he zig-zagged north, approaching to within half a mile of the beach on one tack, and sailing out to sea for two miles on the other tack. He grabbed 20 minute sleeps on the tack out to sea, relying on his faithful fire bell to awaken him, knowing that if he overslept he would end up a long way out to sea and not on the beach.

As the sun rose on the first day of 1995, fatigue was taking its toll. The wind was up and down and reefs were being put in and taken out several times an hour. But there were only 100 miles to go ...

For Isabelle the last day of 1994 brought mixed emotions. Relief that rescue was imminent, for she had been told that she would be lifted off her yacht by helicopter early that morning. Sadness that she was leaving her yacht. But she was overjoyed to hear that a salvage attempt was going to made from Hobart to recover *EPC2*.

In one of the last drops from the plane there were two apples and a carefully packed beer for New Year's Eve 'celebration'. They also dropped two new EPIRB beacons so that before abandoning her yacht, she could activate them to assist the salvage ship in finding *EPC2*. The signals would last a maximum of 60 hours, probably less as the cold temperatures drained the lithium batteries. It had taken nearly three hours for search aircraft to find *EPC2*, so what chance did a salvage vessel have, with its much more limited field of vision at sea level?

*The moment when Isabelle abandoned her yacht and her dreams deep in the Southern Ocean, lifted off by a Sea Hawk helicopter on New Year's Eve.* PHOTO: AUSTRALIAN AIR FORCE/PPL

Isabelle's last night on board was strange, damp and cold. 'A New Year's Eve in the darkness of the sail locker, wrapped in a rescue blanket.' She took photographs of herself and the damaged yacht as a final remembrance.

As dawn lit up her dark world on 31 December another low, noisy fly past brought her up on deck. The wind was blowing 20-25 knots. A new noise filled the sky. 'At sunrise I heard it coming. It happened very quickly.' She activated the EPIRBs. A Sea Hawk helicopter was hovering over the area she had cleared on deck at the front of the yacht. 'An incredible acrobat was hanging from a rope. He made it on to the deck and put a harness around me and we were winched back up together.'

It was 0659 Sydney time on New Year's Eve. Three days after the monster wave had overwhelmed her yacht, Autissier suddenly felt a great pang of sadness as she looked down on the heaving deck of *EPC2*. 'This is the first time I had to leave my boat. It was very difficult. The yacht represents three years of my life, thinking about and preparing for the BOC. After the first leg everything was so wonderful for me. I had a big lead. But I have done a BOC before. I know what can happen. But this time the Indian Ocean was very tough for me … '

Within 30 minutes the helicopter had landed on *HMAS Darwin*, which turned towards Adelaide with an ETA of midday 2 January.

In a ship to shore call to the BOC Race office in Sydney, Isabelle said she was feeling good, an opinion seconded by the medical officers on *HMAS Darwin*. 'I am dressed like a sailor in the Australian Navy,' she said. 'The colours are good for me.' The colour of her fleet air arm jump suit was grey. She was not quite in mourning.

*Seeing her shore crew Serge Viviand, Isabelle rushes to an emotional reunion.*
PHOTO: ADELAIDE ADVERTISER/PPL

On board she showered, ate and slept deeply. Some 24 hours after she had been airlifted aboard, she boarded the helicopter again as the warship approached the Australian coast and was flown to Edinburgh Air Force Base near Adelaide. As she stepped on to dry land for the first time in 37 days after her harrowing ordeal, her smile and expression of relief said it all.

She thanked the Australian defence force members for her rescue. 'I am here because of you and I will never forget that,' she told her rescuers. She was reunited with her shore crew Serge, who presented her with a new pair of dangling earrings, her trademark. Later, she was wearing a T-shirt, a gift from Caroline Adams, which bore the legend: 'I spent New Year's Eve with 200 Aussie sailors.' She had finished the race with only 'my wet passport and my wet credit cards.'

When asked about her future plans Isabelle replied: 'I do not know right now. But I do know I will race again.'

So ended what was undoubtedly one of the most dramatic rescues in the history of ocean yacht racing as the courageous and resolute Frenchwoman twice lost the rig from her yacht in one leg and then found her life in deadly jeopardy. The incident graphically demonstrated how fate and fortune could single out even the best prepared yacht in the race while others less well prepared survived to sail on.

Many lessons would be learned from Isabelle's rescue. Not least was the suspect position reports from the two EPIRBs, transmitting positions with a disparity of up to nine miles. More important was the question of making a yacht more visible to searchers. The white deck of *EPC2* proved almost invisible against the breaking waves. Having a yacht's deck painted in a bright, visible colour, or having a sheet of fluorescent material that could be tied to the deck to make sighting easier, would be a necessity next time around.

Never one to relinquish her dreams while there was any glimmer of hope, Isabelle spoke enthusiastically of the salvage operation being mounted from Hobart to recover her yacht. 'I think the boat can float for a long time. I really hope the salvage operation succeeds,' she said. The rollover in *EPC2* had only increased her faith in the yacht because it had brought her through the crisis. 'You cannot imagine the power of the water; something has to break,' she said. *Petuna Explorer*, a deep sea trawler, left Hobart on New Year's Day, having been commissioned by the insurers of *EPC2* to search for the drifting yacht.

New Year's Eve was also Nigel Rowe's birthday, but as he wryly observed, 'It didn't seem to matter at all with everything else that has been going on lately! But I can't wait to reach Hobart and find a bar that knows how to build a really good dry Martini.'

In the midst of Isabelle's rescue drama early on race day 35, New Year's Eve, Alan Nebauer sailed through Sydney Heads in *Newcastle Australia* to complete his childhood dream of circumnavigating the globe under sail. It was something he had wanted to do since he was eight years old. He finished third in Class II in his yacht named after his hometown and the local businesses that sponsored him. His time was 34d 04h. Alan was having a race within a race with Niah Vaughan, who had beaten him across the line in Cape Town. Alan now trailed Niah by two-and-a-half days at the halfway point of the race.

Vaughan became the ninth sailor and the first Brit to complete the second leg into Sydney. His arrival coincided with the climax of a New Year's Eve fireworks extravaganza over Sydney Harbour. 'It was a spectacular welcome party. To go to all that expense of fireworks just for me. I think it's tremendous of Sydney!' he joked. His time of 34d 22h gave him fourth place in Class II.

The only notable sign of abuse on *Jimroda II*, in the midst of her third BOC circumnavigation, was a broken main boom, repaired with a spinnaker pole splint. Niah was the fifth skipper to have suffered a broken boom on this leg of the race.

'It broke just north of Kerguelen Island,' he said. 'We decided to go north, but not far enough. We surfed down a short, sharp sea, rounded up and the boom went in the water. That was it, she was gone.' Niah had been fortunate on this second leg. The maximum winds he had experienced were 45-50 knots in Bass Strait. His worst ordeal was when the toilet got blocked 14 days from the finish and he had to take it apart while it was full. After that he used a bucket all the way to Sydney.

Fellow Brit Robin Davie had been listening to a ball by ball cricket commentary on the first day of the Sydney Test Match as he tacked and reefed his way north towards the finish line. The rapid fall of English wickets followed by a great fight back by Atherton and Crawley boosted Robin's morale. On his last night at sea a four hour calm was followed by a forecast 30 knot southerly frontal system. With everything set and flying and a great wind from astern, *Cornwall* charged north with a bone in her teeth at 8 knots, rock-hopping along the coast through a night of rain and low cloud. The lights of towns and villages were sometimes barely visible.

By dawn Robin was passing Botany Bay and shortening sail as the wind rose. The Sydney cliffs were in sight between rain squalls as *Cornwall* surfed in through the Heads and across the finish line at 0655. The local Coast Guard patrol reported 50 knot squalls. It was 'a hell of a way to finish a hell of a leg', and as lashing rain and spray soaked the reception committee, Robin was pleased to let them swarm on board to get the sails down and get the tow hitched up. He was more interested in the obligatory fresh milk and coffee ice cream that they had brought with them as he was towed through the harbour under Sydney Bridge.

It was still blowing as they tied up to the dock in downtown Sydney, at Pyrmont Bay Marina next to Darling Harbour. Robin was tucking into his second two litre pack of ice cream and drinking his third litre of fresh milk as he stepped ashore to meet the local media. Having nipped at the heels of Alan Nebauer and Niah Vaughan, Robin was the tenth yachtsman to complete the second leg. His time of 36d 6hr 55m was a terrific accomplishment in a boat ten feet smaller than their 50-footers. He finished just 32 hours behind *Jimroda II*.

In his last BOC race, it had taken Robin 43 days to reach Sydney. In Cape Town he said 'I think there are three days to come off that. Whether there is the luck to do it is another thing.' In the end he had knocked off an amazing five-plus days. He had set a bench mark that other 40-footers would have a tough time to beat in future races.

*Cornwall* was the oldest boat in the fleet and, together with Harry Mitchell's, one of the shortest. Davie had scrimped and saved to sail in his second BOC Challenge, and lack of sponsorship forced him to travel third class. He had come through the terrible storm after Christmas suffering only minor damage. The log transducer had been shattered as he crashed off a wave, the tiller for his self-steering had broken off and his staysail had some bad rips and tears. 'It's a displacement boat, not a skimmer or a surfer, so I can't exceed 8 or 9 knots. Even if I have the occasional faster burst, it doesn't affect my daily average of 180-190 miles. The other thing that's very important is reliability. You always have to have another way of doing something if anything goes wrong. Otherwise you're going to lose that speed and consistency.'

Like others in the race, Robin had been keeping his Achilles heel a secret. His major scare had occurred early on, east of Kerguelen Island at 50° south. He noticed cracks along the stainless steel swages on several of the wire stays that supported the mast. If any serious loading was applied to the rig, the rigging wires could pull out. He rationalised the problem thus: since there was heavy rust staining in the cracks it was clear that the cracks had not happened recently. He could reasonably hope that the stays might hold until Sydney. He marked them with a black dye pen so that he could watch for any clean wire starting to pull out of the swages. He thought out a plan to stay the mast and collected together the ropes and blocks ready for action if required. Then, for the rest of the 3,500 mile voyage to Sydney, he inspected the wires closely every hour, using a torch at night.

Within an hour of tying up at Pyrmont, Robin's first Cornish visitors were on the dock to greet him: Betty Bevans, president of the New South Wales Old Cornwall Society and John Hornby, a prominent retired local yachtsman and old friend from the last BOC race, who was soon lugging several dustbin bags of 'vile,

*Home at last: Australian skipper David Adams embraces his wife after enduring the worst seas he'd ever encountered.*

PHOTO: JON NASH/PPL

stinking horrible laundry and bedding' (Robin's description) to his car for his wife's washing machine.

Such scenes of Aussie hospitality beyond the call of duty were repeated for all the shoestring skippers. Robin's first priority ashore was to take off with Niah Vaughan to sample a good fried breakfast at the local greasy spoon café.

With Robin Davie's arrival in Sydney, the focus of the race now shifted to Hobart, Tasmania, towards which three skippers, all within a couple of hundred miles of each other, were limping like the walking-wounded with damaged steering systems. Nigel Rowe on *Sky Catcher* was due to arrive in Hobart later that afternoon. Arnet Taylor reported: 'We are all mentally fatigued and stay in touch on the radio to make sure everybody is coping.'

For Harry Mitchell, still 2,000-plus miles from Sydney, there had been no such comforting contact. Given his concerns over using too much battery power and not having the regeneration capacity to replace it, his use of long range radio had been absolutely minimal, especially with his young friend Neal Petersen out of the race. Anxious for the latest news on Isabelle, Minoru and Nigel, Harry sent a message to Race HQ, also reminding Terry, 'if I reach Sydney you owe me half a beard.' While the Wind Gods had been trying to collect a few scalps, Harry was busy collecting beards – a reference to his wager whereby Mark Schrader, Jean-Luc Van den Heede and others had agreed to shave off their beards when Harry completed his circumnavigation.

Harry survived another potential calamity when, after the big storm of 27 December, he noticed a smell of gas in the cabin. He suspected one of the cylinders was leaking, but until now it had been too rough to change over to one of six cylinders lashed firmly in racks either side of the heads. Now that things had calmed down, he swapped cylinders. But, worryingly, the smell of gas persisted. Harry systematically checked the length of gas pipe which ran from the cooker behind the settee berth on the port side. To his horror he found that the armoured piping was almost cracked in half where it had been subjected to constant chafe from the motion of the yacht. 'I was sweating when I found it. I could have been blown to kingdom come. "Someone's watching over me", I thought.'

Fortunately, Harry carried a spare length of piping, otherwise there would have been no more hot meals until he arrived in Sydney. There was better luck for Harry on New Year's Day, when he had one of his best ever 24 hour runs, recording 210 miles.

Nigel Rowe arrived in Hobart on Monday 2 January, and reported three priorities on getting ashore, in the following order: 1. A very dry Martini. 2. A steak. 3. A shower. 'But the people who came out to meet me would have preferred number three as number one!' he quipped.

Nigel reflected on the fact that perhaps he had been too cautious in not going far enough south and too conservative with his sail area. 'Perversely it was the cautious approach that put me in the middle of a stunning storm. If I had sailed a little more aggressively, I would have been out of the way.' Nigel had been knocked down three times during his two day nightmare and had felt dwarfed and insignificant against the waves.

In Hobart he had unexpected company alongside *Sky Catcher*. Ex-BOC competitor Don McIntyre, who had sailed *Buttercup* to a Class II finish in the 1990-91 race, was on his way next day to Antarctica for a year's expedition with his wife Margie, taking with them a high-tech prefabricated survival cabin in which they would live for a year. BOC competitors have always been a breed apart.

As Nigel Rowe and his shore manager Skip Miller completed repairs on his self-steering gear, Arnet Taylor was due to arrive in Hobart next day, steering by sail trim. Minoru Saito was 72 hours away from respite having been plagued by his own steering woes.

Arnet, using his wits and a variety of makeshift materials including spare lines, a length of chain and an empty bucket, guided his rudderless yacht into Tasmania's Storm Bay late on the afternoon of 4 January. He was making a rendezvous with a waiting tow vessel stationed just inside the permitted 10-mile tow limit on the River Derwent. Under race rules, he could anchor or accept a tow of 10 miles for repairs, as long as he restarted from the same spot.

Remarkably, Arnet had sailed his yacht the last 1,500 miles without any rudder. 'I rigged spare genoa sheets to port and starboard winches and shackled them to a 70ft length of line, with two fathoms of chain on the end, which I streamed behind the boat. I used this warp primarily to slow the boat down. I also had a small bucket I called "the parking brake" which I could throw over the side! Mostly I used sail trim for steerage. None of it really steered the boat. There was no refinement available, but in combination I had some control,' he reported.

In the 19th century, Hobart was the town that hosted the Yankee whalers and it is still a staunch maritime community. 'This Yankee vessel received a warm welcome,' said Arnet. It was the second time that *Thursday's Child* had diverted to Hobart. During the 1993 Vendée Globe race her then skipper and owner,

Welshman Alan Wynne Thomas, had retired from the race and sailed to Hobart with broken ribs and a partially collapsed lung, following a Southern Ocean knockdown. Many of the same friends who helped Alan out then were standing by to volunteer their assistance in Arnet's hour of need.

A replacement emergency rudder was made out of Tasmanian pine by Arnet's shore crew, Merfyn Owen and Peter Robie, at Ian and Kathy Johnston's workshop. Skip Miller, Nigel's crew gave a hand to work on the rig. An old friend, Bas Gamlin, worked on the wind generator. A new main rudder had been made in Florida by Lars Bergstrom and shipped out to Tasmania. Arnet put his usual good humoured slant on things: 'We continue our programme of injecting dollars into the local maritime community. I think the rumour is out that we are part of an American foreign aid programme. We leave each new port far more prosperous than we found it.'

Meanwhile, 'A Day In The Life of a Skipper Ashore' was chronicled by his project director, Katie Paine. 'After a day aboard assessing the damage, Arnet handed the laundry to the project director and took a nap, thoroughly enjoying the luxury of a hotel's soft bed and clean sheets. Next on the list, television, a hair cut and a quick exploration of the local market and the purchase of a couple of Aussie hats.'

On 6 January, on his 35th day at sea in leg two, Harry Mitchell was continuing his slow but steady progress towards Sydney 1,650 miles away. As *Henry Hornblower* tramped on at 4.6 knots, Harry sat down at the chart table, making himself comfortable in his scrapyard car seat, and began tapping the keys of his laptop computer. In one of his rare communications of any length to Race HQ he relived his experience in the December storm that wreaked havoc with the fleet.

'The storm of December 27 began the day after Perth forecast a storm in my area,' he wrote. 'With the barometer at 865 millibars and the wind building, I stowed my mainsail and set about 10ft of foresail. With the wind at 45 knots by mid morning I hove-to. When the wind reached 50 knots the seas were 30 feet-plus high with the wind gusting to 60. Conditions became diabolical.

'I was in a washing machine with foam everywhere and the wind shrieking in a thick, very low mist. The tops of the waves were whipped off giving a blinding spray which probably saved me from being rolled or pooped. The wind generator blades blew away, the self-steering vane snapped off. I was scared and even afraid of being afraid.

'The wind died down by early evening and the boat came through undamaged and dry. It was only me that had the wet pants. The wind was from the northwest and bitterly cold. I don't wish to go through that again in a hurry,' he concluded.

While Harry sailed east in lighter winds, the crew of the deep sea salvage vessel *Petuna Explorer* reported that eight-metre swells were dampening their efforts to locate Isabelle's abandoned yacht several hundred miles south of Adelaide.

In Hobart's morning newspaper, *The Mercury*, the *Petuna*'s skipper John Peterson was quoted saying that the yacht's EPIRB batteries had 'run down and quit three days previously'. Using a twin engined jet plane for the search next day had proved futile. The salvagers reluctantly announced that they had given up the search, believing the 60ft yacht had either sunk or drifted too far south towards the Antarctic, beyond the range of a feasible salvage operation.

On the evening of his 41st day at sea, on a cold, black night without a hint of summer, Minoru Saito piloted his 50ft yacht up the River Derwent towards

Hobart. He was 'very, very tired', his autopilots having failed about a week after leaving Cape Town. His mechanical windvane had been damaged in a knock-down three weeks before.

'Crazy trip,' said Minoru, who celebrated his 61st birthday that same day. 'Had no good sleep on first leg for two weeks (due to leaks needing constant pumping) and no good sleep on this leg.' He had only been able to leave the helm for occasional half-hour breaks after dropping the mainsail and lashing the wheel. Only then could he get a little sleep and make meals and radio calls. 'Trip not boring, though!' added Saito, who had diverted for Isabelle's position for 30 hours on instructions from Race HQ. 'I had no wind instruments but there was 50-60 knots of wind and with just my mainsail with three reefs I was making 19 knots!'

After a quick turnaround of just over 36 hours, Minoru got underway for the final stretch to Sydney, following in the wake of Nigel Rowe, whom he trailed by six days since the start in Charleston. Nigel was abreast of Gabo Island, enjoying a bumpy ride 'heading across the cobblestones of the Tasman sea'. For the first time at sea since Cape Town, he discarded his thermal jacket and felt the warmth of the sun while contemplating shorts and T-shirt.

With the sun shining and riding a favourable easterly breeze through the Heads, Nigel Rowe finally crossed the Sydney finish line into sixth place in Class II with a time of 45d 10h. He arrived feeling 'bloodied but unbowed', pleased with how *Sky Catcher* had survived such dreadful conditions and satisfied with how he had handled things.

A week after Nigel sailed into Sydney Minoru Saito, looking thin but healthy, crossed the line with a time of 52d 19h. He had suffered five knockdowns during the leg and had hand-steered his 50ft yacht for most of 7,000 miles. He had also been pumping water out of his boat from a leak in the centreboard every day for more than two weeks. 'I am very happy to be here!' he grinned.

Back in Hobart, Arnet Taylor had been ready to set sail, but local salts were concerned about him heading off on Friday the 13th. After an internal conference with his shore support crew Arnet decided that 'on this leg every day was like Friday the 13th, so why fight it?' He eventually set off later that day without incident.

Later 'after an evening of tacking off the beach with very little wind, an anchor in one hand and a rosary in the other', Arnet reported that he was pushing out into the current off the Australian mainland. But the Wind Gods had not finished with the final two BOC competitors yet. On her final morning at sea, *Thursday's Child* suffered a 130° knockdown that laid the mast in the sea. 'I was on the top of the wrong wave. It broke over us,' said Arnet. 'Everything that could break loose down below did break loose. The blades on my wind generator broke and the solar panel on the stern was smashed. It was frustrating. But I'm here,' said Taylor, after he crossed the finish line at six in the evening. His time was 55d 18h. For a man who had never even sailed a transatlantic voyage before the BOC qualifier, sailing halfway around the world alone was victory enough. Half a dozen other BOC sailors were on hand to catch his docklines as the yacht nosed into the marina, offering congratulations and demanding details on how he sailed for two weeks without a rudder. 'You just do what you have to,' Taylor said laconically.

After Bass Strait, Harry Mitchell enjoyed his best night's sail for weeks as he passed Cape Otway. Under a full moon and a clear sky he was running with a 15 knot wind in a flat sea. He could see every unlit rock and island as he went through the narrow passage known as Crocodile's Teeth. 'The barometer dropped slowly to 980. When it drops slowly it's usually going to be a long one. In this case it stayed there for two days and didn't move!' With 50 miles to go, he got caught by a southerly buster.

'So far I have lost a spinnaker pole overboard, bent and broken the main boom support vang, lost all the blades on the wind generator, broken the blade on my windvane and I am now watching the foresail slowly tear apart. Otherwise, still holding together.'

Harry conceded that the two legs so far had been much tougher for him than the 1986 BOC Challenge. Almost seventy days at sea, cursed by the calms of the first leg had left him with a mere five day stopover in Cape Town. On this leg the endless gales, intense cold, and dampness had been hard on his morale. But Harry was a fighter.

Nine hours after Arnet completed leg two, Harry Mitchell took the gun in the early hours of the morning of the 57th day of the race. His delayed start from Cape Town meant this was Harry's 51st day at sea. Both Harry and Arnet had fought strong currents and a northerly gale on their final approach to Sydney. Harry had practised some good seamanship to get his boat to Sydney in one piece. 'He'd been out there longer and suffered more heavy weather than any of us' said Robin Davie. 'He'd also had it tougher with less radio contact than anyone else.'

For Harry it had, so far, truly been the loneliest race. Looking tired and drawn after sleepless nights navigating through fishing fleets and coastal hazards, Harry arrived having lost about 30lb in weight, but he had managed a shave while he was on his way towards Sydney Heads. A crowd had ferried out there to cheer him as he sailed across the finish line. As the welcome party came aboard and took charge of *Henry Hornblower*, Harry revelled in the sights of Sydney Harbour, the city's spectacular skyline aglow by night. The towboat took him past Sydney Opera House, underneath Sydney Bridge and into Darling Harbour. Surrounded by friends and congratulations, Harry felt as if he had woken up on a different planet compared to the empty desolation of the Southern Ocean a few days before.

The moment of arrival in Sydney as he tied up to the dock was a sublime one. To bring a tiny craft safely and alone across 7,000 miles of the most savage and immense ocean in the world brings out qualities deep and unknown within a man. It had been a rite of passage, an ordeal that purged the soul. This was 'the afterwards' that Harry had challenged himself for.

'I don't know,' he told reporter Kate Ford, his elbow locked around a shroud as though he were still at sea. 'At my age you shouldn't be out there in that (weather) by yourself... should be at home enjoying yourself.' Later he was to say: 'I was afraid, the seas were bloody huge. And huge and huge and huge. I really thought, we're not going to survive this thing. What saved me, I think, was that the wind was so strong it blew the tops of the waves off. If they'd been breaking, there's no doubt I would have been swamped. The spume was just dead white. But the wind, in this case, really helped me out.'

Once ashore, Harry was ready for a drink and some human company. Together with Niah and a few other partymakers, he didn't need much persuasion to head

for the all-night Guiness pub just up the road from the BOC dock for a few celebration drinks.

The final straggler of the flock was home. This second leg of the fourth BOC
Challenge had unquestionably brought the worst weather in the history of the
event, which had lived up to its reputation as the toughest yacht race in the
world. None of the skippers escaped unscathed. The first leg winner had lost her
yacht and been fortunate to escape with her life. Mayhem had prevailed in the
mountainous seas with violent knockdowns, dismastings, broken booms,
smashed rudders. It had been hell on high water and the next leg – the third and
longest, through the Southern Ocean around Cape Horn to Punta del Este – was
just seven days away.

# 8 · *Preparing for the Big One*

B y the time the BOC fleet had left Sydney for the Southern Ocean, questions were asked in Parliament about the cost of rescuing Isabelle Autissier from her stricken yacht and revealed a bill of A$5.8 million. Thirty one personnel had been recalled from leave for the operation and the country's defence assets were used for a total of 224 hours.

Senator Jocelyn Newman asked: 'Why hasn't the Government inquired about the insurance held by Ms Autissier and the race organisers to defray at least some of the not inconsiderable cost? The BOC race involves millions of dollars worth of yachts and sponsorships and is contested by professionals. It is only reasonable that professionals would take all possible precautions and some responsibility for their actions.' The Senator was no doubt thinking of Blondie Hasler's entreaty that singlehanded sailors should hazard no rescuers but 'drown like gentlemen'.

When the Australian media questioned the cost of the rescue, Isabelle responded, 'Maybe I am not worth a million dollars ... I don't know. I cannot say anything about it.'

John Hornby, chairman of the Safety Committee of the Yachting Association of New South Wales, wrote a letter expressing the counter argument: 'It's high time the myth concerning the cost of search and rescue is laid to rest. We, the taxpayers, already own the planes and ships and pay the crew's wages ... the only real cost is fuel, stores and liferafts. The incident should be treated as a hands-on exercise for the services concerned and is better than playing "war games", the cost of which is never questioned.'

It was John Hornby who later carried out stalwart work on preparing the yachts of Robin Davie and Harry Mitchell. He was also Robin's host in Sydney. Robin was facing bills upwards of £4,000 before leaving Sydney for the next leg. A rigger's inspection showed that much of *Cornwall*'s standing rigging needed replacing and the radar was unserviceable. The Old Cornwall Society held a fundraising champagne breakfast and a boat supper, where everyone brought their own food and drink and paid Robin $10 to eat it on the dock overlooking the BOC fleet. Funds raised paid for a new radar, fitted the day before the restart.

Preparing Harry's boat in Sydney was a race against time. The cabin was damp and musty and there hadn't been time to strip everything out. Down below was a shambles. There were mouldy old canvas bags full of rope ends, jam jars of nuts and bolts that had long since fused into a solid lump of rust, along with seized

*The final fourteen face the media the day before the start of the longest leg.*
PHOTO: PAUL GELDER

spanners and other tools, and, incongruously, a punctured old lorry tyre's inner tube in the fo'c'sle. Harry was a terrible hoarder who drove a hard bargain when it came to throwing anything away. In the forward watertight compartment under the inspection hatch some 40 gallons of water were pumped out. No one knew how it had got there, least of all Harry, who wasn't unduly worried. The same thing had happened in Cape Town, he said.

'I've lost the silicone,' said Ted Donnelly, one of the volunteer helpers.

'Join the club,' said Harry, 'I've just found my glasses after five days!'

'Is there a place for the junk?' someone asked.

'It's called the boat,' said Harry good humouredly.

Ted's wife, Ineen, had taken all Harry's clothes to be washed, as well as his blackened pots and pans from the galley stove, which was like Fagin's kitchen. The engine had been overheating when Harry was on starboard tack and he had been syphoning the cooling water up by sucking on a pipe with his mouth. One of the helpers was trying to solve the problem.

'How do you keep warm; do you have a gas heater?' someone asked. 'No, when it's cold I fill a hot water bottle and stuff it inside my sailing jacket and huddle down in the bunk to keep the circulation going,' said Harry. He didn't tell us one of his two hot water bottles was leaking until he was on his way out to the start. 'If you believe in an after life Harry's already done most of his purgatory in this world!' said Ted, looking at the spartan conditions below.

On Australia Day, three days before the start of leg three, the BOC skippers were on parade to be presented at the city's official celebrations in Tumbalong Park followed by the Premier's reception. 'A great Aussie honour and at least we weren't shot at like the Duke of Cornwall at last year's do,' noted Robin. The day culminated in a spectacular firework display in Darling Harbour.

Harry, asked about procedure for piercing his ear in anticipation of that gold earring, replied: 'The strategy in my case is pretty well accepted ... that there's no fool like an old fool. For me to say I am thinking ahead would be jumping the gun. This is where I came in in 1986... and where I went out in 1986, at the bottom end of New Zealand. If I can make the effort and not prove myself an idiot, I will. My aim is to see Mark Schrader clean shaven. That will be sufficient motivation to get there.'

There was much humour at the Sydney prize-giving on the last night, with Aussie ex-BOC skipper Ian Kiernan saying, 'For those of you who round Cape Horn it will bring a lot of privileges. For a start you'll be able to piss to windward. You can wear an earring without being gay and you can toast the queen with one foot on the table.' Each skipper was introduced to the accompaniment of their national anthem and tracked by spotlight as they walked to the stage down a long flight of steps from the theatre gallery. By the time Harry, exhausted from his work on the yacht, got halfway, the national anthem had almost played out, but the huge ovation for him continued.

Robin Davie was the dubious recipient of the Omega best 24 hour run in leg two for 197 miles – dubious because the hot shot racers had been too busy to submit their best day's claims, so by default he walked away with the yellow jersey, or in this case, flag. He also won the COMSAT communications award for assisting Neal Petersen after his dismasting.

Isabelle Autissier, still deeply affected by the loss of her yacht and the sudden change from sailor to spectator, admitted that watching the fleet leave Sydney without her would be hard. But staying on was her gesture of thanks. That she had won the hearts of Australians was plain to see from the standing ovation she received that night as she collected a special award for seamanship, shared with Arnet Taylor, who had sailed 1,500 miles without a rudder.

In her impromptu acceptance speech she once again thanked the RAAF and Navy: 'Without you I would not be here today. All of us have bad moments in life and we must overcome them. The other skippers were scared for me. I am sure they understand that my staying on is my way of saying thank you to them. It is all I can do. It would not be right just to say goodbye...' To her fellow competitors all she could add was: 'Enjoy the sea, the skies and the stars. My heart is with you.'

## *Sydney to Punta Del Este, Uruguay (6,914 miles)*

# 9 · And Then There Were Thirteen...

If the second leg of the BOC Challenge had always produced the worst weather conditions in previous races, the third leg was considered to be the 'big one'. The prize of rounding Cape Horn is the ultimate credential for any seafarer, says Robin Knox-Johnston, a former Race Director of the BOC Challenge. Nowhere else on the surface of the globe does the sea flow round the world unchecked by any land barrier. The names on the chart speak volumes: Isla Desolacion, Isla Hope and Isla Deceit. Here the waters of the Southern Ocean are funnelled into a 600 mile gap between Antarctica and the southern-most tip of South America. The seabed rises dramatically from a depth of two miles to a shelf of 600ft. Waves of 120ft, the size of a 20-storey building, can be encountered in this region. Though the race is timed to pass through the Southern Ocean during the summer months, missing the worst storms between April and October, conditions can be savage.

Six of the sailors who sailed out of Sydney Harbour at noon on Sunday 29 January had rounded this legendary landmark before. Of the eight who had not, one, Harry Mitchell, had been trying to lay the ghost of Cape Horn for 50 years. Once the Horn was astern, the fleet would have conquered its biggest psychological hurdle. Meanwhile, the 7,000 mile voyage to Uruguay was potentially the most hazardous leg of the race, taking the fleet deep into the most desolate reaches of the Southern Ocean – past a point of no return, the point on Earth furthest from land. The yachts would be beyond ship and aircraft range for much of the time, and if problems developed, help would have to come from another competitor.

It was a spectre that seemed a long way off as a puff of smoke from a cannon on the deck of the replica ship *HM Bark Endeavour*, signalled the start of the race under blue summer skies over Sydney Harbour. David Adams, whose grand-father was a Cape Horn clipper-ship sailor, found a whisper of wind in the patchy sea breeze that had eluded the others and *True Blue* accelerated to the front of the fleet, streaking through Sydney Heads. With the cheers of hundreds of his fellow countrymen muffled by the sirens and the wind, it was a proud moment for Adams, who had a lead of 22 hours on rival Giovanni Soldini.

Last time he had sailed to Cape Horn in the Challenge, Adams had gone down to 63° south. He described the cold in his 60ft aluminium yacht, *Innkeeper*, as 'like being in the top compartment of a refrigerator'. In the deep south, skippers had experienced 10 days of solid fog when they couldn't see the front of their boats. The only ice reports had come from the yacht in front. Even with radar it was like a blind man running through a mine field. In the freezing waters of the Southern Ocean, life expectancy is a matter of minutes, and cold water saps the strength of the toughest. To minimise the risks for this fourth race, the organisers had established a waypoint at 59° south and 130° west which the skippers had to leave to starboard. 'It's a much better way to race. You're not gambling with lives,' said Adams. But the bigger boats would still be the pathfinders through the ice hazard.

Of all the spectators and competitors at the start, no one was more emotional than Isabelle Autissier. Her disappointment at not being part of the start was tempered only by the fact that Adams, her close friend, was in the lead as she cheered him on.

When the canon fired, Niah Vaughan had just edged *Jimroda II* over the line first in Class II, as he had in Cape Town. But Robin Davie, Nigel Rowe and David Scully were left almost becalmed as everyone else found wind. 'We drifted across the line shouting the usual curses at the Wind Gods before the breeze eventually came to us,' said Robin.

Nigel had looked forward to leg three with a healthy mixture of dread and excitement. As the spectator fleet and Sydney's skyline disappeared astern and the fleet spread across the horizon, a deep melancholy settled over *Sky Catcher*. It had happened at the beginning of each leg of the race so far. The sudden isolation after so much socialising in port and the prospect of another six or seven weeks alone at sea, so soon after the previous leg, was having its effect. Each time it was taking him three or four days to settle into a rhythm again. The storm during leg two that diverted him to Hobart was still a vivid memory. 'It taught me the meaning of gut-wrenching fear and I neither want nor need another lesson... I pray this leg will be kinder to us than the last,' he said in a message to Race HQ.

As the last of the spectator boats turned for home, a solitary BOC yacht remained tied up to the pontoon at Pyrmont, now a haven of tranquillity after the feverish buzz of preparations over the last few days. As the blazing heat of the afternoon sun beat down on the deck of *Henry Hornblower*, Harry Mitchell was down below slumped in his $75 scrapyard car seat in front of the chart table. His preparations had ground to a halt. The sweat poured off him. A friend put the kettle on for a cup of tea. Harry didn't seem to hear what was being said to him. The friend felt his forehead. Harry was feverish and disorientated. Ted, a first-aider who had been working on the boat, was called and diagnosed possible heat exhaustion. Or maybe Harry had caught the same virus that had affected Alan Nebauer.

Back on land after the rhythm of life at sea his sleep patterns had been disrupted. It had been a week of parties and official receptions, as well as hard work on the boat, including a haul out and antifouling. Now he was helped from the yacht and driven the half mile to his hotel room and put to bed. A doctor was telephoned for advice. 'If he's not feeling better after a couple of hours sleep, I'll be happy to come over and check him,' he said. The reluctant patient, on hearing that the doctor charged $120 for a house call, stirred under the sheets and exclaimed: 'Tell him I'll be alright in a couple of hours!' Harry's real fear was that a doctor might tell him to rest up for a week, and by then he would be too far behind to rejoin the race. At the same time he was anxious about the work that remained to be done on *Henry Hornblower*. Time was running out. He agreed to stay in bed provided everyone went back to work on the boat; he'd come down and check for himself later that afternoon.

He also wanted to attend the traditional shore crew party at the marina that evening. Some had joked that Harry had only delayed his start so he could attend another party. That evening at the party Harry and Isabelle, the only BOC skippers in port, heard David Adams' wife, Caroline, and Merfyn Owen sing a poignant duet to the gathering. At 8.30 pm Harry left to get an early night.

Out at sea, as dusk fell, the fleet ran into patches of calm as the wind died away to 3 or 4 knots. It was a slow first night and next day saw the yachts sailing on glassy seas fuelled by a light and fluky easterly breeze. Christophe, the furthest south, moved to the front of the pack and covered just 140 miles in the first 24 hours with Jean-Luc Van den Heede 11 miles astern. In Class II a quartet of skippers renewed their private contest, with David Adams and Giovanni Soldini a mile apart and Alan Nebauer two miles ahead of Niah Vaughan on *Jimroda II*. Minoru Saito had communications and charging problems aboard *Shuten-Dohji II*, which meant that Race HQ could not track his position. Eventually he diverted to Port Kembla 70 miles away.

Back on the Sydney dockside the next day, Harry had regained his rosy disposition and complexion. He had been into town to have his hair cut convict-style. That morning there were a few last minute jobs to be done. He was concerned that in a knockdown he might lose the expensive EPIRB mounted in a white lozenge shaped canister in the cockpit. He tied the distress beacon and its spring-loaded mechanism, designed to release automatically under water, inside the canister and then taped up the outside joint. He would still be able to release it manually, but by disabling the automatic facility it would not, he hoped, set off a false alarm as others had done in the race.

A succession of Harry's fans came by as he completed preparations to leave the dockside, including a couple of 70-year-olds who asked him what his biggest problems were: 'Fatigue and money,' replied Harry. 'We're a bunch of masochists, I don't know what we're proving.' Isabelle Autissier came to wish him luck, embracing him across the guardrails. Next with a kiss was Julia Humberstone. 'Could you take this back to England?' Harry asked her, proffering a presentation box awarded to him at the BOC prizegiving for completing leg two. 'I don't want it to get damaged and if anything happens to me I'd like Diana to have it.'

Shortly after, *Henry Hornblower* was hitched up to a line and towed out of the marina. Those aboard included Skip Miller, John Hornby, who had worked on the yacht, Tanya Mottl, the BOC's Mumm Champagne girl, and myself. As we went under the shadow of Sydney Bridge and passed the opera house, Harry was having a quick teach-in on how to operate the video camcorder given to him by Dan McConnell to shoot some footage for the official BOC film of the race. Harry was in good spirits. He was back to his perky old self and any trepidation he might have felt about heading back into the Southern Ocean was not displayed. We laughed and joked about the leg of ham swinging from the grabrail down in the cabin. It was covered in a swarm of Aussie flies. 'Extra protein,' said Harry.

When we reached Sydney Heads, Mark Schrader came alongside driving the fast inflatable to take everybody off the yacht. As the north shore loomed up, Harry needed to change tack quickly and there was no time for prolonged farewells. We motored alongside, keeping Harry company for a while as he waved back at us blowing his foghorn as he had at every start of a leg. His parting words were: 'Keep an eye on me till I get past the bottom end of New Zealand – that's the first big one!'

'We'll be watching you all the way, Harry,' Mark shouted back. 'I'll be stroking my beard . . . ,' a reminder that Mark was one of several people who had agreed to shave off their beards when Harry completed his circumnavigation. At 1730 local time the BOC fleet was extended by one as Harry sped south in a 10-knot north easterly.

Less than 48 hours after the start of the race the fleet encountered its first storm as a southerly buster came blasting through. 'Beating into a 40 knot gale in the Tasman Sea is not for the faint hearted,' said Robin Davie, as *Cornwall* was chucked around all over the place. The Tasman Sea is widely regarded as one of the most difficult and unpredictable areas of ocean, and in every one of the previous BOC races storms have swept the fleet causing damage to boats and equipment. Robin was feeling tired and somewhat seasick, 'which isn't unusual if bad weather comes soon after a re-start.' In the first hours of an offshore passage bad weather is the last thing a sailor wants. He hasn't got his sea legs, his night vision or established the rhythm of being back at sea.

David Adams was resting on *True Blue* when a vicious 60 knot squall came through. 'They'd told us a change was coming, but I was expecting 30 knots. It just about wiped me out,' he said. 'The headsail tore and the furler got caught and tried to rip the mast out. But it's all okay now.'

On the second night out as the wind began to rise, Nigel Rowe on *Sky Catcher* decided to take a reef in the mainsail. As he looked up he saw a gaping hole in the mainsail which had torn horizontally from luff to leach below the third reef point. The yacht's rudder, which had been fitted with new bearings in Sydney, was already stiff and inclined to stick. For Nigel it was the worst time for things to go wrong. Emotionally, like the others, he was at his most vulnerable during those first few days. In the now developing gale he altered course for the Australian fishing port of Ulladulla – an almost 200 mile beat – to assess his options.

Nagging at the back of Nigel's mind since before the start of the race was the fact that he had been unable to insure *Sky Catcher*, which had soaked up his life's savings. Sailing uninsured troubled him. By the time he got to Ulladulla he was 'ready to throw in the towel'. But after discussing the situation with Race Director Mark Schrader, he postponed any decision on whether or not to continue 'until I knew if continuing was even a possibility'. Meanwhile, he ordered a new mainsail and prepared to haul the boat for rudder repairs.

Minoru, having made a five hour pit-stop at Port Kembla for repairs to his satellite communications system, was also en route to Ulladulla having discovered further electrical problems. Nigel and Minoru eventually arrived in

Ulladulla within 45 minutes of each other on the third night of the race. It would be almost another 48 hours before Minoru rejoined the race.

Out at sea damage reports continued to come in on race day four.

'Blowing dogs off chains,' said David Scully, busy bailing out *Coyote*. His masthead wind instruments had been blown away and he had an 11 foot split in his mainsail between the second and third reef points. Later Scully was answering radio communications with the introduction: 'Sobstad Antarctica'. He reckoned he had put about two miles of stitches in the mainsail and even then he could only raise it to the first reef. 'I sewed it up, but the next day an identical tear opened up right next to it. My stitching held. It was the best looking part of the sail, but I may have to take up quilting if the sail continues to fall apart.'

Without his masthead instruments he described night navigation as like sailing by braille. Two days later Scully's sail was starting to look like a Venetian blind. It was the second time the high-tech sail had delayed him. After the start of leg two in Cape Town, he had limped back in to the Royal Cape Yacht Club when it had torn, and had set off again with a borrowed, secondhand sail. Now the repaired sail flown to Sydney had failed again. Conceding that he couldn't keep up with the sail-mending, Scully decided to divert to Bluff, a fishing port on the southern end of New Zealand. It was a delay he could do without. He was also racing a 'biological clock' to Uruguay. His wife, Veronique, was expecting their second child and he was hoping to reach land in time to fly home in time for the birth.

David Adams was accurate in his observation: 'I bet there's lots of people getting into strife out here... Not much fun, I think I wanna go home!'

Robin Davie, in radio contact with Harry Mitchell, reported that Harry had 'diabolical conditions' and was down to his fourth reef in the mainsail but was 'soldiering on like a good 'un.'

Aboard *Cornwall* Robin was finding the persistent southerly winds very wearing as the yacht crashed to windward, sometimes landing heavily off the backs of swells and waves. He began to fear damage to the rigging or mast might occur. The only comfortable place on the boat was the bunk. He had also succumbed to the same flu bug that had hit Alan Nebauer and Harry in Sydney '... sore throat, headache and feeling like hell warmed up.' He also suffered occasional bouts of seasickness whenever he tried to eat. These had lasted four days until the wind eased. It was not yet as cold as it had been on leg two, but the last few days had seen continuous rain and low clouds. Below decks was damp and covered in heavy condensation which dripped off everything. The hot water bottle was out at night to help keep the bedding dry and the first layers of thermals were helping to keep the cold at bay. To compound his misery the deck speakers for his hi-fi had packed up. 'I'll have the albatrosses on strike if they don't get their heavy rock,' he said.

Arnet Taylor, tussling with 30 knots on the nose in *Thursday's Child*, had observed the leaders 'slamming into it with great abandon' but had backed off himself on the theory that 'I've got five to six weeks to break things. Why do it all the first week?' He was getting more sleep in the first week back at sea than he had during his short stopover in Sydney. 'I don't think I realise how much I miss the human contact until I get in, and then I can't get enough,' he admitted.

Alan Nebauer had spent the day on the phone and in the generator compartment on *Newcastle Australia*, trying to get his power supply going. The charging system that had caused him to put into port after the Cape Town start was testing him again. He switched to a spare alternator but thick black smoke was pouring out of the generator exhaust. Having failed to make repairs he became the second sailor to divert to Bluff, 140 miles to windward. 'The port looks quite shallow in parts,' said Alan, concerned about his four metre draught and literally 'praying for quiet conditions on arrival'. Cindy, his wife, had called a woman who managed traffic control. 'I hope it's not the same woman who put Harry on the beach last time!' warned Alan.

Before the first week of leg three was over Nigel Rowe had reached one of the more difficult decisions in his life as he announced his withdrawal from the BOC Challenge. Encouragement to continue had, he said, bordered on pressure, but most of his friends urged him to take the decision which was right for him and 'to hell with what anyone else might think of it'.

Work on building his new mainsail and the rudder had taken several days and he was now a long way behind the fleet. 'On this leg of the race more than any other I do not think it is prudent for me to carry on. There would be nothing in the 5,000 miles between New Zealand and Cape Horn except other BOC boats, should anything go wrong. Not only would I be at significantly greater risk myself, but I would have to put others at greater risk too in coming to my aid.

'For me sailing has always been a hobby to be enjoyed, not a way of life to be endured. The race has been every bit as tough as I knew it would be, but I have not enjoyed the sailing anywhere near as much as I expected to. There seems little point in continuing to take the risks involved. My participation as a competitor has been an intensely interesting and rewarding experience in other ways, and my respect and admiration for those left in the fleet remains considerable.'

Nigel's romantic dream of a solo circumnavigation that had become a consuming obsession had ended abruptly. He said he felt a bit like Icarus who flew too close to the sun and had his wings burned. 'It is one of those simple truths that the only way to avoid the prospect of failure in life is to take no risks at all, and it has long been my view that avoiding risk is no recipe for a fulfilled life. Besides, failure can be a valuable and enlightening experience.'

Nigel was the seventh skipper in the race to retire. With his departure came the inevitable comment from one fleet watcher: 'I hope 13 in the race isn't a bad omen ...'

David Scully paid his own tribute to the urbane Brit who had bought a certain *élan* to his campaign: 'I will miss Nigel very much. Whenever I was particularly wet, cold and uncomfortable, my spirits were buoyed by reminding myself that, not too far away, someone was opening a bottle of Puligny-Montrachet to the accompaniment of a Rachmaninov concerto. "I wonder what Nigel is having this evening?" I would say to myself, as I spooned down my freeze-dried.'

Over the radio and satcom David Scully had received two offers of a replacement sail from fellow competitors. Isabelle Autissier was willing to loan him a new mainsail she'd planned to fit on *EPC2*, and a secondhand *True Blue* sail was also on offer from David Adams. As leg two entered its second week, Scully arrived in Bluff to be met by David Barnaby, Steve Pettengill's shore manager, who had come to help him recut *True Blue*'s old sail. The sail was somewhat short for *Coyote*'s towering mast 'and I can't get my money back for the unused

(*Above*) Fourteen of the remaining fleet of 18 BOC Challenge yachts sailed across the Cape Town start line in November heading for the treacherous Southern Ocean waters. PHOTO: CEDRIC ROBERTSON/PPL

(*Left*) Work goes on in Cape Town docks to repair Japanese skipper Minoru Saito's *Shuten Dohji II*.
PHOTO: PAUL GELDER

Rig check time for
Robin Davie sailing
*Cornwall*, the oldest,
smallest yacht in the
race. PHOTO: BILLY BLACK

(*Right*) Robin Davie at the bow of *Cornwall*.
PHOTO: BILLY BLACK

(*Below left*) Farewell kiss for Australian skipper Alan Nebauer from his wife, Cindy.
PHOTO: BILLY BLACK

(*Below right*) 'What's all this then?' Harry Mitchell arrived in Cape Town as the fleet left on the second leg for Australia. PHOTO: BILLY BLACK

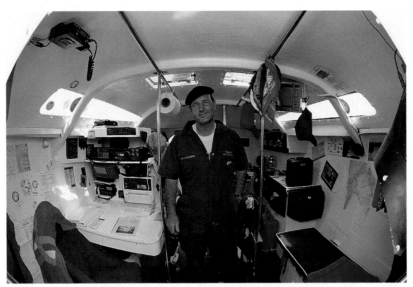

(*Left*) Niah Vaughan, wearing his trademark French beret, aboard *Jimroda ll*. It was the yacht's third BOC Challenge. She was built and skippered by Mike Plant and then Josh Hall. PHOTO: MARK PEPPER

(*Below*) *Cornwall* rides the waves like a rodeo star as Robin Davie arrives in Punta del Este after stepping a new mast in the Falkland Islands. PHOTO: BILLY BLACK

(*Above left*) Wearing
her survival suit and
talking on VHF radio
to rescue planes,
Isabelle Autissier in
her 60ft yacht *EPC2*
after it was rolled,
dismasted for a
second time, and
critically damaged.
PHOTO: ISABELLE
AUTISSIER

(*Above right*)
*True Blue* and
skipper David
Adams, who sailed to the
rescue of Isabelle Autissier when she was
dismasted 1,200 miles from Cape Town.
PHOTO: BILLY BLACK

(*Above*) The shattered cabin roof of *EPC2*
with its five square metre hole which
exploded under water pressure. Isabelle
salvaged a spar as a ridgepole for her
makeshift 'tent'. PHOTO: ISABELLE AUTISSIER

(*Right*) On dry land for the first time in
17 days, Isabelle Autissier is reunited
with her shore crew, Serge Viviand. She
finished the race with only 'my wet
passport and wet credit cards.'
PHOTO: ADELAIDE ADVERTISER/PPL

(*Opposite page, above*) The complex rudder arrangement on *Thursday's Child* which failed, leaving skipper Arnet Taylor to sail 1,500 miles without a rudder. PHOTO: BILLY BLACK

(*Opposite page, below*) After falling asleep, Jean-Luc Van den Heede woke up to find his yacht on the last bit of sand before 50 miles of rocky coastline to the Sydney finish line. Beach strollers watch as a tow line is fixed. PHOTO: HERB MCCORMICK

(*Below*) A relaxed Nigel Rowe sails *Sky Catcher* out of Sydney, next stop Punta del Este. A week later he faced up to one of the more difficult decisions of his life when he withdrew from the race. PHOTO: PAUL GELDER

(*Above*) Harry Mitchell, with his convict haircut, practises with his video camera as *Henry Hornblower* is towed out to Sydney Heads the day after the official start of leg three. One of the last pictures of the intrepid singlehander who was lost at sea 31 days later in a 70 knot storm. PHOTO: PAUL GELDER

(*Left*) David Adams, whose grandfather was a Cape Horner, streaks through Sydney Heads to start leg three to the cheers of hundreds of his fellow countrymen. PHOTO: PAUL GELDER

(*Below*) 'Losing the rudder and making it to Punta was physically, mentally and emotionally the hardest thing I've ever done in my life,' said Alan Nebauer, pictured at the finish of leg three with *Newcastle Australia.* PHOTO: BILLY BLACK

mast length,' lamented Scully. But after a 24-hour stopover, he streaked out of the harbour leaving local fishermen astounded that a sailing boat could go so fast. Scully wasn't wasting time as he began the weary business of catching up. Alan Neubauer was also back in the race having fixed his alternator.

While he had been working on recutting the mainsail, the latest addition to the *Coyote* team had arrived a month prematurely in Paris. Scully shared the happy news with Race HQ: 'Wind is on the beam and we are making 18 knots. La vie est belle... I have been in the *Coyote* cellar, and am blowing the dust off something special with which to welcome my second daughter into the world... Cheers, David.' Suggested names for David and Veronique's new baby girl came from JJ Provoyeur (Tasman) and Arnet Taylor (Bounty, after the island just west of the international dateline).

Christophe Auguin had already crossed the dateline and had spent his second Monday battling to stay ahead of his pursuers. In the first week, the lead among the top Class I boats had changed back and forth almost daily between Christophe, Jean-Luc Van den Heede and Steve Pettengill. Second-placed Jean-Luc said, 'Now that I have passed the dateline it seems to me that I am going back home. Everything seems perfect: nice weather, not too cold, nice wind, nice sea . . . until when?'

In Class II, David Adams and Giovanni Soldini just couldn't seem to shake one another. Adams, who had jokingly remarked on the second leg of the race that 'every morning when I get up, I look outside and there's Giovanni!' found it was happening again. But by race day 11 Giovanni had stretched his lead to 100 miles over David Adams. In a message to Race HQ the nearly bi-lingual Italian said: 'Mai best day is around 290. I learn in last leg ow to go in Southern Ocean. The most important thing is some good seas and a nice bottle of red wine per day. The bottles I ave are leetle only two glasses in each, like on an airplain, so dont tink I am dronk or crazy all the time!! I slept veri well in the last three days so now I am ready for icebergs. I go fast becose I smell home, the Atlantic Ocean, the equator. There I will finish Adams – I hope! Ciai Ciao, Giovanni.'

In a surprising role reversal from the last leg Adams, who had received an ice warning for his area, had other ideas. 'I think Giovanni is pushing too hard and taking risks. It was a pretty wild night with a cross sea pushing us around a fair bit.'

Meanwhile, Race HQ expressed concern that they were not receiving Giovanni's daily position reports and gave him a second warning that, under Race Rule 16.6, he was required to provide a report every 24 hours or a penalty could be imposed.

Sailing in limited visibility south of the 55th parallel, leader Christophe found that his radar was not working and he switched to a safer more northerly course. 'Without radar, sailing in the Southern Ocean is a little stressing. With my new route I think I'll have to sail an extra 200 miles. I'll try to push the boat to compensate.' He did just that, forging ahead into the hazy abyss at an average speed of 11 knots-plus with a run of 307 miles in 26 hours.

At the opposite end of the fleet, on race day 10, tailenders Harry Mitchell and Minoru Saito, at 50° south, were already 1,500 miles behind the leader and faced quite different conditions with 35 knots of wind. Minoru had suffered a knockdown with the loss of his masthead wind instruments. But Harry was raising his glass to celebrate passing a very important personal milestone: the longitude of

the southern tip of New Zealand, where his first BOC Challenge had abruptly ended eight years ago. He had been a tailender then, too, when, hit by the worst of a gale, one wave swept over the decks of *Double Cross* with such force that it twisted the steering wheel pedestal and another sheared part of his windvane. Even though Harry was a clever mechanic it was impossible to carry on without getting the parts welded back together.

In the 1986 race Mark Schrader, now the Race Director, had been a fellow competitor in his 49-footer *Lone Star*. Harry had discussed his options with Mark and decided to put into Bluff, on the south east coast of New Zealand, for repairs. But he had no detailed charts of the area and was further disorientated because a navigation light marking one of the headlands was out of action. On the night of 29 January 1987 Harry sailed *Double Cross* on to a beach at Fortrose, seven miles east of Bluff. It was a night that had haunted him ever since. A night when, for the sake of a few hundred yards, after sailing halfway round the world, he had been robbed of his ambition to become a Cape Horner.

'I was just following local instructions and didn't realise how close I was to shore,' he said later. 'I managed to anchor, but it dragged and the boat was pushed up on the beach.' He realised later that he had sailed right past Bluff Harbour. If he'd turned to port he would have been in harbour by 6.30 pm.

If Harry felt let down by the local advice he had received, he was full of praise for the way the communities at Fortrose and Invercargill rallied round to help him. Two sheep farmers, Alan Strange and Russell Crosby, who saw Harry walking along the beach in a desperate search for help, were the first on the scene. Then another helper, Ray Smith, swam ashore with a big rope. Ian Leask, a fisherman, tried to tow *Double Cross* off the beach with his 56ft boat *Savannah*. Farmers came from all around and had a big meeting to decide how to get the boat off. One brought his excavator down to the beach to help dig a channel for the boat to be towed out to sea on the next high water. 'Everybody, but everybody came down to help me. Without them, I would never have got the boat back afloat,' he said.

After five days *Double Cross* was afloat again, having suffered nothing more than a bent rudder and scratched paintwork. Several boats had run aground along that coastline but Harry's was the only one that had got off. He raided the grog locker and, with all his helpers, had a drink to celebrate. In between tides he had stayed with local farmers and fishermen and had learned how to shear sheep.

The yacht was full of gravel, and without a rudder to steer her Harry took a tow back to Bluff where the rudder and vane gear were all repaired free of charge by the local engineering works. It wasn't until he telephoned Race HQ at Newport to tell them his good news and that he was ready to rejoin the race that Harry realised the consequences of having accepted outside assistance. He had forgotten a basic rule – that no competitor could be towed for more than two miles. Bluff was seven miles west – backwards, as far as Harry was concerned. 'If I'd kept my mouth shut, I might have got away with it,' he joked afterwards. But his resolve suddenly crumbled. 'I was only four days behind the fleet and could have set out again very quickly.' The decision left him devastated.

Some days later Harry, who was staying with Ian Leask, the fisherman who

Opposite: *The night that haunted Harry when his yacht 'double crossed' him on a New Zealand beach in 1986, ending his ambitions to round the Horn.*

had towed his boat, took a taxi to the airport one morning to begin the long haul home to England. He left without saying a word, having sold *Double Cross* to John Hawkins, a photographer on the local newspaper who had admired her. Ten days before he left Sydney on this fourth BOC Harry was reunited with Ian and his wife Meri, who were visiting Sydney for the first time and had come to see the BOC boats. They told Harry, a horologist in his spare time, that the clock he had mended for them was still keeping time.

That night, as Harry enjoyed his happy hour drink, it felt good to have safely passed New Zealand. He reflected on the good fortune of Jean-Luc Van den Heede, whose yacht had successfully been towed five miles off a beach near Sydney. After Harry's incident the towing limit, known as 'Harry's law', had been increased to 10 miles. Ahead now lay new territory. The next land, Cape Horn, was nearly 5,000 miles away.

Now that Diana had sent out a new glass for the brass *Gypsy Moth* oil lamp, which had been broken in a storm on leg two, Harry could stay up a little longer instead of going to bed at dusk to conserve battery power. He had provisioned with plenty of gin and tonics and good Aussie wines for the happy hours ahead. He sat down at the chart table and sent a message to Peter Dunning at Race HQ: 'Tell Terry (Pollard) that if I make it to Punta he would owe me two thirds of his beard, therefore trim it down to a "goaty" till I arrive in Charleston. I think it would make that big square face of his real smart. Something like the ad in Southern Fried Chicken! Otherwise I'm holding on and just coping, Henry the Blower.' He was one step nearer to creating a record as the oldest singlehanded sailor to round Cape Horn.

There was news from two of Harry's close friends, retired BOC skippers, Floyd Romack and Neal Petersen, who had left Cape Town earlier in the week in their yachts bound for Punta del Este and a reunion with their former competitors. They were both planning to rejoin the fleet in an unofficial capacity for the fourth and final leg in April.

On race day 13, Jean-Luc Van den Heede, holding a course deep in the Furious Fifties reported the first iceberg sighting of the leg when he glimpsed the reflected light five miles away. 'My binoculars confirmed it. It was about four miles long, two miles wide and some 39 metres high. I passed two or three miles south and took some pictures.' Two days later Van den Heede spotted another iceberg 'with plenty, plenty, plenty of growlers. Avoid this area by night,' he warned. 'After dark, the white top of each wave seems to be a growler.'

At Race HQ in Charleston communications co-ordinator Larry Brumbach issued a 'fleet broadcast' with the co-ordinates of the sighting. David Adams, commenting that the ice was a lot further north than last time around added, 'Sleep's not going to be on the cards. We'll just be sitting in front of the radar.'

Before the yachts left Sydney, Mark Schrader had warned the skippers that the US Navy and Joint Ice Centre only report on icebergs that are bigger than 15 miles in length. Ironically, Antarctica was about to cast off a giant berg the size of Oxfordshire (1,115 square miles) as rising temperatures in the region triggered a further disintegration of the continent's ice sheets. But for yachtsmen the biggest danger comes from the deadly growlers, chunks of ice the size of a car or double-decker bus that drift mostly below the surface, invisible to radar and the naked eye. Heading south eastwards towards the Antarctic ice mass, Robin Davie and Niah Vaughan were falling in line astern of the Class I boats to let them be the pathfinders.

It was cool at night with thermals, gloves and balaclavas needed, especially on the clear nights when the stabbing beams and shafts of the Southern Ocean lights swept the starlit sky like searchlights. In one of the races within the BOC race, Arnet Taylor and Niah Vaughan had escalated their ongoing wager. A points system was awarded for various goals: first to cross the dateline; first to round Cape Horn; first to see ice of any size; first to stop in the Falklands for a beer. 'Who knows what fate has waiting around the corner,' said Arnet, who would never have guessed there was a beer waiting for him.

As French ace Christophe Auguin set a scorching pace 2,000 miles from Cape Horn at the end of the second week, Harry Mitchell was getting ready to pass from the eastern hemisphere into the western hemisphere as he crossed the international dateline. At 180° west it was now a countdown towards his old adversary, Cape Horn, at 70° west and, eventually, back to his home port in the Hamble at 1° west. He was following in the wake of his heroes, the Smeetons, Chichester, Moitessier, Knox-Johnston and the old Cape Horners, iron men in wooden ships, down what old sailors called Dead Men's Road. Seven miles before he crossed the line Harry sent a message to Race HQ: 'I will hopefully, in the next hour be going back in time, so I have decided to go back 10 years. In future I am to be called Young Henry Hornblower. Otherwise holding on not too bad. Young Henry.'

Like other BOC skippers, Harry had a package of letters and good luck cards from schoolchildren in Charleston who had visited the yachts as part of the BOC's educational Oceanwatch programme. They were from pupils at Men River elementary school, Goose Creek, South Carolina. One evening, with nothing but time on his hands, Harry sat down to read them.

'Dear Mr Mitchell, Brandon and I hope you win the race and *please* try to keep your marbles. We wish we could go with you, but we have to go to school! Good luck.'

'We would like to meet you in person. We have you hanging on our classroom wall. Our teacher Mrs Heartly said you were cute,' signed Amanda and Michael.

'Personally, I would be scared of sharks. Have you ever seen the *Titanic*?' Ryan.

Harry, a grandfather himself, was as amused as he was touched by the letters. In Sydney he had talked to some of the South Carolina children in a computer conference set up by Compuserve.

Five hundred miles ahead of him, Robin Davie, having avoided the brunt of a storm that had hit other yachts, was experiencing 40 knot gusts and had found reefs for the mainsail that he had only read about in books. He eventually dropped *Cornwall*'s mainsail, but it proved a mistaken thing to do on the 13th of the month. The wire halyard ran and disappeared up the mast to land in a heap at his feet. 'We just can't have tightened the clamping screws for the wire properly in Sydney when we serviced the drum winch. Fortunately the topping lift for the boom is designed to be the spare main halyard. Hopefully it will last to Uruguay. Lesson: stay in Sleepy Hollow all day on every 13th of the month.'

# 10 · Fear of Flying

The violent low pressure system barrelling in from the west had overtaken the rear of the fleet. From horizon to horizon there was nothing but a wilderness of foaming seas on a rampaging march eastwards. On deck was no place to stay for long with solid water sweeping the yacht. Alan Nebauer aboard *Newcastle Australia* had encountered 60 knot winds and confused seas. 'It started off with a wave up to the waist filling my new sea boots, followed by a knockdown.' He was badly shaken and it had taken a while for the boat to right herself. Alan had been thrown across the cabin, slamming into the bulkhead next to the navigation station. 'My back feels as if I took a big kidney punch and my whole body aches. I also cut both hands on glass. Several hours later I'm on my hands and knees still cleaning blackberry jam off radios, bulkheads and deckhead. I feel like I'm in a war. I'm slowly waiting as the next front approaches. I'm not up to putting on more sail, let alone taking it down, which is driving me mad! Hopefully I'm far enough north to avoid ice, as I'm not real nimble on the lookout. If I take it easy I'll probably be more active in a day or two. Meanwhile, Niah slips away. Overall I'm pretty disappointed.'

Rivals Giovanni and David Adams, some 70 miles apart, had both spotted their first icebergs. Adams joked: 'It was very tall with the sun on it. Now that I've seen my berg, I can go home.' As Soldini went north, Adams, having honoured the waypoint at 59°, dived south into the notorious Screaming Sixties to become the southernmost competitor.

David Scully, who was having a ride in *Coyote* which he likened to 'being in a front loading washing machine', had also suffered 'a bonus points knockdown' as his wine cellar was up-ended. A bottle shattered on the cabin ceiling and red wine was everywhere. 'I have never seen one bottle go so far. But it could be worse. I still have an unbroken bottle,' reported Scully, who spent most of the day rinsing manuals, charts and clothes.

On *Thursday's Child* Arnet Taylor was under bare poles with 60 knots and had come down below after struggling to get the last of the sail down while watching expensive pieces of his boat break. Outside the gigantic seas were smoking with spray and spume. The wild Southern Ocean weather, with fronts charging through every 18 hours, had given little time for respite. 'There are several marine engineers and other "professionals" that I'd like to have aboard tonight,' thought Taylor, who was nursing the bruises from a severe knockdown which

*Man against machine against the weather. Arnet Taylor, a diminutive figure on the deck of* Thursday's Child, *reefed down for heavy weather.* PHOTO: CEDRIC ROBERTSON/PPL

had underscored the dangers of slack vigilance.

Running before a strong south westerly gale, Arnet had waited for the wind to moderate before jumping up on deck to gybe the boat. He sat on the windward bunk to read for a while. *Thursday's Child* is fitted with two bunks, one port and one starboard. Its previous skipper had broken several ribs after being pitched out of one of the bunks and Arnet had installed lee cloths – canvas slings designed to hold you in as the boat rolls. Normally diligent about using them when he went to sleep, he didn't bother on this occasion, since he was not intending to turn in. Shortly after he dozed off reading, he awoke to find himself flying across the cabin. He landed in a pile on the opposite side while the boat lay on her side with tons of water washing over the deck. The left side of his body hit the nav station bracket on the way across. 'The wind was knocked out of me, and I was afraid I was badly hurt. The boat righted herself and charged off on her merry way while I tried to orient myself. I was starting to get that strong nausea one acquires after being badly shaken up or injured and I knew I had to get secure. I crawled back to my bunk, grabbing a bag of dry Polartec clothes with me. I put up the lee cloths, and burrowed into a pile of dry clothes and my sleeping bag. Within a few minutes I was warmed up, but was still only able to breathe in shallow gasps. I began to wonder what I would do if I was seriously hurt. The nearest islands with any habitation were 1,500 miles north, a pretty little chain known as French

Polynesia. "Ah yes, French doctors and nurses," I thought. It all seemed so just. I dozed off somewhat reassured. After a few hours of rest the sun was up, and I realised that if I didn't move any part of my body, I was not in any deep pain. Try to roll over, however, and it was a different story. I felt as if I'd been in a football scrimmage. But I began to suspect that my internal organs were in better shape than I had feared. Tahiti was out for the time being.'

From his bunk Arnet could view an electronic readout that showed the position, speed and heading of *Thursday's Child*. He realised he was about 80 miles north of his preferred latitude, and had to gybe. It took him over two hours to perform a routine operation which normally took 15 minutes. He was drenched in sweat, despite the cold, wet conditions on deck. 'I went below to the ship's medical kit and found some potent anti-inflammatory cream and an evil looking painkiller and I was back in my bunk for another four hours. As the week went on, I mended, although I'm still not too quick on my feet.' Arnet commiserated with Alan Nebauer over the radio, who had also taken to his bunk for several days with bruises. 'We compared what Alan called our conservative "kindergarten rigs".'

Meanwhile, rival Niah Vaughan was threatening to protest Arnet's use of 'performance enhancing' drugs. Niah was comparing the storms and knockdowns to battles in a war and Arnet had started to call him 'Sarge'. After a night of 70 knot winds, Niah reported: 'Mortared and shelled all night: couldn't dig a hole deep enough to escape.'

The string of rapidly moving frontal systems in the Furious Fifties had also resulted in knockdowns for Harry Mitchell and Robin Davie. Harry told Peter Dunning at Race HQ: 'I've lost the 10 years with strong winds and heavy seas, so it's back to Old Henry Hornblower again!'

Robin Davie had spoken to Harry on the morning radio schedule and found that Harry, too, had been thrown out of his bunk in one knockdown with 'all hell breaking loose in the cabin'. He was okay, though the boat had lost one of its masthead wind instruments. 'Harry is happier with the way the boat is handling, so I think he may be getting over the post-Sydney blues and starting to look forward more positively to Cape Horn,' reported Robin.

*Cornwall*, too, had been knocked on her beam ends twice by breaking seas, smashing the plywood self-steering vane. 'The sunshine cruise is apparently over for the likely lads down here,' said Robin, who a few days earlier, in light westerly winds and clear skies, had opened up *Cornwall*'s hatches for the first time since Sydney. It could have been a sunny summer's day off the Cornish coast. 'I soon had the bedding out on deck airing, whilst I was showering, shaving and shampooing and then getting out a fresh and clean set of clothing. On the radio sked that evening it sounded to me as though very few of us had had much wind, and Niah, Alan and Arnet had all been at the shampoo bottle during the day.

'Now it's very cold and is blasting up to 37 knots in heavy hail, sleet and snow squalls. We all seem to be getting knocked around a bit in this westerly airflow, and have seen the most alarming drop in barometric pressure: about 30 millibars down to 984 millibars in the last 30 hours. We are left holding our breath wondering when, and from where, the blast of storm force winds is going to come.' Even the birds had disappeared looking for better weather...

Steve Pettengill, in third place, had seen the barometer drop to 960 millibars and was battening down in anticipation of an intense low pressure system, while David Scully had his mainsail on deck for repairs and had to go inside frequently to thaw his hands. His rudder post was leaking 'like a flowerpot'.

Minoru Saito was again reduced to hand steering *Shuten-Dohji II* with a broken welding on the bracket of his windvane. It was thought to be repairable, but as Robin said, 'we can only make suggestions'. The language barrier was a problem. 'It's going to be hard to spark up the inventive side of Mino's mind, but we have to persuade him that fixing the windvane is better than a month of standing in the cockpit steering 2,700 miles to Cape Horn. Harry is thinking on the problem and going to have a chat to Mino, too. Hopefully Mino's problems will take Harry's mind off his own slower progress.'

Later Robin was able to pass on the good news that Minoru had made a repair to his self-steering. 'It will work in moderate conditions, up to 30 knots, but is not strong enough for storms.' He also sent Race HQ a status report on Harry: 'Have spoken to the old coot a couple of times today; he's had a good restful 24 hours with good sleep and is sounding in good shape, the best he's sounded since Sydney. Unfortunately, his progress is a bit slow. I wish he'd speed up a bit and keep pace with Minoru. But I think we'll just have to accept Harry going along at Harry's pace and be patient a few extra days until he is safely round the Horn...'

Robin had been right to hold his breath as he encountered brutal conditions on race day 20 with snow squalls from the Antarctic and vicious seas. There was no correct amount of sail to carry. He probably had too much for the 30 knot blasts, but not enough for the calmer winds between. He was in the cockpit in the middle of the night when a squall hit and all seemed pretty good. He turned in for an hour only to be awoken by the boat shaking and then heard a bang.

'I was on my way out of the bunk instantly, stepping straight into my oilskin trousers and boots fireman fashion. *Cornwall* was lurching drunkenly. Something was very wrong as my head came up through the hatch looking for the mast above me. It wasn't there.' It had broken seven feet above the deck and the top half was leaning out over the side of the boat at a crazy angle as *Cornwall* carried on towards Cape Horn in the swirling snow squall.

The dismasting had happened as the yacht rounded up in a snow squall and the poled out headsail backwinded. 'Bang! the mast gave way one foot above the spinnaker pole fittings. A single clean break.' Robin became the third skipper to be dismasted after Neal Petersen and Isabelle Autissier in leg two. It was a surreal scene as *Cornwall*'s deck lights illuminated the sheared mast and sails and the masthead light beamed brightly at a strange sideways angle. 'I didn't know whether to laugh, cry, feel afraid, or just plain cheesed off, but I do remember thinking "Oh well, I suppose it had to be my turn one day, so make the most of it".'

A professional Merchant Marine radio officer, Robin, who had won the outstanding communications award during the second leg of the race, sent a message to Race HQ: '*Cornwall* was dismasted at approx 1000 GMT in a big squall. No assistance required. Light winds between squalls so should be able to sort everything out okay.' He added: 'Down but not out... cheers, Robin.'

The mast had to be got down quickly before it damaged the hull or deck. Luckily, the sheared section had planted itself firmly atop a metal cabin vent, which prevented it spearing a hole through the deck. A quick crawl around revealed little chance of salvaging much of the rig. As Robin eased the genoa sheet the mast lowered itself gently into the rolling swells. For several seconds the masthead light continued to glow before the mast sank into the sea, held only by its wire rigging. He quickly disconnected the attached spinnaker pole which he would need for his jury rig and then, with hacksaw and wire cutters, cut and sawed through every stay and rope until the mast slithered and ground its way over the side plunging down thousands of feet into the depths. At last, *Cornwall* was free. Forty minutes had passed. The snow had stopped, the wind died down and the moon was shining. 'It was hard to appreciate that an hour earlier I had been sailing at full speed towards Cape Horn. Now we were wallowing. I had 2,100 miles to go before rounding the Cape in 12 or 13 days. I turned the wheel to steer *Cornwall* back onto an easterly course, and set the self steering gear to give us an easterly drift at 1.5 knots.'

Down below he put the kettle on, had a quick check around for any damage or leaks and made himself a cup of tea before sending another telex to update Race HQ in Charleston: 'Cleared the decks and cut away the rig. Just having a cup of tea then think I'll turn in until daylight. No damage to hull or decks that I've seen or found yet. Repeat no assistance required. SSB aerial gone so will rig something up tomorrow. Next message in a few hours.'

Peter Dunning at Race HQ replied: 'Message received and understood. We are standing by. Enjoy your cup of tea and steady your nerves. We are at your service. Again good luck, Peter.'

Until daybreak there was nothing more Robin could do. He dozed fitfully with thoughts about jury rigs churning around in his mind. 'A couple of times I climbed on deck just to make sure the mast was gone, hoping it might have all been a bad dream.' Eventually, he fell asleep for four hours and woke to a howling wind and, as he came out of the hatch, the full whiteout glare of a snow squall. 'I realised I'd better come up with a plan to get myself out of here pretty sharply.' With the kettle back on and the porridge cooking he went on deck to inspect the debris. There was superficial damage to the boat with bent stanchions and deck scrapes. He gathered together the ropes, wires and blocks he needed to make a jury rig. He had read many articles on the subject and knew Canadian sailor John Hughes who, in one of the great exploits of the 1986 BOC Challenge, had sailed to the Falklands under jury rig in 45 days, after being dismasted 4,000 miles from the Horn.

'A dismasting must be regarded as all part of the adventure,' thought Robin. By mid morning the snow squalls had died away and the sun had come out as he positioned his two spinnaker poles at the bow of *Cornwall* with a strong lashing at their apex to form an A-frame. 'I needed a strong, well stayed mast and I had to get it right first time. I didn't want to be lowering it to make changes.' It was late in the afternoon by the time he was ready to hoist his rig.

'I had a line from the aft deck to the top of the A-frame around a block to the deck, so that as I lifted the frame onto my shoulders and started to walk it up, I could haul in on the line and take the weight, bringing the frame upright about 20 feet from the bow. A line from the frame to the bow stopped it toppling backwards. I hauled the poles out to the edge of the deck and lashed them securely with the feet on aluminium sheeting I had cut to size. Finally, as it got dark, I connected up the radio antennae that I had taped up the length of the backstay. That evening I was able to talk to Niah, Alan, Harry and Minoru. It was great to

*As Robin improved his jury rig,* Cornwall's *speed increased from 62 to 125 miles a day.*

hear their voices and encouragement.'

Over the next few days Robin refined and strengthened his jury rig, adding extra ropes, stays and guys. 'I knew that storm force, even hurricane force winds and big seas would eventually find me, and I didn't want to lose the rig if we were rolled over. If I was to stay in the race, it needed to be strong enough to carry sail in a gale. One hundred miles a day was not good enough. I had to find 125 miles if I wanted to reach the Falklands, rig a new mast and get to Uruguay in time for the 1 April restart.'

The second day after his dismasting he was ready to hoist sail, and hanked on the upside down staysail from the bow. A moderate 20 knot wind filled the canvas and slowly *Cornwall* surged forward, albeit at only 3 knots. Robin had plenty of food and cooking gas, and although his water might get a bit low, he had a hand-operated watermaker. The yacht's motion felt better for having some sail set. 'She had been whipping about like a snapper before,' he said.

For a few hours the wind came up to 30 knots, and the speed increased to 4.5 knots. 'The rig seemed strong, so I got out the storm jib and set this behind the A-frame as a kind of mainsail without a boom. The speed increased by another knot. Now we were moving. In the first few days I saw my daily 24-hour run rise from 62 miles to 92 on the third day, followed by 125 miles on day five.'

In the first storm *Cornwall* was speeding along at 6 knots, but as the wind increased beyond 40 knots it was time to take down the storm jib. At 60 knots the seas turned to white spume and the yacht surged and strained at over 8 knots. Robin clawed the staysail down onto the foredeck and dragged it back into the cockpit. 'Under bare poles we were doing 6.5 knots with seas breaking all around and over the yacht, but we never felt in any danger. That came later when the wind started to decrease, and as the boat speed slowed we were pushed around by the breaking waves. I thought we were going to roll right over. Everything inside the yacht cascaded and flew across the cabin. I scrambled on deck to see if I still had a jury rig left. Amazed and relieved it was still there, I steered the boat back to its downwind heading and then went below to drag the staysail back up on deck. We were knocked over again. With great urgency I hanked on and hoisted the sail and with 50 knots of wind we took off like a bullet and I had stable steering again. It was clear that speed was my safety, I had to keep *Cornwall* going quickly. Slowing up in the storms was dangerous.'

With two days of big winds Robin covered over 300 miles. The greatest difficulty on board was the violent motion of the yacht. She was whipping around and Robin was black and blue and aching all over from being thrown around. Cooking was difficult with pans flying off the gimballed stove, and on deck he rigged ropes from the bow to the stern as grablines. His bunk was the safest and most comfortable place; even sitting at the chart table was dangerous. In the nine days following his dismasting Robin sailed 840 miles. Back home in Cornwall and in South Carolina his plight was front page news. Race Communications Director Peter Dunning said the outpouring of local support for Robin Davie in Charleston had been fantastic. 'Robin has a lot of friends here and everyone wants him to know they're behind him in his plight.' In Cornwall, Robin's support liaison, Carol Cook, had located a suitable replacement mast and a rigger to go to the Falklands, and was negotiating space on a military flight to the islands from RAF Brize Norton. Peter Morgan from Falmouth made new sails. The total bill, including air freight and the rigger, at £140 a day, was expected to be £22,000. As Niah had pointed out, 'You'll have to do some serious T-shirt selling after the race to pay for that mast.' From the time he had erected his jury rig it would take Robin 24 days to sail into Port Stanley in the Falkland Islands, where the replacement mast would be waiting for him.

David Adams, still in the Screaming Sixties to shorten the distance to Cape Horn, had finally overtaken Giovanni and regained the lead in the small boat division. He was upset to learn of Robin's dismasting. 'Poor Robin, he's been so good on the radio talking to Minoru and Harry, geeing them up all the way. I'll be bloody glad to be out of the Southern Ocean myself. I'm sick of being cold and wet. I took my boots and socks off and my feet are just a mess. The weather hasn't been what I wanted this leg.'

On the same day that Robin raised his jury rig, Christophe Auguin, having already broken a new record for leg three with a day's run of 350.4 miles, rounded Cape Horn more than 300 miles ahead of his nearest competitor, Jean-Luc Van den Heede. Arnet Taylor, meanwhile, had noticed water pouring into *Thursday's Child*'s cabin under the deck-stepped mast. A trip on deck revealed that the mast was twisting dramatically and grinding away at its supports. The base was bent and had opened up like a banana skin with a three-inch crack running up from the mast base and opening to ⅜" with each twist of the mast. Four supporting brackets had sheared or broken loose.

To contain the damage and avoid a dismasting, Arnet strapped the mast in place from three directions with Kevlar line, which he fed to winches in the cockpit so he could adjust the tension. Even with his cat's cradle holding it all together it was still flexing with the rigging loads. Fingers crossed and mainsail down, he adopted a conservative sailing approach to lighten the loads on the rig. 'We are passing through one of the most remote areas in the world and caution is the slogan. But I also have to keep the boat moving or we'll simply be pounded by one gale after another. There is a possibility that we will divert to the Falkland Islands for repairs, however all options remain open. Beaches and bathing suits at Punta del Este was what I had in mind, not more penguins and sheep...'

Robin, in regular touch with *Henry Hornblower* 500 miles astern, heard the consternation in Harry's voice as Harry told him: 'You've sailed as many miles as I have. I thought I was going to catch you up with your jury rig!' Not being left behind all on his own, as he was in the second leg, had been Harry's biggest boost. With Minoru and Robin for company and the miles ticking by, the Horn got closer every day. 'I think the distance when Harry left Sydney was just a massive mental obstacle for him and I must admit, when you leave Sydney, Cape Horn seems a hell of a distance and an eternity away,' noted Robin.

Francis Chichester had said of the Horn: 'It not only scared me, frightened me, but I think it would be fair to say that it terrified me... I told myself for a long time that anyone who tried to round the Horn in a small yacht must be crazy.' Of the eight yachts Chichester knew that had done it, six had capsized or somersaulted before, during or after the passage. Harry was like Chichester, who had declared: 'I hate being frightened, but even more, I detest being prevented by fright.'

In his twenties, Harry had written a letter to Gustav Ericson, owner-manager of the last square rig fleet in the world, to get a job as a deckhand. He took a train to Liverpool to sign on, but arrived too late, after the ship had sailed. Bracing himself now in *Henry Hornblower*'s tiny, shallow cockpit as the wind shrieked and the yacht ploughed eastwards, Harry recalled how the square riggers used to rig a canvas cloth behind the helmsman so he couldn't look back and be frightened by monster waves. Looking back himself that night at the desolation of the Southern Ocean he understood why. The seas that had already repulsed his previous attempt were running wild. From horizon to horizon there was what solo sailor Raud O'Brien had called 'undiluted wilderness on the rampage'. Confused wave trains steamed past, sometimes exploding against the side of *Henry Hornblower*, before surging on for hundreds of miles to dash themselves on some remote, rocky Chilean shoreline.

Down here it was easy to feel like the last man on earth. Harry was in an area of the ocean which is as far from mankind as you can get on the planet. He was a speck on the face of eternity; more out of touch than an astronaut in his space capsule linked to NASA. Indeed, the nearest man-made objects to Harry were probably the satellites hurtling through deep space above him. 'Deep space' in the Southern Ocean seemed as hostile as the void of outer space. It was a place that truly felt like the 'uttermost part of the globe'. Harry, who was often given to quoting poetry or Shakespeare in his contemplative moments, thought of the other skippers out there that night in this crazy globe-girdling epic. All of them alone in their tiny, Herculean efforts. He shivered and retreated below to the relative cosiness of his cabin.

Three weeks and three days after leaving Sydney, Jean-Luc Van den Heede became the second BOC skipper to round the Horn. 'Dark night, but I could see the rock and the light,' said the Frenchman, making his fourth solitary rounding of the sleeping sentinel. A day later Jean-Luc had broken the gooseneck, the fitting that joins the boom to the mast, and spent all night trying to make repairs. 'I break also the top part of the mainsail track in my mast. It is time to arrive!'

Astern of Van den Heede a pack of five yachts separated by 170 miles were scheduled to round the Cape in the next two days. Steve Pettengill and David Adams became the third and fourth sailors to make it round the windswept rock. The last time Pettengill had gone around the Horn it was on the world's largest refrigerated container ship, the *New Zealand Pacific*, which had rescued him and his crewmate from their capsized trimaran *Great American* on Thanksgiving Day 1990. They had been attempting to beat the clipper ship record from San Francisco to Boston on the same yacht in which Steve had set the record from New York to San Francisco. Their trimaran had been twice flipped and dismasted a few hundred miles short of the Horn.

This time Pettengill reported: 'Cape Horn was everything it should be. Dark, overcast, light rain, fog and blowing 40 knots. It was perfect weather with 35-45 knots of wind and I was humming along at 18-25 knots, maybe just a little bit out of control. I was four miles off and could just see the light flash once. I had a long talk with my old dog Frodo. I left his ashes here in 1989 on my first rounding. Perfect place. Frodo always liked a good storm and loved the outdoors. It was good to chat with him again.'

Several hours later Pettengill was followed by David Adams and Giovanni, the first Italian singlehanded sailor to have rounded the three great Capes of the Southern Ocean. But Giovanni was not happy that a computer problem with the race tracking system had reported him a further 80 miles behind Adams.'I am sorry bat your distance tu finis is wrong. I am noit happy at ool! I wold laike very mach if this never happen again! David Adams is probabli 20 miles in front of mi!'

JJ Provoyeur in *Novell South Africa* was next. 'It was misty with lots of wind. I could see the lighthouse through the murk. It was three in the morning and I cracked a beer and toasted the Cape. I had the feeling I had really achieved something. I never thought it would be like that.'

Two days before David Scully reached Cape Horn his autopilots went down. 'I faxed Autohelm, and told them they had three days to figure something out. In the meantime, I would drive the yacht around the Horn. I stopped the boat for half an hour a day to bail out, eat, whatever.' *Coyote* was taking on about four buckets a day through a keel joint. The keel was, in fact, loose in its case. 'It was not structural. It wasn't going to fall out or anything, but it worked a bit and made an incredible screeching noise. I resorted to wearing earplugs down below to drown out the screeching. I eventually drove in some wedges and that helped to stop the noise,' he said. The only good part about the failed autopilots was that it kept Scully on deck and away from the noise.

As *Coyote* came around the Horn it was cloudy, dawn was breaking and the seas were violent. 'I found Cape Horn a frightening place,' said Scully. 'I wanted as many miles between us as possible.' Later he waxed more lyrical: 'Cape Horn is a place where the earth and sea come together and hate each other. The clouds and wind look on and needle them to pound on each other a little harder. I turned that corner and said to myself "I want to get as much distance between me and here as I can in the shortest possible time." ' He shot through the tidal short cut of the Straits of Le Maire. By now, Scully had been awake for three days and had spent a total of 50 hours at the wheel. Autohelm responded with instructions, as promised, and Scully repaired one unit, which worked for a day before going down again. 'I got some good sleep, a couple of good meals. I was making good speed and I figured it was quicker to drive than to stop and fix it again. I figured I could drive for three more days.'

Some 400 miles from the Horn, Arnet Taylor was still nursing *Thursday's Child*'s damaged rig. The crack around the mast had expanded another two inches. 'The mast could fall down in 15 knots of breeze coming off a wave this afternoon, or it may last several thousand miles,' he told Race HQ. His problems were compounded when the port steering cable snapped, turning the yacht broadside to a 20ft breaking wave which rolled her over; Arnet woke up on top of the radios mounted on the roof over his bunk. 'Boy, was I surprised to see the mast still there. The interior looked as if it had been redecorated by Atilla the Hun and the wind generator was wiped out.'

On day 28 of the third leg a stationary high pressure system camped off the east coast of South America spelled paradise for holidaying beach-goers at the resort city of Punta del Este, but slow torture for race leader Christophe Auguin. Less than 200 miles from the finish, he watched his progress slow right down.

Aboard *Newcastle Australia* the same day, Alan Nebauer, who had suffered multiple knockdowns in 70 knots of wind two days earlier, was caught in a 40 knot squall 630 miles west of Cape Horn. He had been on the tail of Niah Vaughan's *Jimroda II*, gradually pulling back the miles. Now Niah had decided he had to make a break to try to keep in front. The two boats were tracking south through an area of reported icebergs to the edge of the Screaming Sixties. On the last radio schedule Alan had been flabbergasted to hear that Niah had gained 30 miles on him, but as Chile weather stations reported snow squalls Niah's yacht was knocked flat, ripping the foot of his headsail.

Then it became Alan's turn. His rig smashed down on to the starboard rail and he became the fourth BOC sailor to be dismasted. The broken mast did remarkably little damage to the yacht. The bow pulpit was twisted and useless and all the starboard stanchions were swept away. The rigging was too thick for bolt cutters, so Alan spent the afternoon hacksawing it off and dumping it over the side. Just as he was clearing it away, he realised one of his spinnaker poles was still attached to the mast and about to disappear over the side. 'I said, "Oh, God, I'm going to need that!" and left the mast while I grabbed at the pole.' In that short time there was a deep gouge where the mast hit the rail. After restoring order, he got a link call to Race HQ in Charleston and told Peter Dunning his news. 'That's too bad, stay in touch,' was the terse reply. Next morning, said Niah, Alan came up on the radio schedule 'distraught and said: "I've lost my rig."' Their duel was over, for the time being.

The rescued spinnaker pole made up one leg of an A-frame rig that Alan used to sail the last 800 miles around Cape Horn to the Falklands. He cut away as much of the mainsail as he could salvage, planning to make new sails if the wind lightened. As it turned out he sailed most of the way using a storm jib and his storm trysail. With this rig, Nebauer managed to occasionally make speeds of 9 knots. 'It's really a bit embarrassing how well I sailed under jury rig. My speed to sail area ratio was a lot better than when everything had been in one piece!'

The next afternoon, reigning BOC champion Christophe Auguin crossed the Punta finish line escorted by dozens of spectator craft and a brace of helicopters. His record time for the 7,200 mile voyage of 29d 16h was 36 hours faster than the previous record holder, Alain Gautier. And this was despite sailing a longer course because of the new waypoint, and his loss of radar. Christophe's maximum wind speeds had been 40 knots and the seas had been 'very easy compared with the previous leg'. No doubt the captain of the rocket ship spared a thought for Harry, with 3,300 miles still to go to Punta.

On *Thursday's Child* Arnet Taylor, carefully nursing his damaged mast, had almost talked himself into by-passing the Falklands when Alan Nebauer came up on the radio to say that he'd been dismasted. 'It was like a message from God,' said Arnet. 'It would have been cataclysmic if my mast had been lost. I would have been out of the race. I decided to go into the Falklands, a couple of days away.' Alan, meanwhile, had received the good news that his local city council in Newcastle, Australia, had agreed to underwrite the cost of a new mast, approving funding of A$30,000.

On race day 32 officials and shore crew of the Yacht Club Punta del Este braced themselves for a wild rush of arrivals as five competitors within 30 miles of each other closed on the finish line. Leading the pack was Steve Pettengill, who had overtaken second-placed Jean-Luc Van den Heede for the first time on the leg and then had fallen behind before regaining the advantage. With 28 miles to go he held a slender three-tenths of a mile lead. It was almost a dead heat and they were expected to come up on the horizon together. While Pettengill and Jean-Luc had been stifled by light headwinds on the approach to Punta, the three yachtsmen astern had a strong southerly breeze to help them catch up. In the seesaw battle that had extended across three quarters of the world, Giovanni on *Kodak* finally had the upper hand and was 18 miles ahead of David Adams on *True Blue*. Soldini was looking for his first individual leg victory of the event. JJ Provoyeur brought up the rear.

When a rain squall came through on their last night at sea, Pettengill stayed north of it, while Jean-Luc decided to stay south. 'I knew the wind was going to switch, so I stood off. I also knew I had my work cut out, so I flew my spinnaker all night until daybreak,' said Pettengill. 'When the wind came it was more easterly and gave me a better wind angle. That was that.' Pettengill crossed the line next morning in second place with a time of 31d 13h. Jean-Luc finished 31 minutes later, admitting he had made a bad decision. 'All my decisions, since the beginning of this race, I make mistakes. I have no luck for three legs. So I think I will have my luck next leg.'

Two hours later Giovanni tasted sweet victory by taking his first individual leg win in the race with 31d 16h. His duelling partner, David Adams, followed him less than 90 minutes later to concede that the Italian had done 'a fantastic job. I think leg four is going to be a ripper. There's a lot in there for both of us.' Finally JJ Provoyeur took the finish flare that afternoon after 31d 19h. 'The sea was kind to us this leg. All except the Tasman and the first days out of Sydney. That was some storm we had, I saw 60 knots of wind.'

The following afternoon David Scully became the seventh finisher with a time of 32d 19h. He had been frustrated on the final stretch by squalls, calms and the wind going around in circles. 'It was just impossible sailing conditions,' he said.

If Scully hadn't been forced into Bluff, New Zealand, for 31 hours to replace his blown mainsail and then been slowed by rudder leaks the story might have been different. Time is measured from the starting gun to the finish, no matter what happens in between, so Scully could take no pleasure in 'what ifs'. But he was still only 29 hours behind second-placed Pettengill and he knew *Coyote* could sail fast.

Almost as soon as his yacht was tied alongside in Punta, Scully was bound to Paris to meet his new daughter, born the night he was recutting the mainsail in Bluff.

# 11 · Missing

T wo hours after David Scully sailed *Coyote* across the finish line in Punta del Este, Harry Mitchell was 12 days away from his goal of Cape Horn when one of the polar orbiting satellites circling the earth every 102 minutes at an altitude of 500 miles picked up a signal from one of the distress beacons on board *Henry Hornblower* in that desolate stretch of the Southern Ocean. The signal was relayed to a ground station in New Zealand. It was 2200 GMT on Thursday 2 March, the 32nd day of leg three. The last satellite communication with Harry had been six hours earlier. The decoded satellite signal from Harry's EPIRB (Emergency Position Indicating Radio Beacon) gave the name of his yacht and his position, 56° 35′ south and 114° 20′ west. It placed him approximately 1,450 miles west of Cape Horn. The New Zealand rescue authorities immediately notified Race HQ in Charleston who went into their well tried emergency procedures.

The EPIRB, an Alden 406 unit, was one of two on board Harry's boat and, at first, was thought to be the one mounted in the cockpit. Race rules require competitors to carry at least two beacons, one attached to, or packaged with, the overboard emergency equipment. The beacons can be activated either by the skipper, or on some yachts the unit is mounted in the cockpit to be deployed automatically if the yacht sinks. Skippers are encouraged not to activate more than one EPIRB at a time. That way when the battery of one EPIRB has drained the second unit can be triggered, giving search and rescue authorities a longer position signal to home in on. Depending on the cold factor, the lithium batteries could last for anything from 72 hours-plus to less than 48 hours. When catastrophe had overtaken Isabelle Autissier's yacht in the second leg of the race she had set off two EPIRBs at the same time. Uncannily that, too, had been on the 32nd day of the leg.

Distress beacons had a history of activating accidentally on this BOC Challenge. A false alarm had been raised from Giovanni Soldini's *Kodak* two hours after the start of the race in Charleston. Arnet Taylor, Neal Petersen and Minoru Saito had all been the subjects of false alarms when waves had swept their cockpits and set off their stern-mounted beacons. In Saito's case, Robin Davie had been awarded an eight hour allowance for sailing to his rescue in leg one.

The fact that the signal from Harry's EPIRB was received at approximately the same time as his satellite INMARSAT-C unit stopped transmitting suggested that perhaps something more serious could have happened. Had he simply suffered another knockdown, which had wiped his aerials off the back of the yacht and activated the EPIRB at the same time? Or had *Henry Hornblower* been overwhelmed by a bigger catastrophe? It was possible the yacht had been rolled over and Harry was lost. Could he have struck a growler? If Harry had taken to his liferaft he would not survive the conditions for long. The best scenario was that the EPIRB had been washed overboard and Harry was sailing on. There were two buttons on his satellite unit that Harry could have hit to broadcast a MAYDAY. But Harry, being 'of the old school' as Schrader put it, probably wouldn't have thought of that, even assuming he had set off the EPIRB.

Speculation was as uncertain and painful as it was endless. All attempts to contact Harry by radio went unanswered. But there was nothing unusual about this, since he was always in the business of conserving his power. At Punta del Este, Race Director Mark Schrader contacted the Marine Rescue Co-ordination Centre (MRCC) in Valparaiso, Chile, where the authorities began investigating possible commercial shipping and military vessels in Harry's vicinity. His closest competitor, Minoru Saito, was some 230 miles west north west of Harry and, crucially, upwind of *Henry Hornblower*.

'Saito will be diverted to Mitchell's location,' announced Schrader. But attempts to contact *Shuten-Dohji II* by radio failed too. Further attempts over the following hours to contact either skipper by SATCOM-C and long-range radio were in vain. Ominous silence reigned over the airwaves from the sailors.

Harry's wife Diana, home in Portsmouth, was notified of the situation. She had lived through enough of Harry's adventures, and misadventures, to be calm and philosophical. That Harry was at the centre of another drama was not new. He had been posted 'missing' or overdue before. On Harry's first solo adventure he was overdue crossing the English Channel, and Diana, then 19 years old, had waited patiently in Cherbourg while Harry was hove-to in a gale in mid-Channel sewing up a torn mainsail. He hadn't told his parents, or the owner of the yacht he had chartered, that this was his singlehanded sailing debut.

By Friday race officials in Charleston and Punta del Este had established regular contact with rescue authorities in Chile, Hawaii and Falmouth, England, in their efforts to find and divert a ship or plane to search for *Henry Hornblower*. Their concern for Harry's welfare was made more acute by reports from meteorologists in France and California which placed Harry and Minoru in an area of severe winds, 'with gusts up to 60-75 knots', at the time the distress signal had been activated. In these conditions any attempts to get search planes to fly over the position were impractical.

Falmouth MRCC alerted the BOC race office to another singlehanded sailor, lone woman Lisa Clayton, sailing the yacht *Spirit of Birmingham* non-stop round the world. Her yacht had been knocked down, too, and she had been reported unconscious for some hours before coming round to find reams of fax messages with the Securité alert for Harry Mitchell. She was willing to sail towards the position of the EPIRB. 'The distance involved is in excess of 400 miles and is upwind,' said Falmouth.' Please confirm that this yacht is not suitable in the prevailing conditions and may be released to continue on passage. We understand that MV *Francisca Schulte* may be proceeding to the area which we consider a more practical search unit.' The BOC Race HQ agreed.

By Friday night Harry had still not checked in with Robin Davie, some 560

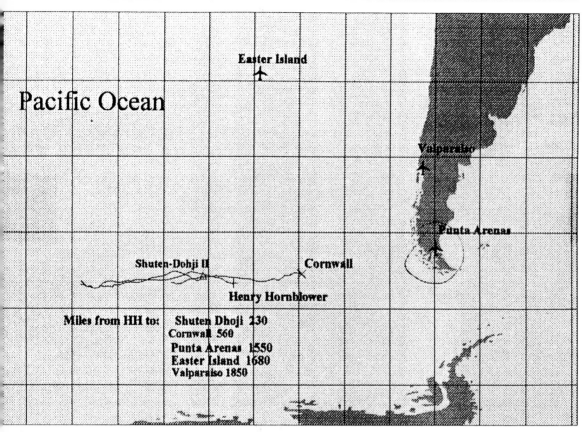

*The worst ocean in the world and the remotest part of the planet; that was where Harry Mitchell's yacht was when his distress beacon was triggered. The map shows his nearest hopes of rescue: other BOC yachts* Shuten Dohji II *(230 miles) and* Cornwall *(560 miles) and the closest airfields.*

miles east of him, on their regular radio schedule. And neither he nor Minoru had made contact via their satellite INMARSAT-C units. Robin, struggling on towards Cape Horn at 5 knots under jury rig, sent a message to Race HQ: 'Alan (Nebauer) and I feel rather helpless at our lack of ability to be able to head back in their direction but with our rigs and the distance involved it would take many days and by then the EPIRB signal would long since have extinguished.' Robin faced the most agonising hours of his voyage so far. Harry had missed every one of Robin's radio skeds in the last 24 hours. But everyone knew that Harry could be the worst person in the fleet for communications. Robin tried again and again to raise Harry and Minoru on the radio. In any other circumstances he would have turned back for his friends. He had remarked before that Harry had enough humour to keep the whole fleet going in a crisis. Now Robin could only hope that Harry, along with his humour, was intact.

On Friday evening Mark Schrader phoned Diana to tell her that a 150m bulk carrier, *Francisca Schulte*, had been diverted to Harry's last known position to assist in the rescue operation. Schrader had spoken to the captain of the freighter, en route to Punta Arenas, Chile, which was 480 miles north west of *Henry*

*Hornblower.* Heavy seas and bad weather were slowing down its progress towards the search area and it was estimated that the ship would not arrive there for almost 36 hours, at 0700 GMT on Sunday morning. Everyone prepared for a long, agonising wait for news. The MRCC in Chile announced its decision not to send up a Chilean Navy plane in the search. They said the signals from the EPIRB continued to be strong and consistent and they were confident the yacht could be located without an aircraft.

In Punta del Este Mark Schrader had to rely on others to tell him about cloud cover and conditions for flying over the search area. His great concern was that if the EPIRB stopped transmitting before the ship arrived, *Henry Hornblower* might never be found. He sent a message to the Chilean rescue authorities: 'He (Mitchell) carried a second EPIRB on board. *If* it is still aboard and *if* he is able to activate it when the first one fails then he will be "visible" for a longer period. However, until someone actually sees the yacht we don't know anything about the situation. It is very possible that the EPIRB battery will fail before the *Francisca Schulte* makes the rendezvous to the last known beacon signal. If that happens it will be extremely difficult, if not impossible, for the ship to find either the yacht or a liferaft. Without visual contact established we won't know the situation. Harry Mitchell is an experienced seaman. He won't go to the liferaft unless that is the only option. In the current weather conditions in the area the liferaft would be dangerous. An over-flight could immediately determine if the ship was looking for a raft or a yacht and could probably determine if Mitchell was alive and well – something of great concern to his family and people all over the world waiting for some news.'

Schrader queried the Chilean rescue authorities' evaluation that it was 'not possible to fly a plane to the distress position'. Was this based on distance involved, the availability of a plane with sufficient range, or concern with the weather over the area? 'I know this is a difficult situation and I want to do everything to help you find Harry Mitchell,' said the frustrated Schrader, who had even checked on Antarctic supply flights over the area.

Robin Davie provided a glimpse of weather conditions at the time, reporting 40 knot winds, confused cross seas and a heavy westerly swell. 'On three or four occasions we have been picked up and chucked sideways onto our beam ends.' It was more like a rodeo than a yacht race, he said.

On the other side of Cape Horn on Friday, Arnet Taylor's shore crew, Welshman Merfyn Owen and American Kate Ford, were on a small plane on the once-a-week flight from Punta Arenas, Chile, to the remote Falkland Islands, to assist with repairs to Taylor's damaged mast. As the plane circled to land at Port Stanley they looked through a gap in the clouds and saw *Thursday's Child* beating up the coast, a pale dot in the spray. By the time they were on the ground, the yacht was tied up in the harbour. With wrecked or abandoned hulks lining the windswept port, the islands were a solemn warning to mariners. The launch used to tow *Thursday's Child* into port tied up to a derelict wooden sailing ship covered in moss. The port was surprisingly busy, with Antarctic survey boats, adventure cruise and fishing boats shuttling in and out daily. But there was room on the leeward side for the BOC boat.

Though it was the middle of summer the air had a wintry chill and smelled of peat furnaces. The half dozen trees on the island were hunchbacked from the

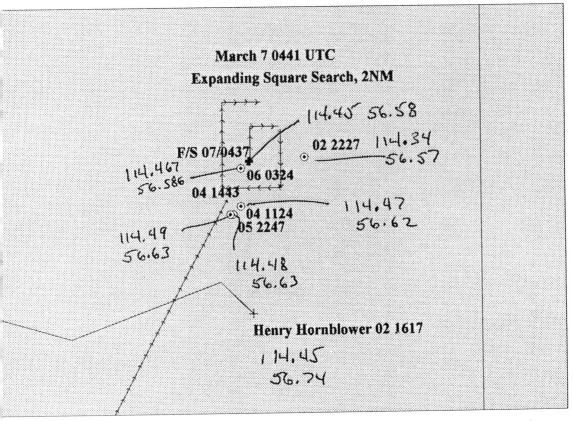

**March 7 0441 UTC**
**Expanding Square Search, 2NM**

114.45 56.58

02 2227 114.34 56.57

F/S 07/0437

114.467 56.586

06 0324

04 1443

04 1124 114.47 56.62

05 2247

114.49 56.63

114.48 56.63

**Henry Hornblower 02 1617**

114.45 56.74

*Five days after Harry's EPIRB was activated this was the search area showing dates, latitude and longitude of various EPIRB signals from March 2 to 6. The final track of* Henry Hornblower *and her last position on March 2, 114° west and 56° south, ends in a cross. The* Francisca Schulte *used two mile spacing for its search at night and fired rocket flares and hand flares.*

southerly winds blowing up from the Antarctic. A close inspection of the mast with Merfyn, a naval architect, told Taylor he had done the right thing to stop in the Falklands. Indeed, he was lucky to have arrived with the mast still up. Its base had bent, leaving about 30 tons of compression focused in two places. The uneven load had made the aluminium crumple like wet cardboard and started the cracks up the sides. Even though Arnet had jury rigged Kevlar lines to control the twist, the mast rotated freely on its base and everything was coated with black aluminium dust where it had ground at the inner fittings and carved a moat in the base. The real danger of this kind of failure was that if the mast gave way, it might jump off the platform and punch a hole in the deck, possibly right through the bottom of the boat.

It was too windy to haul the mast out that day, but between trying to find aluminium welding rods and steel for a new mast base, Arnet, Kate and Merfyn huddled round the long-range radio, and listened anxiously, hoping for news of Harry. They had heard that a merchant ship had been diverted to look for him.

Seventeen hundred miles away the *Francisca Schulte*, nearing the search area early on Sunday morning, spotted a yacht and made contact with the skipper over VHF radio. It was Minoru Saito on *Shuten-Dohji II*, whose last communication with Race HQ had been three days ago. Minoru told the ship that he had suffered a generator failure and had closed down his radio and electronic communications to conserve power. He was not aware that Harry's distress beacon had been set off. He confirmed that he didn't require assistance himself and was proceeding to Punta del Este, though he still had autopilot problems and was handsteering.

In the search area itself at 0500 GMT, weather conditions were described as marginal, with near gale-force winds and three metre seas. At daybreak the master of the *Francisca Schulte*, Capt S Mordovin, reported visibility of only three miles with rain and drizzle.

The grid search pattern for *Henry Hornblower*, based on numerous EPIRB updates over the past 48 hours, was concentrated in a rectangle of about 30 nautical miles by 10 nautical miles. There had been a period of almost 12 hours when no EPIRB signal was received. It was thought this might be due to the low visibility angle of the satellite. The unit was also designed to switch itself off when the battery was too weak to send accurate information. Race HQ in Charleston had noted that the resolution of the signal was poor, indicating that the antenna might be blocked or damaged. The cluster of signals around which the search area was concentrated was something of a mystery too, with a sequence of positions which didn't point to any logical course or pattern of drift. If the EPIRB was still attached to the boat its progress had slowed to a drifting speed of just 1 knot.

By now it was confirmed that the distress beacon signals were not from the EPIRB secured in the cockpit. That was a British-made LO-KATA, which Harry and a helper had taped and sealed up in Sydney to prevent it being accidentally lost overboard in a knockdown. The SOS was from the EPIRB that Harry kept in the cabin. At 1253 GMT that day, around the time the search ship arrived, the EPIRB emitted its final transmission burst. With poor visibility, low clouds and lack of infra-red detection equipment, it had not been possible to send up a search plane over the target area. The ship was conducting an expanding square search using four nautical mile and two nautical mile spacing, depending on the weather conditions and visibility. It was the classic grid search pattern which begins at a central point and expands outward in ever increasing intervals, searching a square of the imaginary grid at a time.

It had taken a Royal Australian Air Force Hercules plane nearly three hours to find Isabelle's 60ft yacht, *ECP2*, which had transmitted signals from two EPIRBs; the pilots had reported that the yacht looked just like another breaking wave in the rough seas. Looking for Harry's 40-foot yacht from the bridge or deck of a ship meant that visibility was severely limited. The crew didn't even know precisely what they were looking for. Was it a dismasted yacht, a liferaft, or just a floating EPIRB that had been washed overboard?

The Master of the *Francisca Schulte* sent a fax to Mark Schrader: 'Assistance at sea is the normal practice of seamen. My crew and I are trying to do our best to locate and rescue this brave man.' At night the ship used two-mile spacing for its search. To attract attention it sounded fog signals, fired hand flares and sent up rocket flares that drifted down on tiny parachutes. The forecast for the search area next day, Monday, was for continued near gale force winds and three metre seas. By now Falmouth MRCC in England were assisting in a drift analysis, based

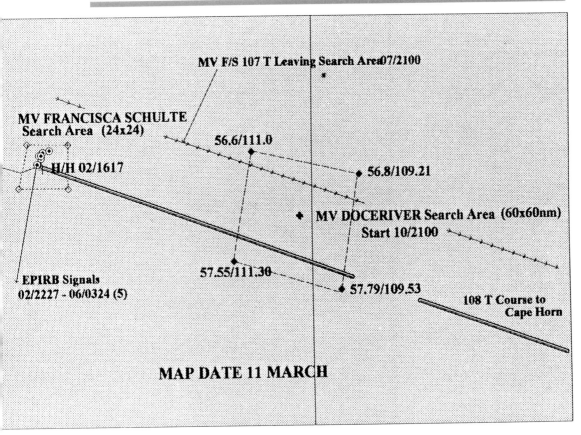

MV F/S 107 T Leaving Search Area 07/2100

MV FRANCISCA SCHULTE
Search Area (24x24)

56.6/111.0

H/H 02/1617

56.8/109.21

MV DOCERIVER Search Area (60x60nm)
Start 10/2100

EPIRB Signals
02/2227 - 06/0324 (5)

57.55/111.30

57.79/109.53

108 T Course to
Cape Horn

MAP DATE 11 MARCH

*Larger-scale chart showing on the left the first 576 square mile search area (with its cluster of EPIRB signals). It was scoured by the Francisca Schulte for 65 hours. 'MV F/S 107 T' at the top shows she abandoned the search at 2100 hours on the 7th, going on a course of 107° true for Cape Horn. The box to the right shows the 3,600 square mile area searched by the MV Doceriver for 36 hours before force 11 winds made it too dangerous for the ship to continue.*

on all the data received, and the assumption that *Henry Hornblower* was disabled, drifting with current and wind, but with some degree of directional control.

There was renewed hope on Tuesday when it was reported that 'two new distress signals' had been picked up from an Alden 406 EPIRB registered to Harry Mitchell. The signals had been recorded some four hours apart by maritime rescue centres in Hawaii and New Zealand and had come 76 hours after the original distress call. The new positions were located due north and within a 3.7 mile radius of the original area. The *Francisca Schulte*, which had been searching an area 45 miles south west, based on current and drift, returned to the site of the new EPIRB signals. Capt Mordovin reported that conditions in the area had deteriorated further with storm force winds of up to 47 knots, seven metre seas, and visibility of four miles with intermittent rain.

Hopes that Harry had set off his second distress beacon were soon dashed when it was realised that the signals weren't new at all. They were 'a last gasp' from the same Alden EPIRB that had been triggered five days before.

Furthermore, it would be some time later before it was realised that the 'two new' positions, to which the *Francisca Schulte* had been diverted, were just a regurgitation of earlier positions held by the satellite's memory. Capt Mordovin in another message to Schrader said: 'I hope we are searching for a lost EPIRB, that all of Mitchell's communication equipment has failed and he is now out of the search area and on the way to Punta del Este. We will search the area once more to be sure.'

Robin Davie sent a message to Race HQ that he had 'fingers, toes and everything else crossed that Harry is "doing a Minoru" and sailing along out of radio contact 400 miles to the east of the search area.' Meanwhile, Schrader commended the master and crew of the *Francisca Schulte* 'for their perseverance and thoroughness. I'm anxious, but hopeful, that all their efforts towards locating Harry will soon be rewarded,' he said.

Later that day the *Francisca Schulte* completed her search of the area and in bad weather and 'heavy seas that could endanger the vessel and crew' she resumed steaming towards her original destination in Chile. Capt Mordovin said that for the next nine hours he would proceed on a heading that would take into account the likely route of Harry's yacht if it was still sailing to Cape Horn. He added: 'My crew and I hope that Harry Mitchell is well. We pray for him.'

A weary Schrader sent a message back thanking the captain and his crew for their efforts 'under extraordinarily difficult conditions'. He asked to be informed when the ship changed course off Harry's possible track. 'It will be helpful for us and comforting for the family to have this information,' he said. The *Francisca Schulte* had spent 65 hours searching for Harry. Meanwhile, rescue centres in Chile, Honolulu and Falmouth were checking for other shipping to divert to the search area.

The problems of co-ordinating the rescue attempt and keeping up to date with each phase of the operation were not helped by the distance and language barrier between Charleston, Punta del Este and Valparaiso and Nigel Rowe, now back on the team of shoreside helpers in Punta, enlisted the help of the British Consul in Valparaiso to improve communications in the search for his old friend Harry. Among the Punta Yacht Club team, Horacio Rosell and Diego Lamas and 'Coco' Lopez helped Schrader as translators.

By Wednesday morning the MRCC centre in Valparaiso had diverted a second commercial vessel, the 270 metre bulk carrier *Doceriver*, en route to Brazil from Newcastle, Australia. Some 600 miles away, she was battling gale force winds and was expected to take two days to reach the search area where conditions were 'foul and worsening'. 'This an anxious time,' said Schrader, 'but I remind myself that Harry is as tough as nails. It is possible that after suffering damage in the horrible conditions of the past week, he is sailing along toward Cape Horn. Harry wouldn't be giving up if he's holding together a disabled yacht, and we're not going to give up either. If circumstances have allowed Harry to survive, it will be with his spirit and sense of humour intact.'

Harry's yacht was equipped for survival conditions with the following list of BOC rules-required emergency equipment: two watertight bulkheads; one four-man liferaft; liferaft grab-bag with flares, food, water, solar still etc; survival exposure suit; a total of 20 parachute, handheld and smoke flares; radar reflector, three bilge pumps; foghorn; flashlight; medical supplies.

*Alan Nebauer in Port Stanley with his A frame rig of spinnaker poles: he'd used up most of his docking lines to secure the frame.* PHOTO: KATE FORD

In the Falklands, the arrival of *Thursday's Child* and *Newcastle Australia* had made the front page in *Penguin News*, the local newspaper. Arnet Taylor and Alan Nebauer were on the list of tourist attractions as at least a quarter of the town flocked to the dockside to see the crazy solo sailors.

Repairs were running behind schedule. For the first three days, it had been too windy to lift out *Thursday's Child*'s rig. Components had also been difficult to obtain. 'These islanders, much like those in other parts of the world, are quite proud of the fact that nobody seems to get ulcers from being stressed by conventional mainland views of time,' said Arnet philosophically. Two engineers, Carl and Andrez, worked late into the night and shared their workshop and welding skills. Although Taylor's campaign was short of funds, in the final balance repairing the rig in the Falklands cost less than replacing it entirely. The islanders were used to making things themselves. Fabricating a new steel mast step for *Thursday's Child* presented an interesting challenge and was done in two days, where it might have taken two weeks in Uruguay.

Alan Nebauer's jury rig – two spinnaker poles lashed in an A frame from his chainplates – had allowed him to make good time around the Horn to the Falklands. His best day's run had been 150 miles. *Thursday's Child*'s crew had gone out in the local launch on a black, blustery night to meet him. 'I caught myself looking for his masthead light a few times, before I reminded myself that he wouldn't have one,' said Kate. 'When Alan waved a torch on deck, we could just see its beam through the swells and spray. His GPS put him right on top of Seal Rocks, two menacing black lumps which guarded the harbour in daylight, but at night they were invisible. He had to feel his way in.'

Alan claimed the coldest hour of the trip from Sydney had been the hour on the helm steering into Port Stanley through the chop. As the sun came up over the Falklands he tied his yacht up alongside *Thursday's Child*. He didn't have much rope left for the docking lines; it had all been used in the jury rig. 'We brought him back to the Warrah Guest House where we were staying,' added Kate. 'He'd only just begun breakfast when his local paper, *The Newcastle Herald* tracked him down for an interview. His wife Cindy didn't even know where he was, but the *Herald* only had to make one phone call.' By 7 am everyone in town knew who Alan was and where he was staying.

Meanwhile, a secondhand mast for Alan and a new one for Robin Davie had been air freighted in 40 foot sections from the UK on the regular military supply flight. Alan retrieved the pieces from the military base in a dump truck and began dismantling his jury rig. Complicating his task was the fact that, according to Arnet Taylor, 682 members of the local adult population of some 900 considered themselves to be correspondents or freelance journalists – and Alan was obliging all interview requests. 'We're going to chain him to his toolbox starting this afternoon,' Taylor threatened. On Friday rigger Anthony Boalch, hired by Robin Davie, flew in from the UK to help put the masts together.

The same day, eight days after the first alert from *Henry Hornblower*, the bulk carrier *Doceriver* arrived in a new search area, 150 miles east south east of the original area. It took into account the likely drift of a disabled vessel. The weather was atrocious as *Doceriver* began to carry out another box search. This time the box was 60 miles by 60 miles – 3,600 square miles.

Meanwhile Robin Davie, one hundred and twenty miles from Cape Horn, had found himself almost becalmed. As darkness fell the wind picked up to gale force with low cloud and heavy rain. Before long the gale gave way to storm force winds and he was clawing down the storm jib that acted as his mainsail. The ride was getting wild as the seas built up and night wore on. 'Great walls of blackness rose behind me. Occasionally they were white as the waves were breaking and we surfed at over 9 knots,' he said. With the wind rising to over 50 knots Robin took down his remaining foresail and ran under bare poles. His speed dropped away and the next breaking wave turned *Cornwall* sideways and knocked her on to her beam ends. 'It was mayhem below. Cassettes and cutlery rained around my head,' Davie said. 'Scrambling on deck *Cornwall* was head into the wind and lying calmly to the seas. It was two hours before dawn and I had been up for 20 hours. I was soaked to the skin from breaking waves and starting to feel cold.'

*Cornwall* was eight miles south of the Horn and drifting slowly eastwards in no danger. Filling his hot water bottle Robin crawled into his sleeping bag to get warm, setting his firebell alarm to wake him every half hour to check his course. 'Soon after first light I felt much better. The wind was still howling at 50 knots and I plotted my position to find that I had passed Cape Horn half an hour before. With heavy rain I couldn't see the Cape visually, or on radar. I felt cheated. I had sailed a long way. But I sure as hell wasn't going back to make sure it was still there!' he added with good humour.

This was not a place to be waiting around in, so Robin was soon crawling across the foredeck dragging the staysail behind him to hoist. Soon *Cornwall* was speeding down the swells at 8 knots. 'I had a big current helping to push me north eastwards towards the Atlantic. As the day wore on the wind gradually fell away and at midnight on race day 41 I was over 100 miles from Cape Horn and becalmed. In the last 24 hours we had covered over 170 miles. Quite incredible.' There were still 300 miles to go to Port Stanley.

The next day, after searching for Harry's yacht for 36 hours, the Chilean rescue authorities released *Doceriver* to continue her passage. Weather conditions in the area had become dangerous. Winds had increased to Force 10-11 with up to 63 knots 'causing structural stress and overloading the main engine propulsion and steering systems' of the ship. The primary search area had now been thoroughly covered twice by the *Francisca Schulte* and a much larger secondary area had been scoured by the *Doceriver*.

Schrader commented: 'We now have to hope Harry is sailing on toward Cape Horn, perhaps under jury rig with no communications equipment.' He also posed some questions to the rescue authorities in Valparaiso, based on the assumption that Harry had sailed out of the search area at his previous average speed of 6 knots and would round the Horn between 14 and 20 March. He asked: 'Do you keep a radar and visual watch at your Cape Horn station? If so, is it possible to keep a very active lookout during these dates? Do you have patrol vessels in the Cape Horn area?' He also asked for sightings of Minoru Saito to be reported. The rescue authorities replied that they had alerted all shipping in the area and would evaluate the possibility of sending additional patrols for the days in question. Optimistically they added: 'We expect good news in the next days.'

But as the days wore on scenarios abounded over what had happened to Harry. There was no shortage of surmise and supposition. For some there remained a slim hope that the EPIRB had been accidentally triggered and Harry was sailing on towards his goal of Cape Horn, sublimely unaware of the massive search and rescue effort being mounted. Those who knew Harry would guess that if anyone could come through a drama like this and confound the sceptics by turning up safe on the other side of Cape Horn, asking 'What's all the fuss about then?', it would be Harry.

That evening, as the *Doceriver* resumed her course for Brazil, Niah Vaughan was five miles away from the finish line at Punta del Este as the sun set over the ocean. A taciturn man, dubbed 'the quiet man of the fleet' at the start of the race, he was not given to showing his emotions. But now he sat down at his laptop computer at the chart table and composed a message to family, friends and supporters back home in Cumbria – his daughter, Paula, the 'Harbour Gang', Waberthwaite schools, the town council, local radio station, museum and even the sea cadets. Emotions flooded though him: elation, deep sorrow, and relief at journey's end. Words couldn't describe what he felt but they were all he had.

'This leg has been one of the great Emotional Experiences,' he typed. 'Frustrations in calms and sheer adrenalin rushes, mixed with tinges of fear in storms and long surfs down large waves. Retirements. Great acts of seamanship. Steering under jury rig for thousands of miles in the Southern Ocean. Knockdowns and lucky escapes in screaming snow squalls. The uncertainty of nightly encounters with icebergs. Hand steering for thousands of miles after

*Niah Vaughan with his instrument platform intact, before it was wiped out in a knockdown after rounding Cape Horn.* PHOTO: PATRICK ROACH

autopilot failures. Great comradeship and banter between skippers on radio skeds. The tragedy, anguish and heartfelt loss of a great old sailor and a very close friend... we still hope and pray. Best regards and love to everyone, Niah.'

As he crossed the finish line, the severity of Niah's voyage was readily apparent to everyone. There was a six foot tear in the mainsail; a four foot rip in the headsail and the stainless steel equipment bridge at the stern of *Jimroda II* was badly crumpled. He had rounded the Horn safely to find himself becalmed between the cape and the Le Maire Straits. A school of dolphins and 30 albatrosses welcomed him back into the Atlantic. An Argentinian trawler came by, the skipper shouting 'Arriba! Arriba!' Niah shouted back 'I need Mucho Gusto!' In a short time he got more than he asked for.

'I was a third of the way through the straits when the wind rose to 50 knots with a 4 knot current against us. You have never seen seas like it in all your life. I was glad it was dark. They were double-storey jobs with the tops collapsing. The self-steering couldn't quite handle them so I took the wheel to assist and stop us rounding up. It was inevitable. In the pitch black an enormous wave rode up and collapsed on the boat. Out of the corner of my eye I saw the windvane hurtling past and then we started to go over. I thought it was just going to be a partial knockdown. Next moment I was under water. Fortunately, I had on my safety harness and had a grip on the wheel. I thought to myself, "We are going all the way!" I went under the water for about ten seconds. By that time the boat had gone through a 120 degree roll. When she came up I was still clinging to the wheel and I started to steer her, knowing that every wave was now a potential knockdown. I then noticed that there was no masthead light. I looked behind me and the stern bridge (instrument platform) was twisted out of recognition. The solar panel frame was half moon shape and one wind generator was scrap. Later I noticed the starboard lower spreader had been half torn off and the guard rail stanchions were badly bent. I was hanging on for grim death and thought "This is it". I couldn't get below to see the radar and we were very close to the Isle of Estados. There were lights behind me: a cruise ship heading for shelter in the lee of the island. I hoped he could see me on his radar. I steered for three hours and was a soggy mess and very, very cold. It was a tough one. The worst part of the trip. I was very fortunate to pull out of it,' said Vaughan, who added 'I don't recommend swimming in the Le Maire Strait, it's very cold.' His time for the leg was 42d 21h.

Hearing reports like this from men like Vaughan, who were not prone to exaggerate, it was not surprising that while some of us were still hoping for the best, many of the skippers, who knew the reality, already feared the worst for Harry Mitchell and didn't think they'd ever see him sport the traditional gold earring for rounding the Horn.

At home in Portsmouth, Harry's wife Diana had received visits and phone calls from the local evening newspaper, radio and television stations all running stories on 'Fears for missing solo yachtsman' and 'Hopes fade for silent mariner'. She had even been given an Answerphone by the BOC Group to filter some of the calls. A letter from Pat Dyer, Chief Executive of the BOC Group, said: 'We watch, wait and pray that the next day will bring some hopeful news. Harry is one of the most popular and admired BOC Challengers. People warm to what we have called his "buccaneering spirit"... you and Harry are in our thoughts and prayers.'

Diana was interviewed by a local reporter on the *Portsmouth News*: 'Hope is eternal,' she said. 'I cannot just stop believing that he is all right. I have to be optimistic, it would not do to be otherwise. I don't know where Harry is, or whether he will be found. He is in the hands of God now...'

In Mark Schrader's race office in Punta del Este a small group assembled each evening at 6pm, including Dan McConnell, Herb McCormick and Nigel Rowe, to raise their glasses to a portrait of Harry Mitchell on the wall and drink a toast to the missing mariner.

Of the five sailors due in Punta del Este, including Harry Mitchell, Arnet Taylor and Alan Nebauer remained in the Falklands, putting the final touches to their rig repairs, while Robin Davie was on his final approach to Port Stanley. There had still been no news of Minoru Saito since his sighting by the *Francisca Schulte* ten days ago.

Arnet, together with his shore crew, Merfyn and Kate, and Alan were all based in the same Port Stanley guesthouse, a village of prefabricated one-storey houses, most painted with reds, blues and greens, which helped to liven up the perpetually grey skyline. A new mast base had been designed for *Thursday's Child* a quarter of an inch taller ('Always looking to increase that power ratio!' said Arnet) and aluminium plates had been made for the rash of cracks along the mast.

'We all hid from the wind as best we could,' said Kate. 'Even Arnie, who'd just come from the Southern Ocean, admitted he'd rather stay below with the diesel heater. We sometimes sneaked away for a long lunch and a swim with the penguins. A day at the beach in the Falklands means a half hour Land Rover trek through the peat bogs, past the mine fields, and peeling off three layers of thermals before you jump in. Our host swam. We hid in our Polartecs!'

Alan had told Arnet that he was drinking too much red wine. Arnet told him: 'It's part of my programme to learn how to sail like a Frenchman.' Alan was concerned it might become a requirement.

The final days in Port Stanley as the season closed down for the southern winter saw a fascinating influx of vessels. There were several small Russian cruise ships, ships from the British Antarctic Survey fleet and one other special visitor: French sailing wizard Phillipe Poupon, who arrived aboard his 40ft cruising boat after several months exploring the frozen southlands. He invited Arnet and crew aboard for drinks.

Anthony Boalch, the rigger whom Robin had hired, soon cobbled together Alan's mast with the ease of experience. He hung it over the boat, measured everything, and then put Andrez to work with the hacksaw.

'The new rig is great,' said Alan, when everything but the backstays were mounted.

'I'm leaving in the morning,' said Arnie.

'I'll be right behind you,' said Alan. As it turned out, Alan was about four hours behind.

Even though the sails were, in Alan's words, 'a bit ordinary', he sailed out of the harbour at 9 knots, with three reefs in the main, a sliver of genoa and the sun setting behind him. The final 1,000 mile sprint to Punta del Este had begun.

'It feels incredible to be sailing with some horsepower again,' said Alan. 'I think I am in shock with the amazing way everything has come together. God is good and I say a humble thank you to all those involved in getting the rig back. It's just incredible to be at the bottom of the planet and re-rigged. I'm looking forward to a fast passage to Punta.' But the young born again Christian would soon have his faith severely tested yet again.

As Alan and Arnet left for Uruguay on race day 44, the Chilean rescue authorities diverted a third Merchant vessel, *Resolution Bay*, through the search zone to look for Harry Mitchell. For almost two weeks conditions in the area had been very bad, with sustained winds of more than 60 knots and seas of 12-15 metres reported by the second search ship, as well as one hundred per cent cloud cover. Now the bad weather had dissipated and visibility was excellent. A fishing fleet was in the area and all ships had been requested to keep watch for *Henry Hornblower* and *Shuten-Dohji II* for the rest of the month of March.

Race HQ, having seemingly exhausted all conventional rescue strategies, now contacted NASA at Cape Canaveral, through COMSAT, to investigate the possibility of the space shuttle or military satellite surveillance over the search area. They were told that NASA would be willing to co-operate but *Endeavour* was not currently orbiting the area and they did not have the right equipment aboard for a search. Objects less than 100 feet long would not be sighted by the space shuttle.

By daybreak next morning, after 45 days at sea, Robin Davie was three miles off the Falklands shore, making his way against headwinds towards Port Stanley. It was slow progress under jury rig, darkness was falling, and it was threatening to rain as a tow launch came out to meet him. Soon he was tied up in Stanley Harbour where he glimpsed familiar faces from his two year stay in the Falklands as a Merchant Navy radio officer. Thirteen years ago Robin had been among the crew of a British Naval tanker which steamed into Port Stanley 24 hours after the ceasefire between Argentina and Britain. His ship was carrying 25,000 tons of aviation fuel for the RAF. He was known in the Falklands as 'Flatdog'.

That evening Robin was home and dry with local coaster captain George Betts, enjoying a hot bath, hot dinner and warm bed. To meet the deadline for the start of leg four, he had set himself a five day deadline to get *Cornwall* rerigged and ready for sea. It was a tight schedule. It took him most of the next day to dismantle and clear away the jury rig while rigger Anthony was busy putting together the new mast, helped by engineers Carl and Andrez. By the second afternoon the new mast step was fitted, when someone came by with a basket of authentic Cornish pasties. As Arnet Taylor's shore crew, Merfyn and Kate, bid farewell and headed for the airport, six helpers carried the mast out onto the dock where the mobile crane hoisted it up at sunset. With darkness falling, a temporary rope stay was set up until the weekend.

Out at sea, less than two days after replacing his mast, Alan Nebauer's nightmarish trip had taken another shocking twist when, 600 miles from the finish line, he lost his rudder. In the early hours of the morning on race day 47 his off-course alarm sounded and the yacht rounded up. 'I thought I had run into a big kelp bed which had already happened several times, stopping the boat and taking ages to untangle. But it was soon apparent that the rudder was having no effect. I checked the cables and discovered that the blade wasn't visible in the water. There were cracks around the lower shaft bearing which indicated impact. The aft compartment was also half-filled with water.'

The young Australian admitted he cried tears of frustration as he put on his survival suit to get into the compartment to repair the leak. Having slowed the intake of water he sent a message to Race HQ: 'Personally I am devastated after

Gull's-eye view from the masthead of J J Provoyeur's *Novell South Africa* flying her spinnaker. PHOTO: BILLY BLACK

*Opposite page, above)* *Coyote* is careened in Punta del Este harbour as skipper David Scully, in the dinghy, gets ready to make repairs to the bent keel. PHOTO: BILLY BLACK

*Opposite page, below)* Italian Giovanni Soldini powers *Kodak* upwind to stay on the tail of his arch rival David Adams in one of the great duels of the BOC Challenge. PHOTO: CARLO BORLENGHI/PPL

*Above)* The lonely sea and the sky: Christophe Auguin on *Sceta Calberson.* PHOTO: JACQUES VAPILLON

*Inset)* Defending BOC champion Christophe Auguin has the victor's crown within his grasp for a second time as he works on his laptop computer at night. PHOTO: JACQUES VAPILLON

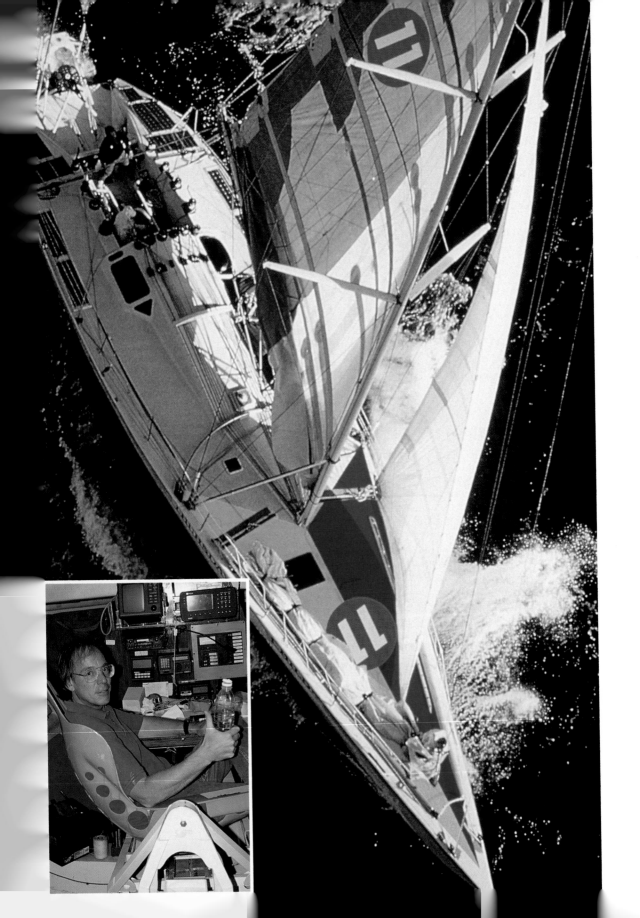

(*Above left*) The 'almost bi-lingual' Giovanni Soldini sits cross-legged at his laptop computer and nav station where he kept in touch with the world. PHOTO: PATRICK ROACH

(*Above right*) The last sailor to arrive in Charleston: Japan's Minoru Saito on *Shuten Dohji II* (Son of a drunk). Minoru planned to sail to England 'to bring Harry Mitchell's soul home'. PHOTO: JACQUES VAPILLON

(*Opposite page*) Three attempts had been made to sail *Thursday's Child* around the world, but only Arnet Taylor succeeded. He had never even sailed across the Atlantic before he sailed around the world. PHOTO: BILLY BLACK

(*Opposite page, inset*) Even the gimballed seat aboard *Thursday's Child* couldn't have saved Arnet Taylor from a painful flight across his cabin in leg three. PHOTO: PAUL GELDER

(*Right*) It wasn't all storms and shrieking wind. There were tranquil tropical sunsets, too. David Adams on *True Blue*. PHOTO: BILLY BLACK

(*Left*) To the victor of Class II, David Adams, an embrace from wife Caroline. Choking back tears at the awards night, the tough Australian said: 'It's a race that gets under your skin and into your bones.' PHOTO: BILLY BLACK

(*Below*) Selling T-shirts to raise funds was how Robin Davie managed to race round the world. For $5 he gave a personal tour of the 40-foot boat which was his home for 197 days. PHOTO: PAUL GELDER

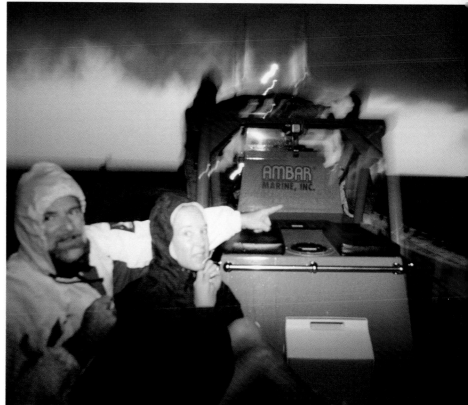

*Above)* Niah Vaughan
finishes the gruelling 27,000
mile marathon with a
patriotic flourish, flying a
huge Union Jack and an even
bigger smile. PHOTO: BILLY BLACK

*Right)* 'She's over there!'
Race director Mark
Schrader, who met every
yacht at every stopover, goes
out to meet Robin Davie's
*Cornwall* for the last time
under menacing black storm
clouds at the Charleston
finish. PHOTO: BILLY BLACK

(*Above*) The three buccaneers. Niah Vaughan (centre) sporting his gold earring for rounding Cape Horn, flanked by Arnet Taylor (left) and Robin Davie. PHOTO: BILLY BLACK

(*Below*) At the Not the BOC Awards night party in Charleston, Diana Mitchell joined in the fun as Harry would have wished. 'Above all else, Harry wanted to be a BOC finisher. If he can't be here, I had to finish the race for him.' PHOTO BILLY BLACK

(*Background*) The gold earring for rounding Cape Horn – the prize that Harry Mitchell valued above all others. PHOTO: PAUL GELDER

*Robin Davie had a race against time in the Falklands to dismantle his jury rig and step a new mast so that he could get to Punta in time to stay in the race.*

PHOTO: KATE FORD

the huge effort by everyone to rig a new mast in the Falklands. What can I say? I am continuing on to Punta with no thought of NOT finishing this BOC by the Grace of God.'

But he was worried. 'I don't think the city of Newcastle can tolerate another disaster. It will set the sceptics on fire...' Neubauer – who had lost his keel in leg one, was forced with generator problems to stop at Simonstown on leg two, and Bluff in this leg, and then lost his mast 20 days ago – was at the nadir of his fortunes. He read his Bible every day after the rudder failure and took heart from a passage in Isaiah: 'It is for my benefit that I suffer so much.' The only saving grace in his situation was that the closest person to him also happened to be the one man in the world who knew all about steering a rudderless ship. Arnet Taylor, 120 miles ahead, had steered *Thursday's Child* for several thousand miles to Australia without a primary rudder. He was soon in radio contact to give expert advice to Nebauer, who turned one of the spinnaker poles (so recently part of his jury rig) into a new rudder, with a washboard as a skeg and limped towards Punta del Este.

The early hours of the morning of race day 50 found Arnet Taylor parked less than ten miles from the Punta finish, waiting for a breeze to take him across the line in *Thursday's Child*, the last of the Class I yachts. He finally took the finish gun at lunchtime to record a time of 50d 15h, including his ten day stop in the Falklands. Despite his enforced stopover in the Falklands to make repairs he had a new worklist for the 11-year-old yacht whose tired systems were showing up after 20,000 miles. There was a cracked boom, a damaged compression pole and more rips in the sails. Merfyn Owen and Peter Robie went out to help bring the yacht into the dockside.

Back in Port Stanley, *Cornwall's* new rigging was in place while, down below, Robin was getting ready for sea with the help of three master mariners: George Betts, Steve Clifton and Dave Hall. Fuel and oil filters were changed, the cooker was ripped apart and rebuilt, the toilet seat changed, and the transmitter rewired up to the new backstay aerial. Robin raided local shops to gather the stores he would need to see him right through to Charleston in May. In third world Uruguay the choice would be much more restricted and expensive. He had one other job to do. Having written nearly 2,000 post cards en route to the Falklands, to commemorate his rounding of Cape Horn and raise funds for *Cornwall*, he presented them to the astonished Falkland Island's Post Office clerk.

By late Monday afternoon he was ready to go, except the Falkland's weather was blowing up to gale force. With an untried mast and rig it seemed prudent to wait until next morning. The extra night's sleep did him good and next morning, with the wind down to a more moderate 20 knots, he was soon speeding north-wards. Having achieved his five day target to re-rig, he now had nine days to sail 1,100 miles. But all was not well the first night when the engine packed up soon after he started charging the batteries.

'I took the starting handle to hand crank the engine and found myself laid out with pulled muscles in my lower back. I was reduced to crawling around the deck on all fours to do all my sail changes and adjustments, and it was very diffi-cult to pull ropes and wind the winches. Down below, even sitting in the chair at the chart table, or lying in the bunk was excruciatingly painful. It proved almost impossible to get out of the bunk once I was in the lying down position. Trying to get in and out of my oilskin trousers, jacket and boots would make a good comedy.'

It would be three days before he could stand straight again, and the engine and generator problems meant cutting back on electricity and communications to conserve dwindling power. There wasn't even enough wind to power up the wind generator. 'All the canaries are lined up on the rail whistling,' he said. 'I'm living in darkness, no lights, only torch light at night, no BBC World Service. My radio and satellite communications have been cut to the barest minimum.' The ex-radio officer had been reduced to silence by his broken generator and an engine firing on one cylinder. 'It was the worst part of the trip. Worse even than being under jury rig,' he said afterwards.

Late on race day 56, Charleston Race HQ received a message from the Falkland Islands Fisheries Department: 'At 2010 GMT today one of our patrol vessels made contact with the yacht *Shuten-Dohji II* about 60 miles west of the Falklands. He (Minoru Saito) is making his way to Punta del Este. At this time he cannot raise his mainsail and his autopilot is not working. Otherwise it appears he is well.'

The sighting of Minoru, from whom nothing had been heard for more than three weeks, boosted hopes for Harry Mitchell. Minoru had rounded Cape Horn without being seen and had no power, no communications and no tracking facilities when he was spotted. 'It is possible the same thing has happened to Harry, although it may not be the most probable thing,' said Race Director Mark Schrader. 'In the absence of finding a wrecked vessel or any evidence, we must assume he could survive. It is not blind optimism, but in the absence of evidence to the contrary it is human nature to hope. He is a tough resourceful guy. If he was in something survivable, he would survive. Diana has lived through a number of Harry's adventures. She's a very strong, brave, philosophical woman. They are a terrific match.'

Next day, in a fading north easterly wind early on the morning of race day 57, Alan Nebauer steered *Newcastle Australia* across the finish line with his makeshift rudder. His elapsed time was 56d 10h. This included his two-day stop in New Zealand, to correct alternator problems, and nine days in the Falklands to step a new mast. 'Losing the rudder and making it to Punta was physically, mentally and emotionally the hardest thing I've ever done in my life,' said the young sailor. 'I thought I was going to lose the boat when I discovered water gushing in the after compartment.'

Nebauer was greeted by fellow Aussies David Adams and Phil Lee, who had already begun work on the new rudder. 'I'm overwhelmed by the support. First I had the whole city of my hometown Newcastle raising money and organising a new rig. Now I have these guys in Punta. It's a pretty unique thing about the BOC that one competitor can help another competitor in this way.' Indeed, the unique spirit and camaraderie of the BOC Challenge was in full force as fellow skippers, shore crews and staff from the Yacht Club Punta del Este rallied to Alan's aid. David Adams and Phil Lee had organised the construction of a new rudder, having contacted the designer of Alan's yacht in Australia, and sourced materials for the job in Uruguay.

Three days before the start of the final leg home, as dawn rose over Punta del Este, Robin Davie's new mast appeared over the horizon surfing the crests of a rolling swell. Robin had stayed up all night and slowed down his progress to arrive at first light. As the official welcome boat came out his first question was: 'Any news on Harry?'

*Cornwall's* black and gold hull bore the scars of her dismasting with white scratches on the port side. Robin stepped on the dockside with a silver trophy-sized goblet of ice cream in one hand and a champagne bottle in the other. The sun came out from behind the clouds as if on cue, putting the reluctant hero in the spotlight. He had become the 11th of the 14 skippers who set out from Sydney to complete the voyage. He had plenty of praise for those who had helped to organise and raise funds for his new mast and sails, especially the host port of Charleston. 'At the end of the day they've basically saved my bacon. I'm just very, very lucky to have found that level of support,' he said, beaming. His time for leg three was 59d 9h.

As skippers made final preparations for the 1 April re-start, and Minoru Saito plugged on towards Punta on his 61st day at sea, Race Director Mark Schrader reaffirmed his hopes for Harry Mitchell. 'We're not ready to give up yet. If Harry has managed to salvage his yacht he could literally survive for months. The incident proves what's been said of the Southern Ocean. It's the worst possible place for something to go wrong and it's also the most likely place for something to go wrong. It doesn't matter if your yacht is 40ft or 60ft, or you're 20 years old or 70, there are conditions out there that will beat you. After we leave Punta we will be in daily touch with MRCC in Chile and notices will go out to shipping every day.'

Before he had even set off from England's south coast the previous summer, Harry had made frequent references to whether he would get round Cape Horn this time. 'Determined to make it?,' he once told me. 'I was determined to make it last time. But it's luck. When I was in the 1976 OSTAR two fellows (Mike McMullen and Mike Flanagan) lost their lives for the first time in the 16 years history of the race. And in the 1986 BOC Challenge Jacques de Roux lost his life. So, am I Jonah somewhere here? Have I got some kind of aura of tragedy about me, a jinx?'

In McMullen's case it was four years later that a small piece of wreckage from his bright yellow trimaran was found washed ashore in Iceland. Harry knew only too well the dangers he was facing. Some had said that it was rash for a man of 70 to set off on such an adventure. Some said that with all his talk of jinxes and not making it back to Charleston, he must have had a death wish. But Harry had a life wish. His doubts came not from any premonition, but rather a recognition that a solo sailor's life hung by a slender thread in the lonely oceans. Harry was the last person to tempt fate. True, he threw caution to the winds. Had those same winds that saved him in the second leg of the race, 'blowing the tops off the waves', now claimed him? While ships were still looking for Harry no one wanted to speculate further.

# 12 · *That Golden Earring ...*

Carnival season was well and truly over in Punta del Este by the time the BOC tailend Charlies arrived in port. One of South America's most glamorous summer resorts for the rich, attracting swarms of upper class Argentinians, the town was quiet with moorings empty and shops closed for the autumn season. It was said that if a tidal wave swept over the narrow peninsula of Punta, half the restaurants in Uruguay would disappear. Bureaucratically the town was part of Maldonado, but economically and socially it was a world apart, with its elegant seaside villas, yachts and expensive restaurants.

For the first time since the start at Charleston, Floyd Romack, who had set off a week late after attending his daughter's wedding, caught up with the fleet. Having been disqualified after reaching Cape Town outside the time limit, he had sailed over to Punta in *Cardiac 88* as had Neal Petersen in his re-masted *Protect Our Sealife* with girlfriend Gwen. They were unofficially joining the fleet to close the circle on their shortened adventure.

David Scully's *Coyote* was the centre of attention as she was heeled over in the harbour to make repairs to her bent keel, which had kept the skipper awake with its screeching when it worked loose in its case. With a halyard running from the pier to the masthead, Scully winched *Coyote* over until one rail was well under water, so he could repair the keel joint from a dinghy. To the crowds on the dockside it was all very unusual. But Scully looked quite accustomed to walking uphill on his sloping deck, though he found the operation a bit hair-raising.

Elsewhere there were hair-raising stories from sailors and crew trying to get equipment for the yachts cleared through customs at Montevideo airport. Arnet Taylor's father arrived at the airport from America with a large consignment of freeze dried food, the packaging sealed and marked 'Do not accept if seals are broken' and 'Food in transit for yacht *Thursday's Child*'. The customs official's thorough 'inspection' included slashing open the packages with a knife. Protests that the food would be ruined were ignored until a Uruguayan friend explained 'He wants money.' A $50 bribe was the price of rescuing the provisions.

For Neal Petersen it was a problem getting new fittings for his roller furler out of customs, and the South African ambassador was called upon to help. Niah Vaughan had a new sail delivered to the airport. It took 36 hours to fly it there from Britain and two weeks and a few dollars more to extract it from customs.

The effort to liberate Arnet Taylor's missing sail involved the Commodore of the Punta del Este Yacht Club, a New Hampshire Congressman and a Uruguayan Whitbread sailor. In true BOC spirit Alan Nebauer had given Taylor one of his headsails which was altered to fit *Thursday's Child*. Finally, hours before the scheduled start, the missing sail turned up. It had been a victim of an international trade problem when it was stopped in Brazil. A friend with connections personally shepherded it through the airport to Montevideo.

Frenchman Jean-Luc Van den Heede stage-managed a continental drama and marched past officialdom to grab his sail from customs – 'maybe that's what you have to do, yell, scream and create a real ruckus,' observed the others.

As the clock ticked on there was a huge collective effort to get the new rudder finished for Alan Nebauer's yacht. Other skippers, including David Scully and JJ Provoyeur, took shifts to grind and shape the core out of wood before fibreglassing, filling, fairing and antifouling the finished shape. 'By the time they finished there was not a drop of epoxy left in Uruguay,' said David Adams, who played no small part in the operation himself. As Kate Ford said: 'In contrast to the America's Cup with its intrigues and espionage, on the BOC Challenge it's not unusual to see crew working on the "wrong" boat, hunched up in an awkward corner to do some moonlight electrical work.'

A Force 10 storm buffeted the Rio del Plata all day on Saturday, hampering last minute preparations on the yachts and causing the race committee to postpone the start for 24 hours. It wasn't called April Fools day for nothing. The irony of a gale delaying a race in which competitors had endured storm after storm was not lost. 'These guys have been through the Southern Ocean, they don't have anything to prove and they don't need to damage their boats,' said one of the race organisers. With the shallow, narrow entrance to Punta del Este's harbour, a short start line and engineless yachts, it would have been a recipe for disaster. It was the most severe storm the local race committee had seen for several years.

Robin Davie said: 'Having arrived a little on the late side compared to everyone else, I'm welcoming the extra 24 hours to sample some steaks and beer.' For Giovanni: 'It is very dangerous for the boat. There is no reason to risk three years hard work in this weather.' Asked what he would do with his day off, he said: 'I think I will go to sleep.'

At the BOC prizegiving in Punta del Este, the skippers had been awarded the gold earring – the prize that Harry had wanted above all others – for rounding the Horn. It was presented in a hand-made silver case engraved with the date on which they had rounded the landmark.

At a private dinner on the final night ashore attended by shore crew, friends and skippers Robin Davie, David Scully, Arnet Taylor, Niah Vaughan and Floyd Romack, glasses were raised for a toast proposed by Andy Darwent: 'Wherever you are Harry, we're thinking of you.'

## *Punta del Este to Charleston (5,751 miles)*

# 13 · Home to Debt and Glory

After the violence of the Southern Ocean the final sprint home through the tradewind belts and across the doldrums would tempt skippers to push their yachts to the limits. The fourth leg of the BOC Challenge could still be tough on boats and gear. It would also test skippers' meteorological skills. The minefield of high pressure systems in the Atlantic can mean that the shortest distance between two points becomes a long zig-zag to stay in the wind. Each yacht received reports from French weather router Meteo Consult, and most had weatherfax maps. Those that could afford it also had real-time satellite pictures beamed to $20,000 receivers. All this technology would shortly be concentrated on penetrating the doldrums north of the Equator at their narrowest point. The trick was to get through quickly before being ensnared by the moving band of calms and wild squalls.

Christophe Auguin in *Sceta Calberson* held an 83 hour lead over second placed Steve Pettengill. The ultra-light *Hunter's Child* was already among the lightest Class I yachts in the fleet, but in Punta del Este Pettengill made further attempts to lighten ship to gain that extra tenth of a knot boat speed. Excess length was cut off each rope aboard, the cabin steps found a new home and he even claimed he'd copied the important pages of his reference books, to avoid carrying the weight of extra pages he wouldn't need. Ashore he had been staying in sailing mode with his alarm clock set to wake him every two hours.

An hour before the rescheduled start on Sunday bad luck struck David Scully for a third time. At the start of leg two his mainsail had torn. On leg three he'd had to divert to New Zealand for a new sail. Now a tow boat rammed into the side of *Coyote*, putting a hole above her waterline ten feet from the bow. It was the last straw, he thought, as he tied up to a buoy and rushed to fit a one-foot-square patch to the hull. But he was still in time to make the start as 11 yachts crossed the line, bouncing over six foot waves as hundreds of spectators watched from the harbour breakwater. Minoru Saito was scheduled to arrive later in the week, and the fleet would also be joined unofficially for the leg home by Floyd Romack on

*Arnet Taylor Senior does some maintenance on his son's yacht* Thursday's Child *in preparaton for the final run home.* PHOTO: BILLY BLACK

*Cardiac 88* and Neal Petersen on *Protect our Sealife* a few hours later.

Handling his 50-foot *True Blue* like a big dinghy, David Adams was first across the line, chasing the Class II prizewinner's cheque of $50,000 to pay off some of his bills. Many of the skippers had left Punta del Este with a flu virus, including Christophe, Robin Davie and Arnet Taylor. In Arnet's case he was sure he had contracted the bug from Niah Vaughan, skipper of *Jimroda II*, whom he accused of practising biological warfare as part of their duel. 'Prior to the start Niah got sick and insisted on enthusiastic displays of affection to spread his infection,' said Taylor. Niah claimed that the virus lacked the stamina of a British bug and must have been imported from America by *Thursday's Child*'s shore crew.

On race day three a power cut paralysed Punta del Este for several hours, and in the pre-dawn hours Race Director Mark Schrader was woken up by someone knocking on the door of his rented house. 'I didn't know the power was out until the knocking woke me up,' said Schrader. 'The man standing at the front door was saying, "El barco! El barco!". As I looked out at the horizon I could see a boat and immediately knew it was Minoru Saito.' After being unable to communicate with race officials for more than a month because of generator problems, the end of Minoru's gruelling 67-day passage from Sydney was in sight.

For the first time race officials received an eye witness account of conditions in the violent storm of 2 March which had caused Harry Mitchell's EPIRB to activate. Minoru said *Shuten Dhohji II* had almost capsized. 'I saw the wind indicator reach 67 knots and then there was nothing. It all blew away.' He lost his autopilot, windvane, radar and steering system in the storm. 'I stayed on deck for 10 or 12 hours and then just went below and waited. It was very, very bad.' Contaminated diesel

*Niah Vaughan's* Jimroda II *bounces through waves left over from storm-force winds at the start of leg four in Punta del Este.* PHOTO: BILLY BLACK

fuel prevented him running the generator that powered his electronics. Eventually he rounded Cape Horn nearly three weeks later, a mile south of the Cape, which he could see clearly. 'The Chilean Navy contact me by radio and say, "Are you panicked?" I say back to them, "Radio no work! Radar no work! Steering no work! I'm okay. Me not panicked, the boat is panicked!"' When asked how he felt to be in Punta del Este Minoru lowered his head and said: 'Sad. Sad that Harry is not here with me...'

Back out at sea, light headwinds hampered progress for the fleet. Giovanni, having gained a 13 mile lead on Adams, suffered a broken forestay and made plans to ship a new one from Italy to the Brazilian port of Vitoria. JJ Provoyeur on *Novell South Africa* reported sailing in sight of both *Kodak* and *True Blue*. 'I'm sandwiched between the two, one mile either side of me. Do you advise me to stay or tack away? I wouldn't want to get caught in the crossfire.'

David Scully also faced rigging problems in the first four days. A 5mm titanium metal strap had snapped in half and he was at the top of his mast mending the tang that held the swivel of the furling headsail in place. 'There was never such a boat for breaking gear,' he said as he celebrated the repair back at sea level with some calvados in his coffee. Later he noticed the headfoil was popping grub screws from a joint high up in the rig. 'This is a technically demanding if not downright frightening repair as it means climbing the headfoil with the sail unfurled,' he said. He had last done it in the Southern Ocean.

*Coyote* had developed other problems too. The fresh water system was growing green scum. The same thing had happened on the last leg, and on arrival in Punta David had flushed the system with a bleach solution. 'Is the water safe to drink?' he asked Race HQ. 'In the last leg I drank a great deal of it and it produced no ill effects other than a craving for young women and a cold beer. Should I regard the green stuff as a health hazard or a diet supplement?' Back in Charleston Peter Dunning advised boiling the water and adding a medical slug of rum in the coffee. To be on the safe side he also passed on the details to the duty doctor in Seattle. Scully was also sailing with the handicap of his 14 ft keel bent five to eight degrees from true. Providing he stayed on the right tack, someone had joked, it could save using water ballast.

Giovanni, who had lengthened his lead over Adams to 47 miles, was holding course for the Brazilian port of Vitoria, north of Rio de Janeiro, to replace his forestay, and drew praise from his rival. 'I can't believe Giovanni. He's without a forestay and he's absolutely flying. According to the weather forecast I'm supposed to have wind, not him.' Later Adams added: 'I have been looking at the position reports and I'm wondering if anyone has told Giovanni he has a broken forestay. I don't understand how his mast is still up there. I know he would have a whole lot of halyards forward to ease the strain but the pounding I've been getting wouldn't have done that any good.' Adams, facing a problem sending messages via his computer, sent one to Race HQ: 'Please don't tell me to read the book because I tore that page out – the book was too heavy.'

On race day seven Giovanni bypassed Vitoria and headed, instead, for Recife to replace his forestay. He had received a telex telling him that the plane bringing his forestay from Spain had left it in Lisbon. His rage was compounded by the fact that he had wasted 24 hours altering course for Vitoria.

The end of the first week of the last leg home found Arnet Taylor and *Thursday's Child* drifting north at half a knot, trapped on the edge of a high pressure bubble 600 miles south east of Rio de Janeiro. 'Too far away to hear any samba music,' lamented Arnet. 'It's about 80° and things could be far worse. I think I'll pack up the remaining thermal clothes today, along with all the winter hats, mittens, and scarves. Knowing all the cold weather is behind us reinforces an optimistic outlook.'

Meanwhile in Punta del Este work had been going on around the clock to get Minoru back in the race. He had received assistance from the yacht club and even the Uruguayan Navy, as well as his Tokyo shore crew. Electronics, radio equipment and self-steering had been repaired from the ravages of his near capsize, and he finally left in light winds on race day seven before a large send-off crowd, many waving Japanese flags.

The predominance of windward work on the final leg ended the advantage that the downwind 50 ft flyers *True Blue* and *Kodak* had enjoyed on the Southern Ocean legs. Now the 60-footers displayed their superior performance with their longer waterline lengths. On race day ten Steve Pettengill on *Hunter's Child* was running hard downwind under spinnaker towards the Equator when the starboard cap shroud, holding up the top section of the mast, broke between the top two spreaders 46 feet above deck. The mast's unusual double-diagonal bracing provided enough initial support to stop the mast breaking. Dropping the spinnaker, Steve grabbed a coil of light Kevlar line and donned his mountain climbing harness to ascend the

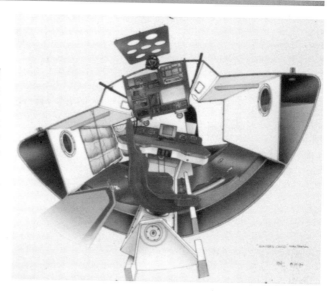

*The high-tech gimballed navigation station aboard Steve Pettengill's Hunter's Child. A stark contrast with Harry Mitchell's scrapyard car seat in which he cat-napped on* Henry Hornblower.

PHOTO: BRUCE ALDERSON

mast. Bouncing over the waves as the sun set he had to work fast to replace the broken wire with multiple turns of rope before the rig collapsed on him.

He climbed to the top spreader nearly 70 feet above deck to loop the rope back down to the middle spreader. Pulling himself up and down the mast in the gathering darkness he got enough turns and cinched them tight with each loop, before winding the assembly even tighter by inserting a spanner into the bundle of lines and twisting it in what sailors' call a Spanish windlass. He returned to deck level bruised, but pleased to see the mast was back in column. 'I'm one lucky guy. I can't believe the mast didn't fall down on me,' he told his wife Patti in a telex home. Over the next couple of days Pettengill spent more than five hours 'banging around in the rigging getting beat up something fierce' as he made sure his jury rig held with a second back-up series of lines.

Sailors have short memories, and for Arnet Taylor being becalmed at sea was more dreadful than any gale he could recall. 'When your fellow competitors a relatively short distance away are streaking off the blood pressure gets notched up. It's worse than being sentenced to attend a festival of Ibsen's plays,' he said.

Giovanni's progress slowed to a crawl, too, as he nursed his broken forestay. But on the evening of Good Friday, race day 12, he made a flying three-hour repair stop in Recife to replace the wire and was back in the race, keeping alive, just, the closest and most exciting race within a race that he and Adams had contested over every one of the 27,000 miles round the world. Twenty-one hours separated the two in overall standings, but Giovanni's forestay problem had allowed Adams to open up a devastating 478 miles advantage.

While fleet leader and reigning BOC champion Christophe Auguin had crossed the Equator, Robin Davie was enduring a slow, tortuous push up the Brazilian coast amidst great squalls and great calms. 'You can never be sure what each cloud mass will bring. There was not a breath of wind at deck level, while 7 knots registered at the masthead anenometer and up in the sky the clouds scudded by in the moonlight – it's just unreal,' he said. 'I seem to be forever putting in and shaking out reefs as the wind goes up and down. It's worth noting that the leading 60-footer passed by here over six days ago. Christophe has 2,086 miles to go to the finish, whilst *Cornwall* is 3,987 miles from Charleston. Believe it or not, we are both in a big hurry to get there!'

In the closest duel in the race Alan Nebauer had Niah Vaughan six miles astern. 'Old Niah is wearing me out. He just won't go away,' said Alan. Later from Niah: 'I woke up this morning after a night of squalls and scanned the horizon. There was a smudge in the distance and as it diminished rapidly it became *Newcastle*.' The two rivals crossed the Equator within hailing distance. Later it was Nebauer's turn to wake up to find 'a funny white boat on my horizon... astern at least.' Niah was excited about a match race all the way to Charleston. 'Why not?' said Alan. 'We've come this far; we may as well hold hands the rest of the way.' Niah had a big flag flying. 'I'm not sure if it's a Union Jack or a Skull and Crossbones. Probably the latter!' thought Alan.

Eight miles north of the Equator Alan put a radio telephone call through to Yarmouth, on the Isle of Wight in England, to speak to one of his special patrons. 'I was going to call before I lost my mast in the Southern Ocean... now I thought, "I'm in her hemisphere, I'll give her a call."' At No 4 Coastguard Cottage Susan Hiscock picked up the phone. As a boy of 17 Alan had found himself anchored next to the Hiscocks' *Wanderer IV* for seven months in Opua, in New Zealand's Bay of Islands. He recognised the yacht immediately, having read all of Eric's books, from *Voyaging Under Sail* to *Come Aboard*. Eric was going blind already. 'They were an inspiration,' said Alan, who forged a special friendship with Susan. She would row over to his boat with biscuits and invitations to dinner. They stayed in touch and met again in 1982 at Coffs Harbour, north of Sydney. Susan would send postcards to Alan from the Hiscocks' ports of call, and when she heard he was putting together a campaign to do the BOC Challenge she sent him a generous cheque. Now she was eager for news as Alan neared the end of his adventure, and praised his rescue of Josh Hall. Alan knew something wasn't quite right, from the manner in which she brushed aside inquiries about herself. A few days after he arrived in Charleston Susan Hiscock lost her battle against cancer and Alan lost a very dear friend.

At the back of the fleet Minoru Saito wondered at the ironic reversal of his weather fortunes. 'Almost no wind. Now very hot in cabin, 90° F. Few weeks ago I had many snowing, hailing, cold front, storm gale, big waves. Very different now.'

At the other end of the fleet, with little more than 1,000 miles to go to the finish line, Christophe Auguin revealed something of his winning strategy: 'This leg for me was very hard at the beginning. I was sick with a fever. I spent much time working on deck. If you want to go fast in the Atlantic you have to work a lot with the sail trim, weather forecast and so on. Sometimes I work 24 hours on deck without sleep. Sometimes it's possible to sleep eight hours a day. Right now I'm sleeping only three hours each night. I try to keep my concentration on sailing this leg. But sometimes I let myself dream that it is possible to win a BOC a second time.'

Robin Davie was having different dreams when he was woken by a high-pitched squeaking noise reverberating throughout the cabin. A pod of 14 pilot whales were swimming alongside, under, in front and astern of *Cornwall*; the biggest was 18 feet. He watched the show for 20 minutes until his fire-bell wake-up alarm, which he'd set 40 minutes earlier, rang. 'It was enough to wake the dead. The whales promptly scattered and disappeared.'

Despite his lead of 500 miles over Giovanni, David Adams still couldn't help look-

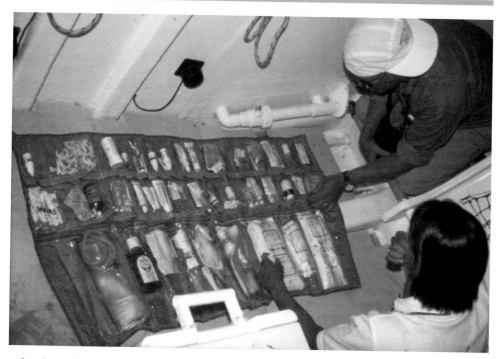

*Checking the medical kit on* Novell South Africa, *which included skin staplers, epoxy dental kit, splints and burns creams.* PHOTO: PAUL GELDER.

ing over his shoulder knowing the wily Italian was doing 10 knots to his 6. Adams had been forced to hand-steer for up to 12 hours a day because fuel problems had limited the use of the generator which charged the autopilot's batteries. On the edge of exhaustion he now altered course for the Caribbean island of Antigua to make repairs. Met by his shore crew Phil Lee at English Harbour, he found he couldn't repair the generator. Instead, they got a second-hand petrol engine set up in the cockpit hooked up to the spare alternator. 'It sounds like having a helicopter in your living room and belching fumes down stairs,' said Adams, who rejoined the race after nine hours to resume his Class II lead. His detour partially opened the door to Giovanni, who had shaved more than 200 miles off Adams' advantage and was now 270 miles astern of him. There were only 1,000 miles left to play catch-up.

The doldrums trap the unsuspecting and the unwary, and whilst Robin Davie was very suspecting and wary he still got caught, suffering two of his slowest days of the entire race. Sixty miles south of the Equator the wind stopped, as though someone had turned the fan off. 'Great storm clouds gathered, towering thousands of feet high, and torrential rains fell amidst a grand thunder and lightening exhibition illuminating the evening sky. We drifted slowly north and I sat in the hatchway throughout the night trimming and adjusting course and sails to keep *Cornwall* moving. For several hours we drifted around in circles. Dawn brought a continued calm and a glassy sea. The sails banged and slatted back and forth. The noon position showed I had sailed only 55 miles, the worst day of the voyage. Unbelievable! I did better under jury rig after I lost the mast. Ahead *Thursday's Child* offered some consolation, having only sailed 41 miles. I paced like a caged lion, having fallen unwittingly into this airless hole. I took a swim to cool off and took some photos as *Cornwall* circled me. A second night of cockpit steering and trimming followed on the oily, windless sea. The fire bell rang every 15 minutes to keep me awake. I drifted across the Equator from the southern to the northern hemisphere and made King Neptune an offering of a miniature bottle of rum in the hope he'd send a bit of wind. Eventually *Cornwall* began to glide across a flat sea at 3 knots as dawn broke. I had done another 55 mile day.'

Christophe, averaging a scorching 12.7 knots, was 336 miles from the finish. 'The second boat is now approximately 400 miles behind me. I suggest this lead can be divided into different parts. One hundred miles is due to the boat itself. Another 100 miles is due to sailing in different weather conditions. Still another 100 miles is due to tactics. Fifty miles is credited to autopilots and 50 miles to my sails ...' He added 'It does not seem real that it's possible that I might win my second BOC. Right now it's still a dream ...'

Scully, skippering that second boat, had the satisfaction of finally learning about his yacht. The first leg had been a lesson in how to race down oceans, instead of across them. In the second and third he'd been handicapped by undersized, borrowed mainsails. 'Finally, equipped with a beautiful new mainsail, I am discovering how to sail *Coyote* to her true potential. And that is exciting. But still,' he added, 'every thought I have of this race produces an echo in my mind that asks how to do it better. Next time.'

Christophe, who had predicted in Punta del Este that he would arrive in Charleston on 27 April, showed his clairvoyance to be as masterly as his sailing when, early on the morning of race day 24, barefoot and smoking a cigarette, he trimmed his sails as the rising sun glowed orange. His nearest competitor was 600 miles away. A fleet of 40 boats had streamed out at dawn from Charleston's marinas to share the moment, as Christophe steered *Sceta Calberson* across the finish line. The wiry Frenchman raised his hands in jubilation. It was all over. 'And then it sank in. Like someone who faces death and sees his life pass before his eyes, I saw the life of the 27,000 mile race flash through my mind in an instant. All 121 days were in my brain,' he said in an interview later with Tony Bartelme, of *The Charleston Post and Courier*. 'I remember all the times, all the problems, the very nice moments. The feeling was enormous.' Christophe had equalled the accomplishment of fellow Frenchman Philippe Jeantot who had won the 1982 and 1986 BOC Challenges. 'When Philippe Jeantot won his first BOC I was just a kid. I was very young,' said Christophe. 'I read about it in a magazine. For me it was a big thing, a dream. And now it is a dream come true.' Now the $100,000 first prize and silver plate were his for a second time.

From the smallest, penultimate boat in the fleet, Robin Davie, who had finally escaped the doldrums, offered his congratulations: 'It's incredible the speeds he's achieved ... it's making some of us look rank amateurs. Having said that, my old girl's gone well and we can't go much faster.' The wild rush began for second place between David Scully, Jean-Luc Van den Heede and Steve Pettengill, all within a few miles of one another. Pettengill, his blue eyes bloodshot red, reported that he was down to his last three cups of coffee and 'may need toothpicks to hold my eyelids open'. But he was not called the 'BOC comeback kid' for nothing. During the weekend he'd gambled that a cold front was coming through and chose to veer away from the group, while the other two headed west, looking for a push from the Gulf Stream. Pettengill's tactics paid off as he overtook *Coyote* and *Vendée Enterprises*.

Soon after dawn the 43-year-old, who got his start in singlehanded racing as a shore crew, sailed across the line to claim the best ever finish by an American sailor in the BOC Challenge. For once luck was with Pettengill. When his cap shroud broke, the mast could easily have come toppling down. The Mr Fixit of the race had finally fixed it with a time for leg four of 27d 19h. His overall elapsed time on the voyage, 128 days, gave him second place overall.

Six hours later, on Sunday afternoon, David Scully roared across the finish line with *Coyote* driven by a strong sea breeze. Watching with tears in her eyes was Helen Davis, who had salvaged *Coyote* after it was found upside down in mid-Atlantic, her fiancé, Mike Plant, lost at sea when the keel fell off. 'Mike would have been proud,' said Helen. Scully's time of 28d 2h from Punta gave him third place on leg three, and an elapsed time round the world of 133 days. Though Scully had beaten Jean-Luc Van den Heede, who followed him into Charleston 44 minutes later, the Frenchman's fourth circumnavigation was faster at 129d 17h, and gave him third place overall in Class I.

Next morning David Adams drove *True Blue* over the line on May Day, and set a new mark for the fastest solo circumnavigation by an Australian singlehander. He had smashed the Class II record of Yves Dupasquier in the 1990 BOC by a remarkable 10d 10h. His time of 29 days for leg four gave him an overall elapsed time of 131 days around the world, three and a half days faster than his fellow countryman Kanga Birtles in the last race. Adams had even beaten three of the 60-footers.

'I'm very, very proud,' he said. 'The guys who have won this 50ft class before are all great blokes. They're top sailors. Mike Plant was a guy I greatly admired, he's the one who probably got me into this sport. It's terrific to have my name mentioned alongside his. And it's terrific that an Aussie is finally taking home a bit of silverware in the BOC Challenge.'

Adams had once confessed: 'The worst part of racing is the finish line. The hardest part is the end. You have to understand, you are totally focused on one thing and suddenly you come back and there is no race. It's a big shock.' As Australian as they come, Adams has shoulders as big as the Outback, but when Herb McCormick had watched the rugged sailor arrive in Sydney back on Christmas Day, the lines etched on his face were caked in salt and his shoulders hunched as he listlessly coiled his lines. McCormick realised the Southern Ocean had nearly broken the veteran sailor. 'The sight of so tough a man pushed to the limits of his endurance is something I'll never forget,' said McCormick.

Fifteen hours after Adams' arrival, in the small hours of a black, breezy and moonless South Carolina night, South African JJ Provoyeur went below to put on his smart Royal Cape Yacht Club blazer and a tie bearing the new South Africa flag. He was going to sail his 60ft yacht *Novell South Africa* across the line in style. His overall elapsed time of 133d 5h round the world was a week faster than his fellow countryman Bertie Reed, sailing the same boat in the last race. JJ's timing was the best ever recorded by a South African competitor in the race, and gave him sixth place overall.

The following day Giovanni Soldini was escorted by a school of frolicking porpoises as he drove *Kodak* past the Charleston finishing buoy to score a second place in Class II. His epic battle with David Adams was finally over and his recorded time from Punta del Este was half an hour short of 31 days. Giovanni's overall time circling the world was 134 days.

*Facing up to one another: David Adams and Giovanni Soldini, who fought one of the great ocean duels in their 50-footers. Adams won the race. Giovanni was award-ed the Spirit of the BOC prize for his competitiveness.* PHOTO: JACQUES VAPILLON

Arnet Taylor, 1,000 miles from the finish line and caught in fickle winds, had reached a low point as he contemplated the enormity of time and resources he had devoted to the BOC Challenge and questioned: 'What in the world possessed me to do this, drifting around alone out here for the better part of a year...?' The feeling passed in a couple of days and he put it down to being part of the psychological strain confronted during an extreme endeavour. Herb McCormick had characterised such incidents as the nautical equivalent of marathon runners 'hitting the wall'. It's the point when all available energy reserves are spent and depression creeps in. Winning or losing becomes irrelevant. The event itself loses all meaning. 'Those who succeed find a way over, around, or through the wall,' said Arnet. 'So far we've been fortunate in finding the right combination to pull through.' The law, accord-ing to McCormick, said: 'There are those who cannot penetrate the wall or trick their way past. These are the losers.'

Taylor had shared a windless piece of ocean with Niah Vaughan and Alan Nebauer for much of the week and 'no amount of wind dances, prayers, or tears seemed to affect things.' It had, he suspected, been the slowest week of the entire race. 'But I don't have the heart to research the ship's archives to confirm this,' he added, as the trio trimmed sail to gain every inch of advantage in the battle to be next into Charleston. Arnet celebrated his 45th birthday on race day 31. 'I hope this is the only birthday I spend on this leg,' he sighed.

Robin Davie, 500 miles astern, had escaped the doldrums and found ideal trade wind conditions, powering north westwards for a week with spray flying over

*Cornwall*'s deck. But he, too, was about to hit a wall of calms. After several days of light winds he realised he'd wandered into Taylor's windless zone and so altered course westwards, taking off into the Caribbean and passing south of Guadeloupe and Dominica. 'What a beautiful day's sailing,' he enthused. 'Nice stern winds, the islands both sides of me, the first land I had seen since Uruguay four weeks ago. The temptation to pull in for a night was very real.' The thought of fresh fruit salad, juicy steaks and chocolate gateaux left him drooling. But it would not be in the spirit of the race.

Alan Nebauer was in high spirits at being one day away from finishing his marathon when *Newcastle Australia* slammed into some Gulf Stream flotsam. He saw a big piece of timber roll out from under the stern and noticed boatspeed was down and the yacht had a disturbed wake. A piece of board was hung up on the rudder. Nebauer had been involved in a similar incident when he hit flotsam and damaged his keel soon after the start of the race. 'After stopping the boat and spending half an hour hanging over the side, in and out of the water as the boat rolled, I managed to dislodge the timber and get moving again. Big relief! There is a bit of paranoia on board when it comes to appendages hitting things. My rudder and keel must be magnetic,' he said.

Alan crossed the line next afternoon to take third place in Class II on the leg with an overall elapsed time of 181 days. There to cheer him in was Josh Hall, whom he had rescued 500 miles off the coast of Brazil seven months ago. Alan sailed less of his original yacht over the line than anyone else – he'd rebuilt his keel in Cape Town, stepped a new mast in the Falklands after sailing round Cape Horn under jury rig, and fitted a new rudder in Punta del Este. 'It looked a few times like we weren't going to make it,' he admitted. 'I'd never had a problem at sea before in my life. I'd sailed 40,000 miles and never even had a broken fitting. But on this voyage I learned stuff at every turn. And that was good.'

In the early hours of the following morning Arnet Taylor was a few miles off the Charleston breakwater facing a demanding final evening at sea as he closed with the coast at 11 knots, working his way through big ships and fishing boats. Earlier in the day, crossing rough Gulf Stream seas, the halyard holding up the lightweight genoa jammed inside the mast, allowing the upper half of the Kevlar sail to unfurl. The sail wouldn't go up and wouldn't come down and with 60 miles to go Arnet wasn't going to risk his neck fixing it. Before he could contain the situation the sail shredded into a series of streamers and flags. He put up a small staysail and tucked two reefs in the main to avoid tangling the working sails with the steamers of sail beating the mast top. 'I was determined to finish that night and reasoned I could straighten things out aloft in the peace of the Ashley River where we would be berthed. With less than an hour to go, I finally realised we were going to successfully make it in without major calamity. I had been holding my breath all week, praying that everything would hold together for the last 1,000 miles. I figured if some mysterious Russians could bend spoons with concentrated willpower, maybe I could do the same to keep things intact for the final miles of the passage.

'The VHF radio started crackling with communications from BOC escort boats and others who graciously got up in the middle of the night to see me in. My father's voice came on from aboard Howard Hoffman's *Sportfisherman*. I passed on my position so they could accompany us the final mile or so and lit a white flare to show my location. I double checked my charts and suddenly we were in the middle of a fleet of boats. I strained to keep one of the two buoys in sight which marked the finish to my 27,000 mile adventure. It would be an ignoble end to pile into one of these. Parachute flares shot off, horns sounded and I knew then that we were across the line. An inflatable chase boat came alongside, and race officials, my shore crew and Dave Scully from *Coyote* tumbled aboard to extend greetings and help me get the sails under control. It was all very moving...'

Even more remarkable was the fact that Taylor, who had never made a major solo ocean passage before the BOC Challenge, had succeeded in sailing *Thursday's Child* around the world where three others had failed. In the 1986 BOC her skipper Warren Luhrs was forced to withdraw after being dismasted. The same happened to Enda O'Coineen, when she was dismasted as *Kilcullen* shortly after the start of the 1990 race. In the 1992-93 Vendée Globe she was sailed as *Cardiff Discovery* by Alan Wynne Thomas, who suffered broken ribs and a collapsed lung in a knockdown and retired to Hobart for medical attention.

Arnet crossed the finish line that morning having circled the world 105 minutes over 200 days. He had met fear and danger with good humour. In a feat of seamanship he had sailed 1,500 miles to Tasmania after his rudder was torn off. 'Basically I had three criteria I wanted to fulfil. One, to make the start. Two, to finish the damn thing. And three, to do respectably competitively. I didn't make it on the third,' he laughed. 'But I got the first two done.'

With *Thursday's Child* safely tied up, the rest of the night was devoted to a dockside beer party. Like others, Taylor had come home to debt as well as glory. Fundraising was high on his agenda after the celebrations. He planned to sail the boat home to New England and sell her. 'She's a classic floating hotrod and has some adventures left in her, I'm sure,' he said.

The finishing gun for Niah Vaughan was fired by Harry Mitchell's wife, Diana, on the afternoon of race day 40. A huge Union Jack streamed from the stern of *Jimroda II* as Niah, wearing his trademark black beret, became the 10th skipper to finish from the 20 who had started out eight months ago. His overall time around the globe of 166 days was good enough for third place overall in Class II and completed the yacht's third circumnavigation in a BOC Challenge. As *Airco Distributor* she had been sailed to a Class II win in 157 days by her builder Mike Plant in the 1986 race. In the 1990 race Josh Hall had matched that time sailing her as *Spirit of Ipswich*. 'She's a fantastic old boat. She's got some 200,000 solo miles now, probably more than any other singlehanded yacht sailing,' said Niah. 'Running before the breeze in the Southern Ocean it felt like she could sail on forever.'

Considering Niah's previous singlehanded racing experience – a race round the cans in Cape Town – he had done remarkably well. In Charleston at the start of the race he had looked at the three sleek new-generation 50-footers *True Blue, Kodak* and *Newcastle Australia* and thought his chances of getting a placing were remote. The yachts were half the weight of *Jimroda II*, had taller rigs and bigger sail plans. Off the wind they would fly. But they also looked lightly built and Niah thought something might break. Alan Nebauer's bad luck became Niah's good fortune as he won the $10,000 third prize.

Three days later Robin Davie neared the end of his second BOC Challenge aboard *Cornwall*. His return to Charleston had what Herb McCormick termed 'grimly exquisite timing'. Record 97° temperatures that day had given way to storm clouds as a tornado-type storm brewed somewhere off the bay. At 7.30 pm the first boats

*After one of the most dramatic finishes of the race, with thunderbolts, waterspouts and 60 knot gusts, Robin Davie arrives in Charleston. His time around the world in the smallest boat was 197 days.* PHOTO: BILLY BLACK

came out to meet *Cornwall* as she cruised towards the line two miles away under her dramatic black and gold spinnaker. The afternoon sun was low in the sky, blotted with equally dramatic and menacing black clouds. Bunky, one of the tow-boat skippers, told Robin that the Coast Guard five miles away was reporting 60 knots of wind. 'Can't be,' thought Robin. But in 30 seconds the wind suddenly died and the sea became dark with something more than night.

The spinnaker lay limp. By the time Robin had pulled the spinnaker sock down the wind had blasted up to 30 knots. He tried to reef the mainsail, but the halyard was ripped from his hand as the sail slipped off its track and flew round the yacht's stern, catching on the windvane. With the finishing buoy of his 27,000 mile marathon almost in sight, Robin was forced to turn back to the open sea under staysail to sort out the mess. The thought flashed through his mind as thunder, lightning bolts, 60 knot gusts and a pair of waterspouts danced before his eyes, that he might lose the mast again. 'Don't let lightning strike twice,' he prayed as he was lashed by rain.

He was annoyed with himself for relaxing and getting caught out. His handheld GPS had stopped working and his other electronic navigation systems were down. With no navigation aids to hand he was considering that the seamanlike thing to do if the storm continued would be to go back out to sea for the night. He finally took the finish gun just after 10 pm that night. 'Wasn't that a shocker!' he said. The storm had hit so quickly that spectator boats hadn't had time to run for cover. One of Robin's Charleston supporters, Bill Moore, who hoped to compete in the next BOC Challenge, had waited so long with Robin's traditional end-of-leg prize of coffee ice cream that it had melted. Robin poured it into a saucepan and drank it, along with four pints of milk, before he was even tied up at the dock.

His overall elapsed time around the world in the smallest, oldest boat left in the fleet was 197 days, two weeks slower than his previous race in *Cornwall*. But he had sailed under jury rig around Cape Horn and had a desperate time finding wind on the last leg. He'd snapped at the heels of the 50-footers and been little more than a day behind them on the two Southern Ocean legs. Now he planned to sell his boat 'to remove the temptation of doing the race again in a 40-footer!' 'It's hard to know what to do next. If we could apply the sustained energy we put into this yacht race in a business environment we would be multimillionaires,' he said. Robin's big remaining ambition would be to compete in the non-stop Vendée Globe round the world race. 'I didn't progress after the last race. I've got to progress after this one. There's got to be a big sorting out of life.'

'And what about Harry Mitchell?' asked Tony Bartelme the reporter from the Charleston newspaper.

'It's a helluva way to die … in a yacht race,' said Robin, who had often stayed with Harry and Diana in Portsmouth when he worked on the cross-Channel ferries. But Harry had been doing what he wanted to do most. 'He was living his dream,' said Robin.

'A helluva way to live,' concluded Tony in his wrap-up piece for his newspaper article.

## Epilogue

# *Any news on Harry Mitchell?*

T he final week in Charleston, which culminated in the BOC Challenge prizegiving, belonged as much to Harry Mitchell as it did to winner Christophe Auguin. At the prizegiving attended by more than 1,000 people a resounding cheer went up every time Harry's picture flashed up on the screen during the slide and video show. In his acceptance speech, Christophe paid tribute to Harry and Mike Plant 'who have given their lives to the ocean'. Class II winner David Adams, his voice breaking with emotion as he thanked his wife, Caroline, and crew for their support, said: 'This is a race that gets under your skin and into your bones,' and, choking back the tears, added, 'If this happens in Australia they think you're running for politics.'

Harry was everywhere in Charleston. Cab drivers ten miles beyond the city limits would catch a glimpse of the BOC logo on a T-shirt and ask: 'Hey, are you with the race? Any news on Harry Mitchell?' Harry's son Paul told me he went to a roadside diner at Folly Beach and got talking to a couple. 'Do you know anything about this BOC yacht race?' he asked. 'Oh yes,' the woman replied. 'Wasn't there a chap who didn't make it back ... Harry Mitchell?' That was all she knew about the race. Nothing about the record-breaking French yachtsman or the individual achievements of the other competitors. At BOC Race HQ at the City Marina Harry's photograph looked across the room. At the home of Eugene Fallaw, his host in Charleston last September, a portrait of 'young Harry' had pride of place on the mantelpiece. Floyd Romack had stayed there with Harry and Diana at the start of the race, but couldn't face going back and checked into a motel instead. In restaurants people swapped 'Harry stories'. This was the man who thought he hadn't made a mark in life?

Down on the dockside at the City Marina, I met ten-year-old Holly Phillips, visiting from the town of LaGrange, Georgia, with her family. She'd heard my English accent and came over. Holly was one of 250,000 students from 1,200 schools throughout America and Canada who had been following the race. Her adopted skipper happened to be Harry Mitchell. As long ago as Christmas, her mother told me, she had been excitedly planning to come to Charleston to meet her hero in his finest hour. The family had decided to come anyway. A few weeks ago Holly had taken part in 'a celebration of Harry's life' at Rosemont Elementary School, attended by 200 students. They planted a tree on the campus in his honour and children brought armfuls of flowers from home. Azaleas, iris, dogwood blossoms and wild flowers were placed at the base of the tree. 'The mound of flowers made a beautiful sight on a perfect spring day,' said teacher Jennifer Daniel. 'Somebody put a golden earring on a branch of the tree. The children were very respectful. But we stressed this was a celebration of the life of a man who had the courage to live his dreams, and not a funeral.'

Holly, who never met Harry, spoke the following words which were written with the help of her teacher: 'Anyone who faces a goal faces an ocean full of challenges, for life is about challenges and how you respond to them. Some challenges are big and some are small. Some you look for, and others just find you. When we measure ourselves against how we handle these challenges, winning takes a back seat. Harry Mitchell followed his dream, set his goals, and must be counted among the winners.'

Elsewhere in Charleston lots of folk were doing things to celebrate Harry's memory. Niah Vaughan had his ear pierced with an ice pick at Charleston Yacht Club and was proudly sporting the gold earring for rounding the Horn. 'This one's for Harry,' he said. Floyd Romack, caught in calms and fearing he might not make it to Charleston before everyone left, berthed *Cardiac 88* at a marina in the Caribbean island of St Maarten and caught a plane, arriving with the comment: 'Nothing goes to windward like a 747!' Floyd was going to name a dish in his New Jersey restaurant after *Henry Hornblower*. He recalled how Harry used to joke with BOC watchers on the docks that his father had got a girl in trouble in America and Floyd was his American half-brother.

Out at sea Minoru Saito was surely the loneliest person left in the BOC Challenge that week. While other skippers, crew and friends gathered at a series of receptions and parties and paraded in downtown Charleston, Minoru was 1,000 miles from the finish line. He sent a message back in his broken English over the telex to say that after finishing in Charleston 'I want to sail to England to bring Harry's soul home. That is my way that I couldn't keep him good.' Minoru had been one of the last to speak to Harry. Three days before his EPIRB was triggered he and Harry had been sailing six miles away from each other in the Southern Ocean and within VHF range. 'We spoke on Channel 16 two times. Robin on *Cornwall* tell me to take a picture, but I haven't a telephoto lens. Now I think having a very big regret,' said Minoru. 'Very mortifying that I could not rescue him ... I still have remorse ... having it until the end of my life.'

The bravest person in Charleston was Diana Mitchell. She had come 'because above all else, Harry wanted to be a BOC finisher. And if he can't be here, I had to be here to finish the race for him. I can't allow myself to be sad,' she said. 'Otherwise I'd drown in a sea of tears.' Harry's son, Paul, and his eldest daughter, Marcia, who lives in Georgia with her husband and two children, were with Diana.

To the man in the street who doesn't follow yacht racing, Harry *was* the BOC Challenge. An adventurer taking up the challenge for its own sake, with no hope of winning. We had witnessed not just the toughest BOC Challenge yet, but the last of its kind. Technology and sponsorship were pushing the race to new limits. The leading yachts were ten per cent faster at every race, and their high-tech designs and third millennium materials had left tailend Charlies like Harry Mitchell too far behind. Progress and safety will take the race literally beyond the reach of the average seat of the pants sailor as it becomes an out and out race for purpose-built boats. As surely as the days of Blondie Hasler's half-crown bet for racing across the Atlantic had been numbered, so Harry Mitchell would be the last of a unique breed to take part in the event. There will never be another BOC Challenge that combines the Captain Fantastique of a cool sailing technician like Christophe Auguin with the buccaneering spirit of a maverick like Harry Mitchell. But it was Harry, the daring romantic, whom the public at large undoubtedly identified with.

The fourth BOC Challenge consumed many people's lives for many months. On Sunday 21 May, the day after the prizegiving, 100 or so people gathered at Charleston's Waterfront Park overlooking Cooper River and the bay where the adventure had begun on a grey September day eight months ago. It was a sunny afternoon with a light breeze and a small white yacht with a blue stripe, not unlike *Henry Hornblower*, sailed backwards and forwards with a Union Jack and the BOC flag flying from the backstay. In Harry's will, his last wish had been to have his ashes scattered on the high seas. 'So maybe everyone meets their destiny,' thought Diana. A retired local minister and Charleston's Port Chaplain spoke a few words before Diana was invited to cast a gold earring, a gift from Harry's Charleston's friends, into the sea. Robin Davie, on a motor boat anchored off the park, lit the fuse of the BOC Civil War cannon which had sounded at the finish for the winners. Now its explosion echoed across the bay for Harry. His son Paul gave a hearty blast on a brass foghorn, as his father had done at the start and finish of every leg. The crowd stepped forward to cast their flowers on the water. People stayed to chat. Later, at an informal cocktail party, Niah Vaughan presented Diana with a Red Duster signed by all the skippers and Josh Hall presented her with the fog horn.

'There's no wreckage, so it's like an unfinished story,' Diana had said. 'I think everyone will have to write their own ending for Harry.' On the last day before I left Charleston, I went with Floyd Romack to pay a call at the BOC Race Communications HQ, a small, anonymous white trailer in a downtown car park, next to the State Ports Authority Warehouse and a few miles away from the hub-bub of the City Marina, where the BOC yachts were berthed. 'The trailer' had been the nerve centre of the BOC Challenge, operating round the clock 24-hours a day and sending messages bouncing off satellites hundreds of miles above the earth. For the solo sailors it had been the centre of their universe, for some their only point of regular contact with the world beyond a lonely stretch of ocean. Life and death dramas had been played out between these four walls when Josh Hall's yacht had sunk and Isabelle and Harry's emergency beacons had sent their distress signals. The race wasn't over yet. Minoru Saito, still several hundred miles from the finish line, was expected in five days or so. Peter Dunning and Larry Brumbach were off duty as Terry Pollard worked the afternoon shift. Terry was another convert whom Harry had persuaded to shave off his beard on the occasion of his circumnavigation. Two photographs of Harry looked down benevolently from the wall. How many telexes had Harry sent here from a hemisphere away, demanding a portion of Terry's beard for each cape he sailed past? Was it all worth it? 'It was probably the greatest adventure of my life – that I had control of,' said Floyd. 'The race is one thing, but it's the people you meet. I liken it to the guys in my platoon squad in Korea. It's like we've all been through different battles in this race but now the war is over. The camaraderie is extraordinary. I can't visualise being without the BOC after this weekend. I can't believe Harry's gone. For Harry and me the BOC was a vehicle for meeting some very fine people.' As we chatted and reminisced about the race, a visitor poked his head around the door: 'Just one more yacht to come in and then it's all over and you guys can go home, I guess?' he said. Floyd Romack looked round, tears streaming down his face. 'No, two yachts,' he corrected. 'They'll always be one boat still to come in … '

*Blowing his horn and chasing Cape Horn dreams, Harry sails out of Charleston on September 17 1994. 'For the rest of your life don't waste any time. Make the best of what you may before you turn into clay,' he told students before he left Australia for the Southern Ocean.* PHOTO: BILLY BLACK

# *Results and Overall Positions on Elapsed Times*

Times given in days, hours and minutes

| Position | Yacht/skipper | Elapsed time legs 1,2,3,4 | Total elapsed time |
|---|---|---|---|
| **CLASS I** | | | |
| 1 | **Christophe Auguin**<br>Sceta Calberson | 42d 04h 58m<br>24d 23h 40m<br>29d 16m 15s<br>24d 20h 17m | 121d 17h 11m |
| 2 | **Steve Pettengill**<br>Hunter's Child | 40d 16h 08m<br>28d 02h 12m<br>32d 13h 42m<br>27d 19h 59m | 128d 04h 03m |
| 3 | **Jean-Luc Van den Heede**<br>Vendée Enterprises | 42d 13h 54m<br>27d 10h 57m<br>32d 14h 13m<br>28d 02h 54m | 129d 17h 59m |
| 4 | **David Scully**<br>Coyote | 43d 19h 34m<br>28d 08h 04m<br>32d 19h 07m<br>28d 02h 10m | 133d 00h 56m |
| 5 | **J J Provoyeur**<br>Novell S Africa | 42d 22h 04m<br>28d 20h 06m<br>31d 19h 14m<br>29d 15h 45m | 133d 05h 11m |
| 6 | **Arnet Taylor**<br>Thursday's Child | 55d 23h 29m*<br>55d 18h 06m<br>50d 15h 22m<br>39d 16h 47h | 200d 01h 45m |

**CLASS II**

| | | | |
|---|---|---|---|
| 1 | **David Adams**<br>True Blue | 42d 09h 50m<br>28d 00h 28m<br>31d 17m 15m+<br>29d 00h 55m | 131d 05h 06m |
| 2 | **Giovanni Soldini**<br>Kodak | 43d 06h 22m<br>28d 02h 27m<br>31d 16h 23m<br>30d 23h 32m | 134d 00h 46m |
| 3 | **Niah Vaughan**<br>Jimroda II | 48d 18h 01m<br>34d 22h 40m<br>42d 21h 04m<br>40d 02h 19m | 166d 16h 06m |
| 4 | **Alan Nebauer**<br>Newcastle Australia | 51d 19h 41m**<br>34d 04h 08m<br>56d 10h 35m<br>39d 03h 21m | 181d 13h 46m |
| 5 | **Robin Davie**<br>Cornwall | 58d 00h 45m***<br>36d 06h 55m<br>59d 09h 22m<br>43d 11h 11m | 197d 04h 15m |
| 6 | **Minoru Saito**<br>Shuten Dohji II | 58d 20h 28m<br>51d 15h 21m+++<br>67d 08h 51m<br>43d 13h 29m | 223d 10h 10m |
| | **Harry Mitchell**<br>Henry Hornblower | 69d 21h 54m<br>51d 05h 11m<br>Lost at sea | |

## RETIRED CLASS I

**Isabelle Autissier**
Ecureuil Poitou Charentes 2   35d 08h 52m
Dismasted, rescued from abandoned yacht on
leg two

**Josh Hall**
Gartmore
Investment Managers   Retired after yacht sank in leg one

**Mark Gatehouse**
Queen Anne's Battery   Retired in leg one

## RETIRED CLASS II

**Nigel Rowe**
Sky Catcher   52d 21h 04m
44d 22h 45m++
Retired on leg three

**Neal Petersen**
Protect Our Sealife   67d 16h 59m
Retired after dismasting on leg two

**Floyd Romack**
Cardiac 88   82d 03h 00m
Retired after leg one

**Simone Bianchetti**
Town of Cervia   67d 09h 33m
Retired with hull leaks on leg two

\*      Includes 56 hour penalty for late arrival in Charleston
\* \*    Includes 5½ hour time allowance for Josh Hall rescue
\* \* \*  Includes 8 hour credit for diverting to Minoru Saito during EPIRB alarm
\+      4 hour credit for diverting to Isabelle Autissier
++     12 hour credit for diverting to Isabelle Autissier
+++    28 hour credit for diverting to Isabelle Autissier

# *Autohelm and the BOC Challenge*

In the longest and loneliest yacht race in the world, the only crew available to a singlehanded skipper is his or her autopilot. Autohelm has been at the forefront as a supplier to the BOC Challenge from the inception of the event in 1982. The level of involvement in the 1994–95 race has been higher than previous races, with more and more of the skippers fitting Autohelm instrumentation and integrated navigation electronics, in addition to Autohelm autopilots.

For this reason we are delighted to be sponsoring *The Loneliest Race,* which so accurately portrays the triumphs, terrors and tragedies that encompass the life of the singlehanded round the world sailor. Of the 20 starters in the latest BOC Challenge this is the equipment which the skippers listed below were accompanied by on their extraordinary 27,000 mile odyssey.

| | | |
|---|---|---|
| Christophe Auguin, *Sceta Calberson* | Primary autopilot | ST7000 |
| | Secondary autopilot | ST7000 |
| | Instruments | ST50 |
| Isabelle Autissier,*Ecureuil Poitou Charentes 2* | Primary autopilot | ST7000 |
| | Secondary autopilot | ST7000 |
| Josh Hall,*Gartmore Investment Managers* | Primary autopilot | ST7000 |
| | Secondary autopilot | ST7000 |
| | Instruments | ST50 |
| | Navigation | ST50 Radar Navcentre 300 |
| Steve Pettingill, *Hunter's Child* | Secondary autopilot | ST7000 |
| | back-up autopilot | ST7000, AH2000 |
| Jean Jacques Provoyeur, *Novell South Africa* | Primary autopilot | ST7000 |
| | Secondary autopilot | ST7000 |
| | Instruments | ST50 |
| David Scully, *Coyote* | Primary autopilot | ST7000 |
| | Secondary autopilot | ST7000 |
| | Back-up autopilot | ST4000W |
| Arnet Taylor, *Thursday's Child* | Primary autopilot | ST7000 |
| | Secondary autopilot | ST4000T/GP |

| | | |
|---|---|---|
| Jean-Luc Van den Heede, *Vendée Enterprises* | Primary autopilot | ST6000 |
| | Secondary autopilot | ST4000T/GP |
| | Back-up autopilot | AH2000 |
| Simone Bianchetti, *Town of Cervia* | Primary autopilot | ST4000T/GP |
| | Secondary autopilot | ST4000T |
| | Back-up autopilot | AH2000 |
| | Instruments | ST50 |
| Robin Davie, *Cornwall* | Primary autopilot | AH3000 |
| | Secondary autopilot | AH2000 |
| | Navigation | ST50 Radar |
| Harry Mitchell, *Henry Hornblower* | Primary autopilot | ST6000 |
| | Secondary autopilot | AH2000 |
| Alan Nebauer, *Newcastle Australia* | Primary autopilot | ST4000W |
| | Instruments | ST50 |
| Neal Petersen, *Protect Our Sealife* | Primary autopilot | ST4000T/GP |
| | Secondary autopilot | AH2000 |
| Nigel Rowe, *Sky Catcher* | Primary autopilot | ST7000 |
| | Secondary autopilot | ST4000T |
| | Back-up autopilot | AH2000 |
| Minoru Saito, *Shuten Dohji II* | Primary autopilot | ST7000 |
| | Secondary autopilot | AH2000 (x2) |
| | Instruments | ST50 |
| Giovanni Soldini, *Kodak* | Primary autopilot | ST4000T/GP |
| | Secondary autopilot | ST4000T |
| | Back-up autopilot | AH2000 |
| Niah Vaughan, *Jimroda II* | Primary autopilot | ST7000 |
| | Secondary autopilot | ST7000 |
| | Back-up autopilot | ST3000 |
| | Navigation | ST50 Radar |

Like the BOC Challenge skippers, Autohelm's equipment was often pushed beyond the limits of this demanding ocean race. Our service engineers, Bob Sims and Steve Moore, were pleased to meet skippers at the stopover ports, where they were able to help with repairs to units which, understandably, had suffered with such gruelling, extended use.

We are immensely grateful to the gallant skippers for putting their ultimate trust in our equipment. It is through the incredible punishment to which our units were exposed that we are able to learn the strengths and weaknesses of our products and develop more sophisticated and reliable equipment for cruising yachtsmen all over the world.

# Index to personalities and boats